Five Texts on the Mediaeval Problem of Universals:
Porphyry, Boethius, Abelard, Duns Scotus, Ockham

Five Texts on the Mediaeval Problem of Universals:
Porphyry, Boethius, Abelard, Duns Scotus, Ockham

Translated and Edited by
Paul Vincent Spade

Hackett Publishing Company, Inc.
Indianapolis/Cambridge

99 98 97 96 95 94   1 2 3 4 5 6

Design by Dan Kirklin

For further information, please contact

Hackett Publishing Company, Inc.
P.O. Box 44937
Indianapolis, Indiana 46244-0937

Library of Congress Cataloging-in-Publication Data

Five texts on the mediaeval problem of universals/Porphyry . . . [et al.]:
    translated, with introduction and notes, by Paul Vincent Spade.
            p.   cm.
        Includes bibliographical references.
        Contents: Isagoge/Porphyry the Phoenician—Boethius, from his
    Second commentary on Porphyry's Isagoge—Peter Abelard, from the
    "Glosses on Porphyry" . . . —Six questions on individuation/John
    Duns Scotus—Five questions on universals/William of Ockham.
        ISBN 0-87220-250-X (alk. paper)   ISBN 0-87220-249-6 (pbk.)
        1. Universals (Philosophy)—Early works to 1800.   2. Philosophy,
    Medieval.   I. Porphyry, ca. 234–ca. 305.   II. Spade, Paul Vincent.
    III. Title: 5 texts on mediaeval problem of universals.
    B105.U5F58   1994   93-45554
    111.'.2—dc20   CIP

The paper used in this publication meets the minimum requirements of
American National Standard for Information Sciences—Permanence of Paper
for Printed Library Materials, ANSI Z39-48-1984.

∞

Contents

Introduction

I

It is easy to motivate the problem of universals. Consider these two capital letters: **A A**. Ignore everything else about them and for now observe only that they are of the same color; they are both black.

As you look at the two letters, how many colors do you see? Two different answers are plausible. You may want to say you see only *one* color here, blackness. You see it twice, once in each of the two capitals, but it is the same color in both cases. After all, did I not just say the two letters were "*of the same color*"? Isn't that obvious by just looking at them? This single blackness is the kind of entity that is *repeatable*, found intact in both letters at the same time; it is what philosophers call a "universal." If this is your answer, then you believe in the reality of at least one universal, and are in that sense a "realist" on the question.

But now reset your mental apparatus and look at the two letters again. On second glance, isn't it obvious that you see *two* colors here, two blacknesses: the blackness of the first **A**, *this* blackness, and then the blackness of the second **A**, *that* blackness? The two colors look exactly alike, yes, but aren't they visually as distinct as the two letters themselves? If this is your answer, then you do not believe in the reality of universals (at least not in this case) and are a "nominalist" on the question.[1] The problem of universals is in effect the problem of deciding between these answers.[2]

There is much at stake in this problem. Universals, if they exist, behave in ontologically very peculiar ways. Some of those ways are brought out in the texts translated below. Historically, the strongest arguments in favor of nominalism have always been that such peculiarities amount to metaphysical impossibilities, that realism is an incoherent theory. Whatever you think of

1. The origin of the term 'nominalism' is very obscure. See Courtenay. (Full bibliographical information for items cited in the text and notes may be found in the Bibliography at the end of this volume.) Sometimes the term 'conceptualism' is used to distinguish one subcase of what I here call "nominalism." There is such a distinction to be made, but I do not find it especially helpful in dealing with the philosophical issues raised by the problem of universals.

2. I emphasize that this is only for motivation. You could say you believe in a universal blackness, but just do not *see* it in the two letters.

those arguments, it is true that realists have always had the most explaining to do in metaphysics.

On the other hand, nominalists have always had to deal with the epistemological difficulties their theories raise. After all, much of our knowledge—all of it, in fact, except such utterly singular bits as "Cicero is Tully" or "This is here now"—proceeds in terms of *general* words and concepts. We say "All men are mortal," thereby grouping Socrates and Plato together and calling them by the same name. If there are no universals, then what real basis can there possibly be for such a grouping? Isn't it utterly arbitrary—perhaps pragmatically useful, a matter of cultural conditioning, but ultimately *not* a reflection of the way things really are? In short, doesn't nominalism make all general knowledge impossible? Whatever you think of these considerations, it is true that nominalists have always had the most explaining to do in epistemology.

Nominalists have no special difficulty with metaphysics; their ontology is lean and trim. Their problem is in explaining how we can *know* the world is the way they say it is. By contrast, realists have no special difficulty with epistemology; if universals are real, they are available to provide a basis for general knowledge. Their problem is in explaining how the world can *be* the way they say they know it is.

I do not mean to claim that the difficulties on either side of this problem are unanswerable ones. Perhaps a suitably sophisticated and nuanced theory will be able to handle them all. (Let us hope so; otherwise philosophy is in big trouble!) But I do mean to say that this is where the pressure-points are in the problem of universals. Alert readers will be able to verify this for themselves in the texts below.

II

It is well known that the problem of universals was widely discussed in mediaeval philosophy—indeed, some would say it was discussed then with a level of insight and rigor it has never enjoyed since. The five texts translated in this volume include the most influential and some of the most sophisticated treatments of the problem in the whole Middle Ages.

The first text is Porphyry's *Isagoge*, translated here in its entirety. Porphyry was a third-century Greek neo-Platonist, a pupil and the biographer of Plotinus, and the one who arranged Plotinus's writings into six groups of nine essays (the "*Enneads*"). His *Isagoge* (the word means "Introduction") is nominally addressed to his student, the Roman senator Chrysaorius, and is intended as an introduction to Aristotle's *Categories*. But it does not directly deal with the categories at all; instead, it discusses the notions of genus, species, difference, property, and accident—the five so-called "predicables." In so doing, it fixed much of the vocabulary for subsequent mediaeval discussions.

Despite its importance in this respect, perhaps the main influence of the *Isagoge* lies not in what it says, about the predicables or anything else, but in what it does *not* say. For in his introductory remarks, Porphyry raises but then modestly refuses to answer three questions about the metaphysical status of universals, saying only that they belong to "another, greater investigation" (**P (2)**).[3] It is this brief passage that raised the problem of universals in the form in which it was first discussed in the Middle Ages. It contains some of the most consequential lines in the entire history of philosophy.

Porphyry's silence means that there really is no detailed theory of universals in the *Isagoge*—or for that matter in his other writings. Taken by himself, therefore, Porphyry would not have been a very important figure in the history of our problem. But he cannot be taken by himself. His importance lies in the fact that his *Isagoge* was translated into Latin in the early Middle Ages and used as the occasion for discussing the problem of universals directly and in detail. It was as though commentators found his silence intolerable and were irresistibly drawn into the very questions Porphyry himself had declined to discuss.

The most important of these early mediaeval discussions is undoubtedly Boethius's. Boethius (c. 480–524/5) knew Greek, both the language and the culture, at a time when such knowledge was dying out in the Latin world. He translated most of Aristotle's logical writings into Latin (although only the *Categories* and *On Interpretation* circulated widely before the twelfth century), and in fact through his translations and commentaries was probably the single most important source for early mediaeval knowledge of Greek philosophy.

In addition to works of Aristotle, Boethius also translated Porphyry's *Isagoge* and wrote *two* commentaries on it. (His first commentary was based on an earlier translation by Marius Victorinus, who is known to readers of Augustine's *Confessions* VIII. 2 & 4.) Although Boethius addressed the problem of universals in several places, the discussion in his *Second Commentary on Porphyry* was the longest and probably the most influential. The relevant portion of that commentary is translated below. Not surprisingly, it is the passage where Boethius discusses Porphyry's three unanswered questions.

---

3. For an explanation of references given in this form, see the Note on the Text, below.

Boethius expounds a theory sometimes called "moderate realism." Despite the name, it is not a realism at all in the sense described above. The theory denies the reality of universals, but goes on to address the resulting epistemological problems by holding that nevertheless our general concepts and terms do have a firm basis in reality. The link is provided by what Boethius calls "division" or "abstraction."

In the course of Boethius's treatment, he provides an admirable definition of what a universal is supposed to be, a definition that makes explicit what I left at the motivational level in my little experiment with capital letters above. A universal (Boethius says "genus," but the point can be generalized) is something common to or shared by several things (a) as a whole, not part by part as a pie is shared by all who take a slice; (b) simultaneously, not in succession as a used car is possessed wholly by all its owners, but one after another; and (c) in such a way that it enters into the metaphysical make-up of what it is common to, not in the merely external way a sporting event, say, is wholly and simultaneously present to all its spectators. (See **B** (14)–(18).) Clause (c) is of course the one that requires further work.

This definition gives one of the two main notions in terms of which the mediaeval discussions proceeded. The other comes from Aristotle's *On Interpretation* 7, 17^a38-^b1: "Among things, some are universal while others are singular. By 'universal' I mean what is apt to be predicated of many, by 'singular' what is not. For example, man is a universal, Callias a singular." This text too was available to the Middle Ages, in Boethius's translation. Notice that it is put entirely in terms of predication.

In an obvious sense, of course, *terms* are predicated, and some of them are predicated *of many* things. But they are not what the problem of universals is concerned with. Is this linguistic relation of predication a reflection of a more basic metaphysical relation among extralinguistic entities, a relation such that if it holds the corresponding linguistic predication is true? If so, then there seems little reason not to call this metaphysical relation a kind of "predication" as well. If some extralinguistic entities are then "predicated of many" in this way, they can reasonably be called "universals."

There are thus at least two versions of the problem of universals in the Middle Ages. On Boethius's definition, the question is whether there exist things fitting that definition. On the Aristotelian definition, the question is whether only terms or also extralinguistic entities are "predicated of many." In both cases an affirmative answer is realism, a negative one nominalism.

In practice, these two forms of realism and nominalism often went together in the Middle Ages. A realist in one sense tended to be a realist in the other sense as well, and so too for nominalism. This is not surprising, since the kind of "sharing" or "commonness" Boethius was talking about is perhaps the most plausible candidate for the extralinguistic relation of "predication" that realism in the Aristotelian sense requires.

But there were exceptions and, if I am right, Peter Abelard was one of them. Abelard (1079–1142) was a brilliant but cantankerous philosopher and theologian. His career came at the very end of the early Middle Ages, just before mediaeval philosophy was permanently transformed by a rush of new translations from Greek and Arabic sources, eventually including almost all the rest of Aristotle's writings.

Abelard wrote on the problem of universals in several places. The most well known of them is in the "Glosses on Porphyry" in his *Logica 'ingredientibus'*. Once again the relevant passage is a discussion of Porphyry's three unanswered questions.

After considering and rejecting several theories current in his own day, Abelard sets out his own view. The correct interpretation of this view is a matter of considerable disagreement. But it is plain that throughout the discussion Abelard is operating mainly in terms of the Aristotelian notion of a universal. At least as I read the passage, Abelard embraces a strict nominalism in the Aristotelian sense: ". . . it remains to ascribe this kind of universality *only to words*" (A (63)). But he also argues that there is a real basis for our universal terms. It is what he calls a *status* (A (91)–(92)), and is *not* "predicated of many." Thus if I am correct, Abelard is a nominalist in the Aristotelian sense but a realist in the Boethian sense.

By the time of the last two authors represented below, John Duns Scotus (c. 1265–1308) and William of Ockham (c. 1285–1347), philosophy had become a specialized and highly technical academic discipline, carried on almost exclusively in a university context. These last two texts are here translated into English for the first time, and are by far the longest and most intricate in this volume. Specialists and nonspecialists alike will find them especially difficult. Here are some things you should know before reading them:

First, we are no longer dealing directly with Porphyry or with commentaries on his *Isagoge*. Porphyry and Boethius are still there, of course, but they are in the background. Instead the two texts are excerpts from enormous commentaries on the *Sentences* of Peter Lombard (c. 1095–1160). Lombard was a theologian at Paris, and in 1157/8 completed a systematic survey of patristic and other authors' views on theological topics. The work was known as his *Sentences* (in the quasi-judicial sense of "verdict"). This excellent work became an official textbook of theology at Paris and elsewhere in the thirteenth century and afterwards. It was divided into four books, and each book was further divided into "distinctions." Commentaries on it often took the form of a series of "questions" on the various distinctions of the text, as with the two passages translated below.

Second, it is important to understand this "question"-format itself. The "question" was a stylized format for discussing theoretical matters in mediaeval universities. The format began with a statement of the issue, usually in the form of a yes/no question. Then a series of arguments would be presented *pro* and *con*. (Think of the prosecution and the defense in a court of law.) The author would then "resolve" the question by giving his own view, and finally respond to the arguments for the losing side. Readers of Thomas Aquinas's *Summa theologiae* will be familiar with this format. By the time of Scotus and Ockham, this skeletal structure admitted of many variations. (For instance, in the passage from Scotus below, q. 6 is embedded in the structure of q. 5.)

The reader must constantly be aware of where he or she is in this structure. A very common error among new students of mediaeval philosophy is to quote a passage as expressing an author's doctrine when in fact he is only stating an objection he will then go on to reject and refute.

In the passage from Scotus translated below, Scotus does not ask whether there are universals. Instead he asks what it is that makes (material) things *individual*. In q. 1 he considers the answer that nothing "makes" things individual. They are individual all by themselves; they so to speak "just come that way." This is the nominalist doctrine Ockham would later defend. Scotus rejects it and thereby commits himself to some form of realism.

In q. 2 he considers Henry of Ghent's theory, that things are individuated by a twofold negation. Something *x* is "individual" insofar as it is *not* anything else *y* and insofar as it is *not* internally subdivided in the sense in which a mere "heap" or "pile" is subdivided. A heap is not an individual in the metaphysical sense Scotus is talking about. In q. 3 he considers Giles of Rome's theory that *actual existence* is what individuates things, and in q. 4 the theory that *quantity* (in particular, size and shape) does it. (Compare modern talk of individuation in terms of a thing's spatio-temporal coordinates.) In q. 5 Scotus considers the theory of *matter* as the principle of individuation.

Scotus argues against all these theories that in every case they propose something that itself stands in need of individuation and so cannot be what individuates. Both Socrates and Plato are *not* anything else and *not* internally subdivided in the relevant way. Both therefore have the kind of twofold negation Henry of Ghent was discussing. Why then does this twofold negation produce Socrates in the one case but Plato in the other? Again, actual existence is simply too general to do the job; *all* individuals exist, after all. The same goes for quantity and matter.

Again, Scotus argues against all these candidates (except matter in q. 5) that they are just ontologically "too late" to individuate. It is true that individuals have the kind of twofold negation Henry of Ghent proposed. But that is not the explanation we are looking for; on the contrary, it is what must be explained! Again, existence is what actualizes an *individualized* nature; it cannot therefore be what individuates it. So too, quantity is an accident and is therefore ontologically parasitic on individual substances, not the other way around.

Finally, in q. 6, Scotus gives us his own theory. The principle of individuation is some special entity that is none of those considered above. Against Henry of Ghent, it is something positive. Against Giles of Rome, it must be part of *what* the individual is, not its existence (which instead answers the question *whether* it is). Against the theory of quantity, it must somehow combine with the specific nature to form a *substantial* unity, not a merely accidental unity. And above all, against the theory of matter, it cannot itself need to be individuated—it must be "by itself a 'this'." This mysterious factor, whatever it is, is what Scotus calls the "individual difference" and what later came to be known as *haecceity* (= "thisness").

William of Ockham knew this discussion in Scotus and took it very seriously. In the text translated below, Ockham starts from a very strongly realist theory and then considers a series of progressively less realist theories. But he ultimately rejects them all for an uncompromising nominalism. In q. 4 (the first in the series), Ockham's main target appears to be his contemporary Walter Burley.[4] According to Burley, the universal is not a product of the mind; it is really in things that share it, one and the same in all of them, but is "really distinct" from them. The universal *man* in Socrates and Plato, for instance, is as distinct from them as they are from one another. The second theory he considers (q. 5) is like the first except that according to it the universal is *not* one and the same in all the individuals that share in it. It is "multiplied," in much the same way the impression of a signet-ring is "multiplied" according to the number of times you stamp it on different blobs of sealing wax. (The metaphor was a common one, although Ockham does not use it explicitly here.) It is worth pointing out that these first two theories are very reminiscent of the two previous theories Abelard had considered in his "Glosses on Porphyry," although of course many refinements and complications have been added.

4. See Walter Burley, 3rb–7rb.

In q. 6 Ockham discusses Scotus's theory in detail. For Scotus, the universal is not "really distinct" from the individuals sharing in it, but only distinct by some lesser kind of distinction—the famous "formal distinction." Nevertheless, the distinction is not merely a product of the mind. Ockham quotes long passages *verbatim* from Scotus, including many from the text translated in this volume, and seems to be taking great pains to represent Scotus's theory accurately and fairly. Nevertheless, he rejects it.

In q. 7 Ockham considers several versions of an even less realist theory according to which universals are not distinct from their individuals in *any* mind-independent way at all—either by a "real distinction" or by a "formal distinction." The only distinction between the individual and the universal is a mere "distinction of reason." One variant of this theory—the view of a certain Henry of Harclay—sounds very much like a theory already discussed by Abelard (the second variation of the second main theory he discusses [A (47), (56)–(59)]).

Although for Henry of Harclay there is absolutely nothing common or shared in reality, nevertheless—like all the other theories Ockham has considered—Henry still finds some basis in reality for grounding a universal concept in experience of *a single thing*. And that is too realistic for Ockham. For him, no universal concept can ever be derived from a single experience. It takes at least *two* experiences, which are then compared with one another, before we can get a universal concept.

In q. 8, Ockham draws his conclusions from all this. Universals are *not* outside the mind at all; they are concepts *in* the mind. They are "universal" only in the Aristotelian sense of being "predicated of many." Nothing at all is universal in the Boethian sense of being "common" in the metaphysically appropriate way.

But what kind of thing is a universal concept? Ockham discusses several theories that he says are "probable." One is a theory according to which a universal concept is a "*fictum*"—an intentional object, distinct from the act of thinking about it, and having a different kind of reality than do things in the Aristotelian categories. Alternatively, a universal concept might have the same kind of reality things in the categories do. In particular, it might be a real *quality* inhering in the soul. Ockham discusses several things such a quality might be, but the possibility he seems to take most seriously is that the universal concept is *identical* with the very act of thinking. The universal concept *animal*, for example, is just the act of thinking of all animals. It is not the animals themselves or something metaphysically *in* animals. And it is not some intentional object of the act of thinking; it is simply the act itself. This is what is known as the "*intellectio*"-theory.

In the passage translated here, Ockham does not decide among the theories he says are "probable." Nevertheless, he seems to lean toward the *fictum*-theory. Later on, however, Ockham rejected the *fictum*-theory in favor of the *intellectio*-theory. The person who caused him to change his mind seems to have been one Walter Chatton, a fellow Franciscan with Ockham and almost certainly an acquaintance of his.[5]

One finds traces of this change of heart in the passage translated here. Ockham later went back over the first book of his *Commentary on the Sentences*, revising and correcting it and in general putting it in the form in which he wanted it to circulate. (Such an author-revised text is called an "*Ordinatio*.") In the course of these revisions, he added several passages, including some at the end of q. 8 in which he definitely seems to favor the *intellectio*-theory.

III

Much of the material translated below is dense and forbidding. No translation can turn it into smooth conversational English without distorting it beyond recognition. And nothing short of a full commentary will enable the nonspecialist to untangle many of the arguments. Fortunately, help is readily available in the secondary literature.

For Porphyry's *Isagoge*, the reader may want to consult Gracia, *Introduction to the Problem of Individuation in the Early Middle Ages*, Ch. 2.1. On Boethius, the rest of Gracia's Ch. 2 provides a clear account. Ch. 4 discusses Abelard's views, but a fuller account may be found in Tweedale, *Abailard on Universals*, and especially in King, *Peter Abailard and the Problem of Universals*. King is also extremely valuable for identifying and making sense of the various other theories Abelard discusses. For Scotus, Wolter, *The Philosophical Theology of John Duns Scotus*, Chs. 1, 2, & 4 are very helpful. Ch. 4, in particular, directly analyzes the passage translated here. For Ockham, the most authoritative study is definitely Adams, *William Ockham*, especially Chs. 1–4 & 16. For the context of both Scotus and Ockham, the reader may find Wippel, *The Metaphysical Thought of Godfrey of Fontaines* very useful; I did.

But the single most helpful resource for concepts, terminology, doctrines, and arguments is doubtless Norman Kretzmann, *et al.*, *The Cambridge History of Later Medieval Philosophy*. Ch. 20, "Universals in the early fourteenth century," is especially valuable. Readers of these translations who come across something unfamiliar are advised to consult the index to the *Cambridge*

---

5. The relevant text is edited in Gál, "Gualterus de Chatton."

History. In some cases I have inserted a reference to the *Cambridge History* directly into my translation. Readers should also be aware of the *Glossary* at the end of the present volume.

Note that 'the Philosopher' is an honorific title given to Aristotle, while 'the Commentator' refers to Averroes (1126–98), the great Muslim commentator on Aristotle.

Note on the Text

I have translated Porphyry's *Isagoge* from the Busse edition. The passage from Boethius's *Second Commentary on Porphyry* is from Book I, Chs. 10–11, of the Brandt edition (159.3–167.20). The text from Abelard's "Glosses on Porphyry" in his *Logica 'ingredientibus'* is taken from fascicule I of the Geyer edition of *Peter Abelards philosophische Schriften* (7.25–32.12), with corrections from King. The passage from Scotus is taken from the Vatican edition of his *Opera omnia* (7. 391–494). The text from Ockham is from the Franciscan Institute edition of his *Opera philosophica* (2. 99.7–292.6).

For the sake of cross-referencing, I have numbered the paragraphs. The Latin edition of Scotus has its own section numbers, which I found it convenient to adopt in this translation even though a numbered section of the Latin sometimes includes more than one paragraph of the English. All other paragraph numbering is my own. The numbering is restarted at the beginning of each new text—except for Ockham, where because of the length of the text I restarted the numbering with each new question. Cross-references *within* a text (for Ockham, within a question) are given by simply citing the paragraph number. Cross-references *between* texts are given according to the following code: **P** = Porphyry, **B** = Boethius, **A** = Abelard, **S** = Scotus, **O** = Ockham. In each case the code is followed by the paragraph number—or, for Ockham, by the question and paragraph number. Cross-references between questions in the Ockham text are given simply by question and paragraph number. The following additional codes are also used in references: **K** = Kretzmann, *et al.*, *The Cambridge History of Later Medieval Philosophy*. **OP** = William of Ockham, *Opera philosophica*. **OT** = William of Ockham, *Opera theologica*. **W** = the Wadding edition of Scotus's *Opera omnia*. All other references to Scotus's Latin text are to the Vatican edition of his *Opera omnia*.

To keep footnotes to a minimum, I have incorporated as many references and cross-references as possible into the text itself, enclosed in square brackets. I have also used square brackets to signal occasional words or phrases of my own that are not in the Latin (or Greek), but that I have supplied as a kind of commentary where I thought it was necessary. On the other hand, I have felt free to insert words I thought were clearly implied in the original text, even if not explicitly present there, without flagging them by square brackets or otherwise. Those familiar with these texts in the original languages will know that sometimes, particularly with Scotus and Ockham, the writing is exceedingly compressed; to mark each word supplied by the translator would be to scatter brackets all over the page. Apart from such insertions, all intentional departures from the editions are signalled in the footnotes. In the passage from Ockham, I have used pointed brackets to enclose material Ockham added later in revising his *Ordinatio*.

Asterisks in the text indicate terms found in the *Glossary* (sometimes only in a related form). Such terms that appear frequently are marked with an asterisk only in troublesome occurrences.

Mediaeval authors sometimes divide texts in ways that are not ours. And even where we divide them the same way, mediaeval authors sometimes just give the wrong reference. In all such cases I have included the correct reference, according to the modern division, after an equal sign in square brackets. For example "Ch. 4 [= 3]."

When Boethius or Abelard quotes Porphyry, I have translated directly from *their Latin* rather than merely repeat my translation of Porphyry's Greek. On the other hand, when Ockham quotes Scotus at length, I have simply given a cross-reference to the original passage in my translation of Scotus. In these cases Ockham's quotations are virtually *verbatim* (except for a few points I have flagged), and no useful purpose would be served by printing the same text twice.

I have on the whole adopted a fairly literal approach to translating this material. I find this both desirable in itself and necessary in order to preserve nuances of the original. In my experience, it is almost always possible with texts like this to translate literally and accurately into readable but not necessarily easy English.

The reader should be aware of the following facts that affect these translations. First, word-order is important. By the time of Ockham, and to some extent earlier, a convention had developed of reading the scope of words as extending *to the right* (in speech: *later*). Nothing to the left of a quantifier or negation, for example, was governed by it. This was a *regimentation* of Latin for technical purposes, not a reflection of "ordinary usage." It sometimes led to formulations that sound just as convoluted in Latin as their translations do in English. The same thing happens today in technical English: "Than every number there is a greater, even though there is no number greater than every number."

Second, the word 'thing' is a technical term for Abelard, Scotus, and Ockham, and so is not available to the translator to serve as a neutral "fill"--word. The same goes for 'entity', which in the text from Scotus appears to mean not just anything that is a reality but rather what anything that is a reality *does*. (See S (34).) In the translation of their texts, I have avoided these terms except where (a) they are explicitly present in the Latin, (b) the context makes it plain that their technical use in the translation does not distort the overall sense, or else (c) where the context is obviously not a technical one at all, and there is no danger of the terms' being taken in a wrong sense. (I have been less scrupulous in the texts of Porphyry and Boethius, where the words are not such technical terms.) For "fill"-words, I have had to resort to 'item', 'factor', 'feature', and the like. For example, "really distinct through some features intrinsic to them." The result is sometimes less than graceful. On the other hand, the words 'something', 'everything', 'nothing', etc., should be regarded as neutral terms that do *not* imply "thing" in the technical sense.

'Differ' likewise has a technical sense, particularly in the later texts. Items that differ agree in some higher genus. To "differ" is not the same as being "diverse"; the categories are diverse from one another, but do not differ from one another since they are the highest genera. I have observed this terminological convention throughout, except in passages where the terms are obviously not being used rigorously. See P (39)–(41).

I have not found a satisfactory translation for '*fictum*' as used by Ockham. 'Fiction' implies falsehood, which is not always appropriate. So does 'figment', which also has the disadvantage of meaning an *impossible* object for Ockham (*e. g.*, a vacuum). 'Contrivance' and 'fabrication', while they convey the right idea, are simply too fancy for regular use. I have resolved just to leave '*fictum*' untranslated in Ockham's text, and to let its meaning be fixed by the context. For the verb '*fingere*', the root of '*fictum*', I have generally used 'to contrive' or 'to fashion'. Readers should be aware of this etymological connection when they see 'contrive' or 'fashion' in the context of the *fictum*-theory.

'*Ratio*' is a notorious problem. I have not tried to translate it consistently on all occurrences, and have used 'reason', 'notion', 'aspect', or other words as seemed best for the occasion.

Finally, I have translated forms of '*plures*' as 'several' (*i. e.*, two or more) and of '*multi*' as 'many'. The reader should not take 'several' as implying a great number. ('A plurality of', although correct for '*plures*', was too awkward for regular use.)

Porphyry the Phoenician,
the Pupil of Plotinus of Lycopolis

Isagoge

(1) Since, Chrysaorius,[1] to teach about Aristotle's *Categories* it is necessary to know what genus and difference are, as well as species, property, and accident, and since reflection on these things is useful for giving definitions, and in general for matters pertaining to division and demonstration, therefore I shall give you a brief account and shall try in a few words, as in the manner of an introduction, to go over what our elders said about these things. I shall abstain from deeper enquiries and aim, as appropriate, at the simpler ones.

(2) For example, I shall beg off saying anything about (a) whether genera and species are real or are situated in bare thoughts alone, (b) whether as real they are bodies or incorporeals, and (c) whether they are separated or in sensibles and have their reality in connection with them. Such business is profound, and requires another, greater investigation. Instead I shall now try to show you how the ancients, the Peripatetics among them most of all, interpreted genus and species and the other matters before us in a more logical fashion.

On genus

(3) It seems that neither 'genus' nor 'species' is said in a single sense. For (a) the collection of things related somehow to one thing and to one another is called a "genus." In accordance with this meaning, the Heraclids are called a genus because of their being derived from one person—that is to say, from Heracles[2]—and because of the multitude of people who somehow have a kinship to one another derived from him and are called by a name that separates them from other genera.

(4) (b) In another sense too the origin of each person's birth, whether the one who begot him or the place in which he was born, is called his "genus." For in this way we say that Orestes has his genus from Tantalus, but Hyllus

---

1. A Roman senator and student of Porphyry's.
2. One sense of the Greek *genos* is "race, descendant of."

from Heracles, and again that Pindar is Theban by genus, but Plato Athenian.[3] For the country is a kind of origin of each person's birth, just as his father is.

(5) This latter sense of the word seems to be a common one. For those who come down from the race of Heracles are called Heraclids,[4] and those from Cecrops, together with their kin, are called Cecropids.[5]

(6) The origin of each person's birth was above called a "genus," and after these the multitude of things that come from one origin, like the Heraclids. Dividing that group off and separating them from others, we said the whole collection of Heraclids is a genus.

(7) (c) In yet another way, that to which a species is subordinated is called a "genus." Perhaps this is said because of the similarity with the former senses. For such a genus is also a kind of *origin* for the things under it, and seems also to *include* the whole multitude contained under it.

(8) Now although 'genus' is said in these three ways, discussion among philosophers concerns the third. They describe this sense and set it out by saying that a genus is what is predicated, with respect to what the thing is, of several things differing in species. For example, animal. For among predicates, some are said of one thing only, for example individuals like 'Socrates', and 'he' and 'this'. Others are said of several things, such as genera, species, differences, properties, and common accidents, although not accidents that are proper to something.[6]

(9) An example of genus is 'animal'; an example of species, 'man'; an example of difference, 'rational'; an example of property, 'risible'; examples of accident, 'white', 'black', 'sitting'.

(10) Genera then differ from what are predicable of one thing only, since genera are given as being predicated of several. Again, among what are predicable of several, genera differ from species because species, even though they are predicated of several, are yet not predicated of what differ in species but only in number. For 'man', which is a species, is predicated of Socrates and Plato, who do not differ from one another in species but only in number.

---

3. In these last two examples, *genos* might be translated "stock."

4. The same example was used to illustrate sense (a). But the point is not the same. In sense (a) it is the Heraclids, descended from Heracles, who together make up the genus. In sense (b) it is Heracles himself, who is the origin or genus of the Heraclids. See also (6).

5. *I. e.*, Athenians. Legend had it that the first king of Athens was a certain Cecrops.

6. For example the common accident blackness, but not *this instance* of blackness possessed by this black thing.

But 'animal', which is a genus, is predicated of man and ox and horse, which differ from one another also in species, not just in number.

(11) Again, genus differs from property because property is predicated of only the one species it is the property of and of the individuals under the species, as 'risible' is predicated only of man and of particular men. But genus is predicated not only of one species but of several differing species.

(12) Again, genus differs from difference and from common accidents because even though differences and common accidents are predicated of several things differing in species, yet they are not predicated with respect to what the thing is. For when we ask about the respect in which these are predicated, we say they are predicated not with respect to *what* the thing is but rather with respect to *what manner* of thing it is. For to the question *what manner* of thing a man is, we say "rational." And to the question what manner of thing a crow is, we say "black." (Rational is a difference, and black an accident.) But when we are asked *what* a man is, we answer "animal." (The genus of man was animal.)

(13) So the fact that genus is said of many things distinguishes it from individuals, which are predicated of one alone, while its being predicated of what differ in species distinguishes genus from what are predicated as species or as properties. And its being predicated with respect to what a thing is separates it from differences and common accidents, each of which is predicated of what it is predicated of, not with respect to what the thing is but with respect to what manner of thing it is or in what disposition.

(14) Thus the given outline of the notion of genus is neither too broad nor too narrow.

On species

(15) (a) 'Species' is said of each thing's form. As has been said: "First a species worthy of sovereignty."[7]

(16) (b) What is under a given genus is also called a species. In this sense we usually call man a species of animal (animal being the genus), white a species of color, and triangle a species of figure.

(17) Now if in giving an account of the genus we mentioned the species—by saying "predicated with respect to what the thing is, of several things differing in species"—and we call "species" what is under the given genus, then we must acknowledge that since both genus is the genus of

---

7. Euripides, *Aeolus* 15. 2. 'Species' in this sense refers to a thing's physical shape.

something and species is the species of something, each of the other, both must be used in the definitions of both.

(18) Therefore, they give the following account of species: (c) Species is what is arranged under the genus and is what the genus is predicated of with respect to what the thing is.

(19) Again: (d) Species is what is predicated, with respect to what the thing is, of several things differing in number.

(20) The last account is of the *most* specific species and of what is *only* a species, whereas the others [(a)–(c)] are also of species that are not most specific ones.

(21) This statement can be clarified as follows: In each category some things are most general and again others most specific, and yet others are between the most general and the most specific. The most general is that above which there is no other genus that transcends it. The most specific is that after which there is no other, subordinate species. What are between the most general and the most specific are all the others. These, the same things, are both genera and species, taken in relation to one or the other.[8]

(22) Let us clarify the above statement for just one category.[9] Substance itself is a genus. Under this is body, and under body animate body, under which animal, under animal rational animal, under which man. Under man are Socrates and Plato and the particular men.

(23) Of these, substance is the most general and the one that is only a genus. Man is the most specific and the one that is only a species. Body is a species of substance but a genus of animate body. Animate body is a species of body but a genus of animal. Again, animal is a species of animate body but a genus of rational animal. Rational animal is a species of animal but a genus of man. Now man is a species of rational animal, but no longer a genus—of particular men. Instead it is a species only. Everything prior to individuals and predicated immediately of them is a species only, no longer a genus.

(24) Therefore, just as substance, being the highest, was a most general genus because there is nothing prior to it, so too man, being a species after which there is no species or any of what can be cut up into species, but only individuals (for Socrates and Plato and this white thing are individuals), is a species only, both the last species and, as we say, the "most specific."

(25) What are in between are species of what is prior to them, but genera

8. *I. e.*, a species in relation to the most general genus, a genus in relation to the most specific species.

9. The rest of paragraph (22) contains the so-called "Porphyrian tree."

of what comes after. Thus they stand in two relations, **(a)** the one to things prior to them, in virtue of which relation they are said to be species of those things, and **(b)** the other to things after them, in virtue of which relation they are said to be genera of those things.

(26) The two extremes each have one relation only. For the most general genus has **(b)** the relation to things under it, since it is the highest genus of them all. But it no longer has **(a)** the relation to things prior to itself, since it is highest, both as the first origin and, as we said, that above which there is no other genus that transcends it.

(27) The most specific species also has one relation only, **(a)** the one to things prior to itself, of which it is a species. But it does not have the other relation, **(b)** to things after it, even though it is called a species of individuals. Rather it is called a species of individuals because it includes them, and again it is called a species of what are prior to it because it is included by them.

(28) Thus they define the most general genus as **(i)** that which, although it is a genus, is not a species, and again, as **(ii)** that above which there is no other genus that transcends it. The most specific species they define as **(i)** that which, although it is a species, is not a genus, and **(ii)** that which, although it is a species, we cannot divide further into species, and as **(iii)** that which is predicated, with respect to what the thing is, of several things differing in number.

(29) What are between the two extremes they call "subordinate" genera and species. Each of them they hold to be both a genus and a species, taken in relation to the one extreme or the other. The genera prior to the most specific species, going up to the most general genus, are called both species and subordinate genera. For example, Agamemnon, from Atreus, from Pelops, from Tantalus, and in the end from Zeus. Now as for genealogies, they lead up to one thing—to Zeus, let us say—to the origin in most cases. But with genera and species this is not so. For being, as Aristotle says, [*Metaphysics* III. 3, 998^{b}22], is not one common genus of all things; neither are all things "homogeneous" in accordance with one highest genus.

(30) Instead let us posit the ten first genera as ten first principles, as in the *Categories*. If then one calls all things "beings," he will do so equivocally, Aristotle says, but not univocally. For if being were one genus common to all, all things would be called "beings" univocally. But since there are instead ten first genera, the community among them is in name only, not at all in a definition that goes with that name.

(31) Therefore, the most general genera are ten. The most specific species are of a certain number too, surely not infinite. But individuals, which come after the most specific species, are infinite. That is why Plato exhorts us

[*Philebus*, 16c–18d, *Politicus*, 262a–c] to stop after going down from the most general to the most specific, to go down through the intermediary levels and to divide by differences. He tells us to leave the infinite [individuals] alone. For there is no knowledge of them.

(32) So in going down to the most specific species we must proceed by division through a multitude. But in going up to the most general genera we must gather the multitude into one. For species (and genus even more) is a combination of many things into one nature. By contrast particulars and singulars always divide the one into a multitude. The many men are one by participation in the species, but the one common man, the species, is made several by its individuals. For the individual is always divisive, but what is common combines and unites.

(33) Now given what each of genus and species is, and given that whereas the genus is one the species are several (for the division of a genus is always into several species), the genus is always predicated of the species, and all the higher things are predicated of those beneath them. But the species is predicated neither of the genus immediately above it nor of higher ones. For it does not go both ways. Either equals must be predicated of equals, like hinnibility* of horses, or else greaters of lessers, like animal of man. But lessers are never predicated of greaters. For you must never say animal is a man, as you may say man is an animal.

(34) Whatever the species is predicated of, the genus of that species will of necessity be predicated of them too, and the genus of the genus, on up to the most general genus. For if it is true to say Socrates is a man, man an animal, animal a substance, then it is also true to say Socrates is an animal and a substance.

(35) Thus since the higher are always predicated of the lower, the species will be predicated of the individual, the genus both of the species and of the individual, and the most general genus both of the genus or genera—if there are several, intermediary subordinate genera—and also of the species and of the individual. For the most general genus is said of all the genera and species and individuals under it, while the genus prior to the most specific species is said of all the most specific species and of individuals, and what is only a species is said of all the individuals. But the individual is said of only one of the particulars.

(36) Socrates is called an individual, and so is this white thing and the one who is approaching, the son of Sophroniscus (if Socrates is his only son). Such things are called individuals because each of them consists of characteristics the collection of which can never be the same for anything else. For the characteristics of Socrates cannot be the same for any other particular.

But the characteristics of man—I mean, of man in general—are the same for several things, or rather for *all* particular men insofar as they are men.

(37) The individual then is included under the species and the species under the genus. For the genus is a kind of whole and the individual a part, while the species is both a whole and a part, although a part of one thing and the whole not *of* another thing but rather *in* other things. For the whole is in the parts.

(38) Therefore, we have discussed genus and species, what most general genus is, what most specific species are, which genera are the same as species, what individuals are, and in how many ways 'genus' and 'species' are said.

On difference

(39) 'Difference' is said broadly, properly, and most properly. In the broad sense one thing is said to "differ" from another when it is distinguished in any way by an otherness, either from itself or from something else. For Socrates is said to differ from Plato by an otherness. And he is said to differ from himself as a child and as a grown man, as doing something or as having stopped doing it. Indeed, he always differs from himself in such othernesses of disposition.

(40) In the proper sense one thing is said to "differ" from another when the one differs from the other by an inseparable accident. An inseparable accident is, for example, greenness of the eyes, hookedness of the nose, or a hardened scar from a wound.

(41) In the most proper sense one thing is said to "differ" from another when it is distinguished by a specific difference. For example, man is distinguished from horse by a specific difference: the quality rational.

(42) In general, every difference when added to something varies it. But differences in the broad and the proper senses only make it otherwise, whereas differences in the most proper sense make it other.[10] For some differences

---

10. Socrates as a child is "otherwise" than he is as a grown man, but he is "other" than a horse. In the former case numerical identity is preserved; in the latter it is not. But there is more involved. In virtue of the rest of (42), it is clear that by 'other' Porphyry here means *interspecific* differentiation, not *intraspecific* differentiation. The latter appears to have been overlooked in (42), although it was explicitly included in (39) as an example of "difference" in the broad sense. In (42), the contrast seems to be between specific difference ("other") on the one hand, and merely accidental differences that do not affect a thing's individuality ("otherwise") on the other. Numerical difference is not discussed.

make a thing otherwise, while others make it other. The ones that make it other are called "specific" differences, whereas those that make a thing otherwise are called just "differences." For when the difference "irrational" comes to animal, it makes it other. But the difference "being moved" makes a thing only otherwise than resting. Hence the former makes it other; the latter only makes it otherwise. It is in accordance with the differences that make a thing other that there arise the divisions of genera into species, and that definitions are given, since definitions are made up of a genus and such differences. But it is in accordance with differences that only make a thing otherwise that mere othernesses and changes of disposition arise.

(43) So beginning again from the top, we must say that among differences some are separable and others inseparable. Being moved and resting, being healthy and being ill, and any differences like these, are separable, whereas being green-eyed, or snub-nosed, or rational or irrational are inseparable.

(44) Among inseparable differences some belong by themselves, some by accident. Rational belongs by itself to man, and mortal and being capable of knowing do too. But being hook-nosed or snub-nosed belongs by accident and not by itself.

(45) Differences that belong by themselves are included in the definition of the substance and make the thing other, but those that belong by accident are not included in the definition of the substance. Neither do they make the thing other, but rather otherwise. Those that belong by themselves do not admit of more and less, but those that belong by accident, even if they are inseparable, acquire an intension and remission.* The genus is not predicated more and less of whatever it is a genus of, and neither are the differences of the genus, by which it is divided. For these differences are what complete the definition of each, and the being of each thing is one and does not admit of either a remission or an intension. But being hook-nosed or snub-nosed, or being colored in such and such a way, are intended and remitted.

(46) Thus we have seen three species of "difference." Some are (a) separable, while some are inseparable. Again of the inseparable ones some are (b) by themselves and others (c) by accident. Again among differences by themselves there are some in accordance with which we divide genera into species, and some in accordance with which the divided genera are "specified."[11] For instance, given that all the differences that belong to animal

---

11. *I. e.*, made into species. The distinction here is between "constitutive" and "divisive" differences. In the formula *species = genus + difference*, the difference is a "constitutive" difference of the species but a "divisive" difference of the genus. The most general genera have only "divisive" differences, while the most specific species have only "constitutive" differences. All other genera and species have both.

by themselves are: animate and sensate, rational and irrational, mortal and immortal, the difference "animate and sensate" is constitutive of the substance animal (for animal is animate, sensate substance), but the difference "mortal and immortal," and the difference "rational and irrational" are divisive differences of animal (for we divide genera into species by means of them).

(**47**) These divisive differences of the genera are completing and constituting differences of the species. For animal is partitioned both by the difference rational and irrational, and again by the difference mortal and immortal. The differences mortal and rational are constitutive of man, while the differences rational and immortal are constitutive of god,[12] and the differences irrational and mortal are constitutive of irrational animals. So too, since the difference animate and inanimate and the difference sensate and insensate are divisive of the highest substance, therefore the differences animate and sensate, taken together with substance, complete the genus animal, whereas the differences animate and insensate complete the genus plant. Thus while the same differences taken one way are constitutive and in another way are divisive, they are all called "specific" differences.

(**48**) The main usefulness of these inseparable differences that belong by themselves—but not of inseparable differences that belong by accident, and still less of separable differences—is for the divisions of genera and for definitions.

(**49**) They define differences by saying: Difference is that by which the species surpasses the genus. For man has more than animal: he also has rational and mortal. Animal is not *none* of these, since if it were, where would the species get their differences? But neither does animal have them all, since then the same thing will have opposites at the same time. Rather, as they think, it *potentially* has all the differences of things under it but none of them *actually*. In this way, neither does anything come from non-beings nor will opposites belong to the same thing at the same time.

(**50**) They also define it like this: Difference is what is predicated, with respect to what manner of thing each is, of several things differing in species. For rational and mortal, when predicated of man, are said with respect to what *manner* of thing man is, not with respect to *what* he is. If we are asked what man is, it is proper to say "an animal." But when we inquire what *manner* of animal, the proper reply we shall give is "a rational and mortal one."

(**51**) Just as things consist of matter and form, or have a structure analogous to matter and form—for instance a statue is made up of matter (the bronze)

---

12. Not God (with a capital 'G'). Porphyry was a pagan and a polytheist.

and form (the shape)—so too the specific man in common consists of an analogue of matter (the genus) and of form (the difference). The whole, rational-mortal-animal, is man—just as for the statue.

(52) They also describe such differences as follows: Difference is what naturally separates what are under the same genus. For rational and irrational divide man from horse, which are under the same genus animal.

(53) They describe them also like this: Difference is that by which each thing differs. For man and horse do not differ according to genus, for both we and the irrational animals are mortal animals. But when rational is added, it divides us from them. Both we and the gods are rational, but when mortal is added it divides us from them.

(54) In working through the facts about difference, they do not say difference is just anything that separates things under the same genus, but rather whichever of such factors contributes to the being of such a thing, and what is a part of what the thing was to be. The aptitude for sailing is not a difference of man even if it is a property of man. For we might say some animals have an aptitude for sailing whereas others do not, and we might separate the former from the others. But the aptitude for sailing does not contribute to completing the substance, and is not a part of that substance, but only a "fitness" of it for sailing, since it is not like what are properly called "specific" differences. Specific differences then are the ones that make another species and the ones taken up into what a thing was to be.

(55) So much then about difference.

On property

(56) They divide property in four ways: **(a)** What belongs accidentally **(i)** to one species only, even if not to all of it, as practicing medicine or doing geometry does to man. **(b)** What belongs accidentally **(ii)** to all of a species, even if not to it alone, as being a biped does to man. **(c)** What belongs **(ii)** to all of a species and **(i)** to it alone and at the same time, as growing grey-haired in old age does to man. **(d)** The fourth kind of property: that in which belonging **(i)** to only one species, **(ii)** to all of it, and **(iii)** always, all go together, as risibility does to man. For even if he is not always laughing he is nevertheless called "risible," not because he always is laughing but because he has an aptitude for laughing. This aptitude always belongs to him innately, as hinnibility does to a horse. They say that these are properties in the strict sense, because it goes both ways: If a horse then hinnibility, and if hinnibility then a horse.

On accident

(57) Accident is what comes and goes without the destruction of the substrate. It is divided into two kinds. One kind of accident is separable and the other is inseparable. Thus sleeping is a separable accident, whereas being black is an inseparable accident of the crow and the Ethiopian. Nevertheless a white crow and an Ethiopian who has lost his color can be conceived without the destruction of the substrate.

(58) They also define accident as follows: Accident is what admits of belonging or not belonging to the same thing, or what is neither a genus nor a difference nor a species nor a property, but always has its reality in a substrate.

(59) All the proposed terms have been defined—that is to say, genus, species, difference, property, and accident. We must now say what common features belong to them, and what are the properties of each.

On the community among the five words

(60) Being predicated of several things is common to all of them. But genus is predicated of species and of individuals, and so is difference, whereas species is predicated only of the individuals under it. Property is predicated of the species it is the property of, and of the individuals under the species. Accident is predicated of species and of individuals.

(61) For animal is predicated of horses and oxen, which are species, and of this horse and this ox, which are individuals. Irrational is predicated of horses and oxen, and of particulars. A species, such as man, is predicated of particulars only. A property, such as risibility, is predicated both of man and of particular men. Black, which is an inseparable accident, is predicated of the species of crows and of the particulars, whereas being moved, which is a separable accident, is predicated of man and of horse—primarily of the individuals, and in a secondary sense of the species that include the individuals.

On the community between genus and difference

(62) Including species is common to genus and difference. For the difference also includes species, even if not all that genera do. Rational, even though it does not include irrational things as animal does, nevertheless includes man and god, which are species.

(63) Whatever is predicated of a genus as genus is also predicated of the species under that genus, while whatever is predicated of a difference as difference will also be predicated of the species arising from that difference. For substance and animate are predicated of the genus animal as a genus, but they are also predicated of all the species under animal, down even to individuals. And since rational is a difference, being possessed of reason is predicated of rational as a difference. But being possessed of reason will be predicated not only of rational but also of the species under rational.

(64) It is also a common feature that when either the genus or the difference is destroyed, the things under it are destroyed too. For just as if there is no animal there is no horse or man, so too if rational does not exist there will be no animal possessed of reason.

On the difference between genus and difference

(65) It is a property of genus to be predicated of more things than difference, species, property and accident are. For animal is predicated of man, horse, bird, and snake, but quadruped is predicated only of those animals that have four feet, while man is predicated only of individuals, hinnibility only of horse and of particular horses, and accident likewise is predicated of fewer things than animal is. One must here take difference in the sense of the ones by which the genus is partitioned, not the ones that complete the substance of the genus. Again, the genus includes the difference potentially; for animal: rational and irrational.

(66) Again, genera are prior to the differences under them, because the former destroy the latter along with themselves, but are not destroyed along with the latter. For if animal is destroyed, rational and irrational are destroyed along with it. But differences never destroy the genus along with themselves. For even if all its differences were destroyed, animate sensate substance is still conceived, and that was the genus.

(67) Again, genus is predicated with respect to what the thing is, whereas difference is predicated with respect to what manner of thing it is, as has been said [(12)].

(68) Again, for each species there is one genus, like animal for man. But there are several differences, like rational, mortal, receptive of intellect, and knowledge, which divide [man] from the other animals.

(69) Also genus is like matter while difference is like form.

(70) Although there are still other common features and properties of genus and species, let these suffice.

On the community between genus and species

(71) Genus and species, as has been said [(60)], have in common being predicated of several things. (Let us here take species as species only, not also as genus, if the same thing should be both species and genus.) It is also common to them to be prior to what they are predicated of, and for each of them to be a certain "whole."

On the difference between genus and species

(72) They differ in that the genus contains the species, while the species are contained by and do not contain the genera. For the genus covers more than the species does.

(73) Again, genera must be posited in advance and, when informed by specific differences, complete the species. Hence genera are prior by nature. Also, they destroy the species along with themselves, but are not destroyed along with the species. If there is a species there is certainly the genus, but if there is a genus it by no means follows that there is the species.

(74) Genera are also predicated univocally of the species under them, but species are never predicated of the genera.

(75) Again, genera surpass species by including the species under themselves, while species by their differences surpass genera.

(76) Again, neither could a species become a most general genus nor could a genus become a most specific species.

On the community between genus and property

(77) It is a common feature of genus and property that they follow from species. For if man then animal, and if man then risible.

(78) Also, the genus is predicated equally of its species, and the property is predicated equally of the individuals that share in it. For man and ox are equally animal, and Anytus and Meletus are equally risible.

(79) It is also a common feature to be predicated univocally, genus of its species, and property of the things it is a property of.

On the difference between genus and property

(80) They differ because genus is prior, while property is posterior. For animal must first be, and only then be divided by its differences and properties.

(81) Genus is predicated of several species, but property only of the one species it is a property of.

(82) Property is predicated reciprocally of the species it is the property of, but genus is not predicated reciprocally of anything. For it does not follow: If animal then man, or if animal then risible. But if man then risible, and conversely.

(83) Again, a property belongs to the whole species it is a property of, and only and always to that. But a genus, while it belongs to the whole species it is a genus of, and always so belongs, nevertheless does not also belong *only* to that.

(84) Again, when properties are destroyed they do not destroy the genera along with them, whereas when genera are destroyed the species the properties belong to are destroyed along with the genera, with the result that when the species the properties belong to are destroyed, the properties themselves are destroyed along with them.

On the community between genus and accident

(85) It is a common feature of genus and accident, whether separable or inseparable, to be predicated of several things, as has been said [(60)]. For being moved is predicated of several things, and black is predicated of crows, Ethiopians, and some inanimate things.

On the difference between genus and accident

(86) Genus differs from accident because genus is prior to the species, whereas accidents are posterior to the species. For even if we take an inseparable accident, nevertheless what it is accidental to is prior to the accident itself.

(87) Also, the participants in a genus participate equally, while participants in an accident do not participate equally. For participation in accidents admits of intension and remission, while participation in genera never does.

(88) Accidents have their reality primarily in individuals, but genera and species are by nature prior to individual substances.

(89) Genera are also predicated of the things under them with respect to what the thing is, while accidents are predicated with respect to what manner of thing each is, or how it is disposed. For when asked "What manner of thing is the Ethiopian?" you will say "Black." And when asked "How is Socrates disposed?" you will say he is sitting or walking.

(90) We have said how genus differs from the other four. But it happens

that each of the others also differs from the other four. Thus since there are five, each one of which differs from the other four, four times five, [it would seem that] all the differences add up to twenty.

(91) But this is not so. Rather, since when things are counted in sequence, those in the second place have one difference less, because one difference has already been counted, while those in third place have two differences less, those in fourth place three, those in fifth place four, therefore all the differences add up to ten: four plus three plus two plus one. For genus differs from difference and species and property and accident; the differences therefore are four. Now it was already said how difference differs from genus, when it was said how genus differs from it [(65)–(69)]. But it remains to be said how it differs from species and property and accident; they add up to three. Again it has already been said[13] how species differs from difference, when it has been said how difference differs from species. And it was already said how species differs from genus, when it was said how genus differs from species [(72)–(76)]. Thus it remains to be said how it differs from property and accident; and these differences therefore are two. How property differs from accident is still to be counted. For it has already been said[14] how it differs from species and difference and genus, in the explanation of their difference with respect to it.

(92) Therefore, taking the four differences of genus with respect to the others, the three of difference, the two of species, and the one of property with respect to accident, all of them together will be ten, of which we have already explained four, the ones that are the differences of genus with respect to the others.

On the community between difference and species

(93) It is common to difference and species to be participated equally. For particular men participate equally both in man and in the difference rational. It is also common to them to be always present in what participate in them. For Socrates is always rational and Socrates is always a man.

On the difference between species and difference

(94) It is a property of difference to be predicated with respect to what manner of thing its subject is, while species is predicated with respect to

13. That is, it *will* have already been said. See (94)–(97).
14. Again, it *will* already have been said in the case of species (109)–(112) and difference (100)–(101). For genus, see (80)–(84).

what the thing is. For even if man should be taken [sometimes] as a manner of thing, it is not absolutely a manner of thing, but only insofar as differences added to the genus give man its reality.[15]

(95) Again, the difference is often observed in several species, as having four feet is observed in a great many animals differing in species. But species is only in the individuals under that species.

(96) Again, difference is prior to the species made in accordance with it. For when rational is destroyed it destroys man along with it. But when man is destroyed it does not destroy rational, since there is still god.

(97) Again, difference is put together with another difference. For rational and mortal are put together to make man a reality. But species is not put together with species so that another species results. For a certain horse breeds with a certain ass and generates a mule. But horse simply joined to ass would never yield mule.

On the community between difference and property

(98) Difference and property have as a common feature being participated equally by their participants. For rational things are all equally rational, and risible things risible.

(99) Also, being present always and in the whole species is common to them both. For even if a biped is maimed, nevertheless 'always' is said with respect to its being naturally apt [to have two feet], as [man] also has "being always risible" because of a natural aptitude, not because he is always laughing.

On the difference between property and difference

(100) It is a property of difference that it frequently is said of several species, as rational is said both of god and of man. But property is said only of the one species it is a property of.

(101) Also, difference follows from the things it is a difference of, but it does not go both ways. Properties however are predicated reciprocally of the things they are properties of, because it does go both ways in that case.

15. The term 'man' expresses *what* Socrates is. But it may in a sense also be said to express what *manner* of animal we are talking about: a rational and mortal one. From the point of view of the genus the species expresses what manner of thing is involved, but from the point of view of the individual it expresses *what* the thing is.

On the community between difference and accident

(102) It is common to difference and accident to be said of several things, while it is common to difference in relation to inseparable accidents to be present always and in the whole species. For biped is always present in all crows, and black likewise.

On the properties of difference and accident

(103) They differ in that the difference includes but is not included. For rational includes man. Accidents however in one way include because they are in several things, but in another way they are included because the substrates admit not just of one accident but of several.

(104) Also, difference is not increased or decreased, whereas accidents do admit of more and less.

(105) Also, opposite differences are not mixed with one another, but opposite accidents can mix together.

(106) Such then are the common features and the peculiarities of difference with respect to the others.

(107) How species differs from genus and difference was explained in what we said about how genus differs from the others [(72)–(76)] and about how difference differs from the others [(94)–(97)].

On the community between species and property

(108) It is common to species and property to be predicated reciprocally of one another. For if man then risible, and if risible then man. It has often been said already that risible is to be taken from the natural aptitude to laugh [(56), (99)]. For species are equally in their participants, and properties are equally in the things they are properties of.

On the difference between species and property

(109) Species differs from property because a species can be the genus of other things, but a property cannot be a property of other things.

(110) Also, species has its reality prior to property, while property follows after species. For man must exist in order to be risible.

(111) Again, species is always actually present in the substrate, but property is sometimes present only potentially. For Socrates is always actually a man, but he is not always laughing, even if he is always naturally apt to be risible.

(112) Again, what have different definitions are themselves different. Now the definition of species is: being under the genus and being predicated, with respect to what the thing is, of several things differing in number, and whatever other such definitions there are. But the definition of property is to be present always and only in the species and in the whole of it.

On the community between species and accident

(113) It is common to species and accident to be predicated of several things. But there are few other common features, because accident and what it is accidental to are distinguished from one another in the highest degree.

On the difference between them

(114) The properties of each are: of species, to be predicated, with respect to what the thing is, of what it is a species of; of accident, to be predicated with respect to what manner of thing the subject is, or how it is disposed.

(115) Also, each substance participates in one species but in several accidents, both separable and inseparable.

(116) Also, species are conceived before accidents are, even if they are inseparable ones. (For the substrate has to exist in order for anything to be accidental to it.) But accidents naturally arise later and have an adventitious nature.

(117) Also, participation in the species is equal, but participation in an accident is not equal even if it is an inseparable accident. For one Ethiopian might have a color either remitted or intended with respect to blackness more than another Ethiopian does.

(118) It remains now to speak about property and accident. For it has already been explained how property differed from species [(109)–(112)], difference [(100)–(101)], and genus [(80)–(84)].

On the community between property and inseparable accident

(119) It is common to property and to inseparable accident that without them what they are observed in have no reality. For just as man has no reality without risible, so the Ethiopian would have no reality without black.

(120) Also, just as property is present in the whole species and always, so too is inseparable accident.

On the difference between them

(121) But they differ because property is present in only one species, like risible in man, while inseparable accident, for instance black, is present not only in the Ethiopian but also in crow and coal and ebony and certain other things. Therefore, property is predicated reciprocally of what it is a property of and is equally a property of all its participants, whereas inseparable accident is not predicated reciprocally.

(122) Also, participation in properties is equal, but one participation in accidents is more and another is less.

(123) There are other common features too, as well as peculiarities, of the things discussed above, but these are enough for distinguishing among them and for displaying the common features.

Boethius

From His Second Commentary on Porphyry's *Isagoge*

[Porphyry's Text[1]]

(1) "As for genera and species," he says, "I shall decline for the present to say **(a)** whether they subsist or are posited in bare understandings only, **(b)** whether, if they subsist, they are corporeal or incorporeal, and **(c)** whether they are separated from sensibles or posited in sensibles and agree with them. For that is a most exalted matter, and requires a longer investigation."

[Commentary]

(2) I omit the more exalted questions, he says, in order not to disturb the beginnings and first fruits of the reader whose mind takes these matters in at the wrong time. But in order not to make the reader overlook them altogether, so that he would think there is nothing more hidden here than what Porphyry himself had said, he adds a mention of the very matter about which he promises to delay pursuing the question. He does this in order not to swamp the reader in any way by treating these matters in an obscure and exhaustive fashion, and yet so that the reader, strengthened by knowledge, might understand what it is that could rightly be asked about.

(3) The questions he promises to say nothing about are both very useful and also mysterious. They have been attempted by learned men, but have not been solved by many of them. The first of them is as follows:

(4) For everything the mind understands, it either intellectually conceives what exists constituted in the nature of things, and describes it to itself by reason, or else the mind paints for itself by empty imagination what does not exist. Therefore, the question is: To which kind does the understanding of genus and the other predicables belong? Do we understand species and genera as we do things that exist, from which we take true understanding?

1. Compare **P** (2).

Or do we delude ourselves when we form for ourselves, by the vain thought of the mind, things that do not exist?

(5) If it is settled that they do exist, and if we say the understanding of them is conceived from things that do exist, then another, greater and more difficult question raises a doubt, since there appears to be the greatest difficulty in discerning and understanding the nature of genus itself. Because everything that exists is necessarily either corporeal or incorporeal, genus and species will have to be in one of these groups. Therefore, to which kind does what is called genus belong? Is it corporeal or rather incorporeal? The question what it is cannot be carefully considered unless it is known which of these groups it should be placed in.

(6) But not even when this question has been resolved will every doubt be eliminated. For there is still something that, if genus and species are said to be incorporeal, blocks and holds back the intelligence and insists on being solved: Do they subsist in connection with bodies, or do they appear to be incorporeal subsistences over and above bodies?

(7) For there are in fact two kinds of forms of incorporeals. Some can exist apart from bodies, and endure in their incorporeality separated from bodies. For instance, God, the mind, and the soul. But others, even though they are incorporeal, nevertheless cannot exist apart from bodies. For instance, the line or the surface, or number or single qualities—which, although we declare them to be incorporeal since they are not spread out in three dimensions at all, nevertheless so exist in bodies that they cannot be torn away or separated from them, or else if they *are* separated from bodies, do not persist at all.

(8) It is hard for Porphyry himself to resolve these questions. For the time being, he declines the task. Nevertheless I shall undertake it in such a way that I not leave the reader's mind troubled about them, and so that I myself do not devote time and labor to matters outside the order of the job I have taken on.

(9) First then, I shall set out a few points regarding the dilemma raised by the question. After that, I shall try to untie that same knot of doubt, and to explain it.

[The problem]

(10) Genera and species either exist and subsist or are formed by the understanding and by thought alone.

[The argument against universals]

(11) But genera and species cannot exist. This is understood on the following grounds. Everything that is common to several things at one time cannot

be one. What is common is "of many," especially when one and the same thing is *as a whole* in many things at one time. For no matter how many species there are, their genus is one in all of them. Not in such a way that each single species snatches so to speak some part of it. Rather all the single species have the whole genus at one time. This is why the whole genus cannot be posited as one in several singulars at one time. For it cannot happen that although it is a whole in several things at one time, nevertheless in itself it is one in number.

(12) But if this is so, then a genus cannot be one. Hence it is nothing at all. For everything that exists exists for the reason that it is one. The same can be said about species.

(13) But even if genus and species do exist, but are multiple and not one in number, there will be no last genus. It will have another genus placed above it, including that multiplicity in the word expressing its one name. For just as several animals have a certain similar something, yet are not the same, and for that reason their genera are sought out, so too a genus that is in several things, and is therefore multiple, has a likeness of what is a genus. But this likeness is not one [in number], because it is in several things. For that reason, another genus *of* that genus is also to be searched for. And when that has been found, then for the same reason as was said above, once more a third genus is tracked down. And the argument necessarily goes on to infinity, since this procedure has no end.

(14) Now if a genus is one in number, it cannot be common to many. For one thing, if it is common, is either:

(15) Common by parts. In that case *the whole* is not common. Instead its *parts* belong to single things. Or:

(16) Over time, it passes into the use of those who have it, so that it is common like a slave or a horse. Or:

(17) It is common at one time to all, yet not so that it constitutes the substance of what it is common to. For example, a stage-play, or some spectacle, which is common to all the spectators.

(18) But genus can be common to its species in none of these ways. For it is supposed to be common in such a way that both the whole of it is in all its singulars, and at one time, and also it is able to constitute and form the substance of what it is common to.

(19) Therefore, if it is neither one because it is common, nor many because another genus too is to be sought for that multitude, it will be seen that genus does not exist at all. And the same is to be understood for the other predicables.

[The argument for universals]

(20) Suppose genera and species and the rest are grasped only by under-standings. Then since every understanding arises from a subject thing either as that thing is disposed or as the thing is not disposed (for no understanding can arise from *no* subject), therefore suppose the understanding of genus and species and the rest comes from the subject thing in such a way as the thing understood *is* disposed. In that case, they are not posited in the understanding alone, but are also there in true reality. And once again it must be asked what their nature is. The question above tracked this down.

(21) On the other hand, if the understanding of genus and the rest is taken from the thing, but *not* in such a way as the thing subjected to the understanding is disposed, then that understanding must be empty. It is taken from a thing, granted, but not as the thing is disposed. For what is understood otherwise than the thing is is false.

(22) So therefore, because genus and species do not exist, and the under-standing of them when they are understood is not true, there is no doubt but that all this careful arguing over the five predicables is to be discarded. It is not inquiring about a thing that exists, or about a thing about which something true can be understood or stated.

[The solution]

(23) For the present, this is the question about the matters at hand. We shall solve it, agreeing with Alexander [of Aphrodisias], by reasoning like this:

(24) We do not say it is necessary for every understanding that arises from a subject, but not as that subject itself is disposed, to be seen as false and empty. False opinion rather than intelligence occurs only in those cases that arise from composition. If one puts and joins together by the understanding what nature does not allow to be joined, no one fails to realize that that is false. For example, if someone joins a horse and a man in imagination, and portrays a centaur.

(25) But if this understanding arises from division and from abstraction, then the thing is not disposed the way it is understood, and yet that under-standing is not false at all.

(26) For there are several kinds of things that have their being in others, from which they either cannot be separated at all or, if they are separated, there is no way they can subsist. To make this clear by a widely known

example, a line is something in a body. And what it is it owes to the body. That is, it keeps its being through the body. This is explained as follows. If it is separated from the body, it does not subsist. Who by any sense faculty ever grasped a line separated from a body? But the mind, when it grasps in itself confused and mixed up things from the senses, distinguishes them by its own power and thought.

(27) The sense faculty delivers to us, together with the bodies themselves, all incorporeal things like this that have their being in bodies. But the mind, which has the power both to put together what is disjoined and to uncouple what is put together, distinguishes what are delivered to it by the senses, confused and conjoined to bodies, in such a way that it gazes on and sees the incorporeal nature by itself and apart from the bodies in which it is made concrete. For there are distinctive peculiarities of incorporeals mixed with bodies, even if they are separated from bodies.

(28) Therefore, genera and species and the rest are found either in incorporeal things or else in what are corporeal. If the mind finds them in incorporeal things, it at once has an incorporeal understanding of the genus. But if it observes the genera and species of corporeal things, then as is its habit, it removes the nature of those incorporeals from the bodies, and looks upon it, alone and pure, as it is a form in itself. In this way, when the mind takes on these things all mixed up with bodies, it divides out the incorporeals and gazes on them and considers them.

(29) Therefore, no one should say we are thinking falsely about the line because we grasp it by the mind, as if it were beyond bodies, even though it cannot exist beyond bodies. For not every understanding is to be regarded as false that is grasped from subject things otherwise than as they themselves are disposed. Rather, as was said above [(24)], the one that does this by putting things together is false, as when someone joins a man and a horse and thinks a centaur exists. But the understanding that does this by divisions and abstractions and taking things away from the things they exist in, not only is not false, but is alone able to find out what is properly true.

(30) Therefore, things like this exist in corporeals and sensibles, but they are understood apart from sensibles, so that their nature can be gazed on and their distinguishing peculiarity comprehended. For this reason, when genera and species are thought, their likeness is gathered from the single things they exist in. For example, from single men, dissimilar among themselves, the likeness of humanity is gathered. This likeness, thought by the mind and gazed at truly, is the species. Again, the likeness of these diverse species, which likeness cannot exist except in these species or in their individuals, makes a genus when it is considered.

(31) And so these things exist in singulars, but are thought of as universals. Species is to be regarded as nothing else than the thought gathered from the substantial likeness of individuals that are unlike in number. Genus, on the other hand, is the thought gathered from the likeness of species. This likeness becomes sensible when it exists in singulars, and becomes intelligible when it is in universals. In the same way, when it is sensible it stays in singulars, but when it is understood it becomes universal. They subsist therefore in the realm of sensibles, but are understood apart from bodies.

(32) For it is not ruled out that two things that are conceptually diverse should be in the same subject, like a convex line and a concave one. Since these things are bounded by diverse definitions, the understanding of them is diverse. Yet they are always found in the same subject. For the same line is concave as is convex. So too, for genera and species—that is, for singularity and universality—there is one subject. But it is universal in one way, when it is thought, and singular in another, when it is sensed in the things in which it has its being.

(33) Now that these matters are finished, every question is answered, I think.

(34) [**Reply to (1a):**] For genera and species subsist in one way, but are understood in another.

(35) [**Reply to (1b):**] They are incorporeal, but subsist in sensibles, joined to sensibles. They are understood, however, as subsisting by themselves, and as not having their being in others.

(36) [**Reply to (1c):**] But Plato thinks genera and species and the rest are not only understood as universals, but also exist and subsist apart from bodies. Aristotle, however, thinks they are understood as incorporeal and universal, but subsist in sensibles.

(37) I did not regard it as appropriate to decide between their views. For that belongs to a higher philosophy. But we have carefully followed out Aristotle's view here, not because we would recommend it the most, but because this book, [the *Isagoge*], is written about the *Categories*, of which Aristotle is the author.

Peter Abelard

From the "Glosses on Porphyry" in His *Logica 'ingredientibus'*

(1) "For the present about genera" [**P** (2), **B** (1)]. He settles what those higher questions are, although he does not solve them. And the cause is given for both facts: the fact that he passes over inquiring into them, and the fact that nevertheless he does make mention of them.

(2) He does not discuss them, because the unskilled reader will not be strong enough to inquire into them and grasp them. But he does mention them in order not to make the reader overlook them. For if he had kept silent about them altogether the reader, thinking there was absolutely nothing more to be asked about them, would entirely disregard their investigation.

(3) There are three questions, as Boethius says [**B** (3)] "mysterious" and "very useful" ones, attempted by not a few philosophers, but solved by few of them.

(4) The first is this: "Do genera and species subsist, or are they posited only in," etc.? As if he said: "Do they have true being, or do they reside in opinion only?"

(5) The second is: "If it is granted that they truly are, are they corporeal essences or incorporeal?"

(6) The third: "Are they separated from sensibles or posited in sensibles?" For there are two species of incorporeals. Some of them, such as God and the soul, can endure in their incorporeality outside sensibles. But others, such as a line without any subject body, are entirely unable to be outside the sensibles they are in.

(7) He passes over these questions, saying "As for genera and species, I shall decline for the present to say (a) whether they subsist," etc., "or (b) whether, if they subsist, they are corporeal or incorporeal, and whether (c)," when they are called "incorporeal," they are separated "from sensibles," etc., [or posited in sensibles] "and agree with them" [**P** (2), **B** (1)].

(8) This can be taken in different senses. For we can take it as if it says: "About genera and species I shall decline to say what the answers are to the three questions given above, and about certain other questions that agree with them"—that is, with these three questions.

(9) For other, similarly difficult questions too can be raised about these same genera and species. For instance, the question about the common cause of the imposition* of universal names. That question is: "Diverse things agree according to *what*?" Or also the question about the *understanding* of universal names, by which understanding no *thing* appears to be conceived. Neither does it appear that any *thing* is dealt with by a universal word. There are many other difficult questions as well.

(10) Again [see (8)], we can analyze the words 'and agree with them' in such a way that we add a fourth question: Do genera and species, as long as they are genera and species, necessarily have some thing subject to them by nomination?* Or alternatively, even if the things named are destroyed, can the universal consist even then of the understanding's signification alone? For example, the name 'rose' when there are no roses to which it is common.

(11) We shall argue these questions more thoroughly below. But first let us follow the letter of Porphyry's *Prologue*. Note that when he says "for the present"—that is, in the present treatise—he hints in a way that the reader may expect these questions to be answered elsewhere.

(12) "For that is a most exalted matter" [P (2), B (1)]. He sets out the cause why he refrains from these questions here: namely, because treating of them is "a most exalted matter" for the reader who cannot reach that far. He immediately establishes [that this is his meaning, when he says] "and requires a longer investigation." For although the author is able to solve them, the reader is not able to inquire about these questions. ["It requires,"] I say, "a longer investigation" than yours, [the reader's], is.

(13) "Rather what" [P (2)]. After showing us what he is *not* going to talk about, he tells us what he does set out [in the remainder of the *Isagoge*]: what "the ancients"—not in age but in judgment[1]—"discussed about these matters"—namely, genera and species—"and about the" other three questions just "proposed, in a probable way"—that is, with likelihood. That is to say, the points on which everyone concurred and about which there was no disagreement. For in answering the questions above, some people thought one way and others another. Thus Boethius [B (36)] mentions that Aristotle said genera and species subsist only in sensibles but are understood outside sensibles, while Plato said they not only are understood outside sensibles but also exist there. "And of these ancients," I say, and "the Peripatetics most

---

1. This might mean either: (a) those who are not necessarily old in years, but who nevertheless have a mature judgment; or (b) the "ancients," not necessarily those who actually lived in ancient times, but *anyone* who shares their views (= judgments).

of all," that is to say, one party among these ancients. (He is calling "Peripatet-ics" the dialecticians—that is, all those who argue.)

(14) Note too that the features appropriate to prologues can be found in this one. For Boethius, in his *Commentary on Cicero's Topics* [22], says: "Every prologue intended to prepare the listener, as is said in rhetorical writings, either tries to win his *good will*, or prepares his *attention*, or produces in him an *aptitude for being taught*." It is appropriate for one of these three, or several of them together, to be in every prologue. Two of them can be noted in this one: first, the *aptitude for being taught*, where he gives a foretaste of his subject matter, which is the five predicables; and second, *attention*, where he recommends his treatise about what the ancients established for teaching these five predicables [**P** (1)], on the grounds of its fourfold utility.[2] Alterna-tively, *attention* can be found where he promises to proceed in an introductory manner. There is no need for *good will* here, where there is no knowledge that will be found hateful to whoever needs Porphyry's treatment of it.[3]

(15) But now, as we promised, let us return to the questions posed above and carefully examine and answer them. Because it is plain that genera and species are universals, and that in the discussion of them Porphyry touches on the nature of all universals in general, let us here distinguish the characteristics of all universals together from the characteristics of singulars, and let us exam-ine whether these characteristics belong only to words or also to things.

(16) Aristotle defines the universal in *On Interpretation* [7, 17^{a}39–40] as "what is naturally apt to be predicated of several." But Porphyry defines the singular—that is, the individual—as "what is predicated of one only" [**P** (8)].

(17) Authority seems to attribute this both to things and to words. Aristotle himself attributes it to things, where just before the definition of a universal [(16)], he states [*On Interpretation* 7, 17^{a}38–40]: "Now because, among *things*, some are universals and others singulars—now I call 'universal' what is natu-rally apt to be predicated of several, but I call 'singular' what is not," etc.

(18) Porphyry too, when he says a species is made up of genus and difference,[4] ascribes these to the nature of *things*.

2. **P** (1) says the *Isagoge* is needed (a) in order to teach about Aristotle's *Categories*, and is also useful for (b) giving definitions, and for matters pertaining to (c) division and to (d) demonstration.

3. The sentence is convoluted, but the point is clear. This isn't a court of law. The reader's good will can be *assumed*, or else he wouldn't be reading the *Isagoge* in the first place.

4. The edition of Abelard cites Boethius's translation of **P** (47). But while this passage seems to fit Abelard's description of the location, it does not explicitly say what Abelard says it does.

(19) From these passages it is plain that *things* themselves are contained under the name 'universal'.

(20) But *names* are also called "universals." Thus Aristotle says [*Categories* 5, 3ᵇ19–21], "Genus determines a quality with respect to a substance. For it *signifies* what kind of a thing the substance is." And Boethius in his book *On Division* [885C] says "It is very useful to know that a genus is in a way one likeness of many species, a likeness that shows the substantial agreement of all of them." Now "signifying" or "showing" belongs to words, but "being signified" belongs to things.

(21) And again he says [*ibid.*, 886B], "The word 'name' is predicated of several names and in a way is a species containing individuals under it." It is not *properly* called a species, since it is not a substantial but an accidental word. But there is no doubt it *is* a universal, and the definition of a universal [(16)] fits it. On the basis of this passage, it is proven that words too are universals. To them alone is the task of being the predicate terms of propositions ascribed.

(22) Since both things and words seem to be called universals, it must be asked how the definition of a universal can be adapted to things. For no thing or collection of things seems to be predicated of several singly, which the characteristic feature of a universal demands. For even though this people, or this house, or Socrates, is said of all its parts together, yet no one ever calls them universals, since their predication does not reach to singulars.[5] Now *one* thing is predicated of several much less than a collection is. So let us hear how they call either one thing or a collection a "universal," and let us set out all the views of everyone.

[First theory]

(23) Some people take "universal thing" in such a way that they set up *essentially the same* substance in things diverse from one another through forms. This substance is the "material essence" of the singulars it is in. It is one in itself, and diverse only through the forms of its inferiors.* If these forms happened to be separated from it, there would be no difference at all among the things that are in fact distinct from one another only by the diversity of forms. For the matter is entirely the same essentially.

(24) For example in single, numerically distinct men there is the same

---

5. Let the parts of a house be the roof, the walls, and the floor. Then the house can in a sense be predicated of all its parts together (we can truly say "The roof and the walls and the floor *are* the house"). But it cannot be predicated of them singly (we cannot truly say "The roof is the house").

substance *man*, which becomes Plato here through these accidents and Socrates there through those accidents.

(25) Porphyry seems to agree completely with these people when he says [**P (32)**], "Several men are one by participation in the species, but the one and common man is made several in its particulars." And again, he says [**P (36)**], "Such things are called individuals because each of them consists of characteristics the collection of which is not found in anything else."

(26) Likewise, they also posit one and essentially the same substance *animal* in single animals that differ in species. They draw this substance into diverse species by taking on diverse differences. For example, if out of this wax I make on the one hand a statue of a man and on the other a statue of an ox, by adapting diverse forms to entirely the same essence that remains the same throughout.

(27) But it makes a difference in the example that the same wax does not make up the two statues at the same time, as is allowed in the case of a universal—that is, the universal is common, Boethius says [**B (18)**], in such a way that the same whole is *at the same time* in diverse things, of which it constitutes the substance materially. Although *in itself* it is universal, the same whole is singular through *advening forms*. By nature it subsists in itself, without those advening forms, but in no way does it actually persist without them. It is universal in its nature, but singular in actuality. It is understood in the simplicity of its universality as incorporeal and nonsensible, but the same whole subsists in actuality through its accidents as corporeal and sensible. As Boethius testifies [**B (31)**], the same things subsist as singulars and are understood as universals.

[Objections to the first theory]

(28) This is one of two views. Although most authorities appear to agree with it, the philosophy of nature contradicts it in all respects.

(29) [**Objection 1:**] For if essentially the same thing exists in several singulars, then even though diverse forms occupy it, this substance brought about by these forms must be [identical with] that one occupied by those forms. For example the *animal* formed by *rationality* is the *animal* formed by *irrationality*. Thus, *rational animal* is *irrational animal*. And so contraries reside together in the same thing. In fact, they are not contraries any more at all when they coincide in entirely the same essence at once. For example, whiteness and blackness would not be contraries if they happened to occur together in this one thing, even though the thing would be white from one source and black from another, in the same way it is white from one source and hard from another—namely, from whiteness and hardness. For diverse contraries cannot inhere in the same thing at once, even in theory, as relatives and lots of other things can. Thus Aristotle, in the chapter on *Relation*,[6] shows that *great* and *small* inhere together in diverse respects in the same thing. Nevertheless he proves that they are not contraries, just *because* they are together in the same thing.

(30) [**Reply 1:**] But perhaps it will be said, according to this theory, that rationality and irrationality are no less contraries because they are found in this way in the same thing—that is, in the same *genus* or in the same *species*—unless they are based in the same *individual*.

(31) [**Refutation of reply 1:** But that they *are* based in the same individual] is shown as follows: Rationality and irrationality are truly in the same individual, because they are in Socrates. Now the fact that they are together in Socrates is proved on the grounds that they are together in Socrates and Browny.[7] But Socrates and Browny are [identical with] Socrates. Socrates and Browny really *are* Socrates, because Socrates is Socrates and Browny[8]—that is, because Socrates is Socrates and Socrates is Browny. That Socrates really *is* Browny is shown as follows, following this view:

(32) Whatever is in Socrates other than the advening[9] forms of Socrates is what is in Browny other than the advening forms of Browny.[10] But whatever is in Browny other than the advening forms of Browny just *is* Browny.[11] Thus, whatever is in Socrates other than the advening forms of Socrates is Browny. But if that is so, then since Socrates himself is what is other than the advening forms of Socrates,[12] Socrates himself is Browny.

(33) The fact that what we assumed above is true, namely that whatever is in Browny other than the advening forms of Browny just *is* Browny, is

6. The reference is to the *Categories*, but the passage is not in the chapter on relation (Ch. 7), as Abelard says, but instead in the chapter on quantity, Ch. 6, 5^b33-6^a9.

7. *Burnellus* or *Brunellus* (= "Browny") is the name of an ass, the paradigm of an irrational animal. The example is a favorite one in Abelard.

8. The point of this step of the argument is merely to perform a simple conversion: If x is y and z, then y and z are x. The real work of the argument is still to come.

9. Throughout this and the next paragraph, I have interpreted Abelard's "forms" as the "advening" forms of (27). I do not think the interpretation is controversial, but the reader should be notified.

10. That is, *animality* is in both of them.

11. On this step, see (33).

12. Presumably this is so for the same reason that whatever is in Browny other than the advening forms of Browny just *is* Browny. Again, see (33).

plain because **(a)** the *forms* of Browny are not Browny, since in that case accidents would be substance, and **(b)** neither are the matter and the forms of Browny together Browny, since in that case one would have to grant that body and something *already* a body are body.[13]

(34) [**Reply 2:**] Some people, looking for a way out of this problem, criticize only the words of the proposition '*Rational animal* is *irrational animal*', not the judgment. They say [*animal*] is indeed both but this fact is not properly shown by the words '*Rational animal* is *irrational animal*'. For the thing [*animal*], although it is the same, is called "rational" on one basis and "irrational" on another—that is, from opposite forms.

(35) [**Refutation of reply 2:**] But surely forms attached to the same thing[14] at exactly the same time no longer stand in opposition to one another.[15]

(36) Furthermore, they do not criticize *these* propositions: 'A rational animal is a mortal animal' or 'A white animal is a walking animal',[16] on the grounds that the animal is not mortal *insofar as* it is rational and does not walk *insofar as* it is white. Rather they maintain these propositions as entirely true because *the same* animal has both features at once, even though the reason is different in each case. Otherwise they would not admit that any animal is a man, since nothing is a man *insofar as* it is an animal.

(37) [**Objection 2:**] Furthermore in accordance with what the above theory holds, there are only ten essences for all things: the ten most general genera. For in each of the categories there is found only one essence, which is made diverse (as was said [**(23)**]) only through the forms of its inferiors and would have no variety at all without them. Therefore, just as all substances are basically the same, so too for qualities and quantities, etc. Since therefore Socrates and Plato have in themselves things from each of the categories, but these things are basically the same, it follows that all the forms

13. There is a textual problem in this sentence, the crucial sentence of the argument. I have followed the reading in King, Ch. 6, § 4. The argument in **(31)**–**(33)** is a notoriously obscure one and subject to many interpretations. For a very sensible discussion, see King, Ch. 6.

14. Conjecturing '*eidem*' for the edition's '*eis*'.

15. Thus the problem has not been avoided. Either there cannot simultaneously be rational animals and irrational animals, or else rationality and irrationality are not contraries. Neither alternative is acceptable.

16. Latin's lack of an indefinite article makes it sometimes hard to decide whether it is better to translate with or without one. Here it seems smoother to include it. But the reader should understand that the Latin syntax here is exactly the same as in '*Rational animal* is *irrational animal*' in **(34)**.

of the one are also forms of the other. The forms in themselves are not in essence diverse from one another, and neither are the substances they are attached to. For example, the quality of the one and the quality of the other, since each is basically *quality*. Therefore, Socrates and Plato are no more diverse from one another because of the nature of qualities than they are because of the nature of substance. For there is only one essence of their substance, just as there is only one essence of their qualities too. For the same reason neither does quantity make a difference between them, since it too is the same. Nor do the other categories. Thus no difference can arise from their forms, which are not diverse in themselves any more than their substances are.

(38) [**Objection 3:**] Further, how would we regard there as being a numerical "many" among substances, if there were only a diversity of advening forms with what is basically the same subject substance persisting? For we do not call *Socrates* "numerically many" because of his taking on many forms.

(39) [**Objection 4:**] Neither can it be maintained that those who hold this first theory mean for individuals to be produced through their accidents. For if individuals draw their being from accidents, then surely accidents are naturally prior to individuals, just as differences are naturally prior to the species they bring into being. For just as *man* is distinguished by being informed by a difference, so they call Socrates ["Socrates"] from his taking on accidents. Thus Socrates cannot exist apart from his accidents, any more than *man* can exist apart from its differences. So Socrates is not the underlying foundation for the accidents, just as *man* is not the underlying foundation for its differences. But if accidents are not in individual substances as in subjects, they are surely not in universal substances. For Aristotle shows [*Categories* 5, 2ᵃ34–ᵇ6] that, in all cases, whatever is in secondary substances as in subjects, the same things are in primary substances as in subjects.

(40) So from these considerations it is plain that the theory in which what is basically the same essence is said to be in diverse things at once is completely lacking in reason.

[Second theory]

(41) Thus other people with a different theory of universality, who get closer to the true theory of the matter, say single things not only are diverse from one another by their advening forms, but are discrete "personally"* in their essences, and what is in one thing is in no way in any other, whether

it is matter or form in the thing. They cannot subsist any the less discrete in their essences even when their forms are removed, because their "personal" discreteness (that is, the discreteness according to which this one is not that one) does not arise from those forms but is from the very diversity of the essence, just as the forms themselves are diverse from one another *in themselves*. Otherwise the diversity of forms would go on to infinity, so that one would have to assume yet others to account for the diversity of other forms.

(42) Porphyry made note of a difference like this between a most general genus and a most specific species when he said [P (28)], "Further, neither would a species ever become a most general genus or a genus a most specific species." As if he were to say: "This is the difference between them, that the essence of this is not the essence of that."

(43) So too the discreteness of the categories does not depend on any forms that produce it, but only on the diversification of each proper essence.

(44) But since these people want all things to be diverse from one another in such a way that none of them participates either *essentially* the same matter or *essentially* the same form with another, and yet they still retain a universal in *things*, they call things that are discrete "the same," not *essentially* but *indifferently*. For example, single men who are in themselves discrete they call "the same *in man*"—that is, they *do not differ* in the nature of humanity. The same things they call singular according to their discreteness they call universal according to their "indifference" and the agreement of likeness.

(45) [Variation 1:] But there is disagreement here too. Some people take the universal *thing* as consisting only in a *collection* of several things. They do not at all call Socrates and Plato by themselves a "species"; rather they call all men collected together the "species" *man*, and all animals taken together the "genus" *animal*, and so on for other cases.

(46) Boethius seems to agree with them [B (31)]: "Species is to be regarded as nothing else than the thought gathered from the substantial likeness of individuals. Genus, on the other hand, is the thought gathered from the likeness of species." When he says "gathered from the likeness," he implies a gathering of *several* things. Otherwise genus and species would in no way have any "predication of *several*" or a "containing *many* in a universal thing," and there would be no fewer universals than singulars.

(47) [Variation 2:] But there are other people who not only call all men collected together the "species," but also *single* men *insofar as they are men*. When they say the *thing* that is Socrates is predicated of several, they are taking this in a metaphorical sense, as if they were saying several men are "the same" as (that is, "agree" with) him, or he with several men. With respect to the number of *things*, they maintain as many species as individuals,

and as many genera. But with respect to *similarity* of natures, they assign a lesser number of universals than of singulars. All men are both *many* by their personal discreteness and also *one* by the likeness of humanity. The same men are judged to be diverse from themselves with respect to discreteness and likeness. For example, Socrates insofar as he is a man is divided from himself insofar as he is Socrates. The same thing could not be its own genus or species unless it had *some* difference from itself; what are relatives should be opposites in at least *some* respect.

[Arguments against the various forms of the second theory]

(48) Now let us first refute the theory stated above about a "collection" [(45)]. Let us ask how the whole collection of men taken together, which is said to be one species, is able to be *predicated* of several so that it is a universal, and yet the whole collection is not *said of* single things. If it is granted that the collection is predicated of diverse things through its *parts*—that is, insofar as its single parts are fitted to themselves[17]—that has nothing to do with the kind of community a universal has. The universal, as Boethius bears witness [B (18)], is supposed to be in each of its singulars *as a whole*. In this respect a universal is distinguished from the kind of common thing that is common by parts, like a field, the different parts of which belong to different people.

(49) Furthermore, Socrates too would likewise be "said of" several through his diverse parts. So *he* would be a universal too.

(50) Further, *any* plurality of men taken together would rightly be called a "universal," since the definition of a universal would fit them likewise. Or any such random collection would even be called a *species*, so that the whole collection of men would already include many species.

(51) Likewise, we would end up calling any collection whatever of bodies and spirits one universal "substance," so that since the whole collection of substances is one most general genus, it would follow that when any one substance is taken away while the rest remain, [we would have a most general genus. And since this holds for *any* substance], we would have many most general genera among substances.

(52) But perhaps it will be said in reply that no collection included in a most general genus is itself a most general genus.

(53) But I still object that if when one of the substances is separated, the remaining collection is not a most general genus and yet the universal *sub-*

17. *I. e.*, the "collection" is predicated *part by part* of all the members *of* the collection.

stance still endures, then that remaining collection has to be a *species* of substance and has to have a coequal species under the same genus. But what coequal species can there be opposite to it? For either the latter species of substance is straightforwardly contained in the former, or else it shares some individuals with it, as *rational animal* does with *mortal animal*.

(54) Further, every universal is naturally prior to its own individuals. But a collection of any things whatever is an integral whole with respect to the singulars of which it is constituted, and is naturally posterior to the things out of which it is put together.

(55) Further, Boethius in his *On Division* [879D] gives the following difference between an integral whole and a universal: The part is not the same as the integral whole, whereas the species *is* the same as the genus. But how can the whole collection of men be the same as the multitude of animals?

(56) It now remains for us to attack those [(47)] who call "universal" the single individuals *insofar as* they agree with others, and who grant that the same things are predicated of several, not in such a way that the several *are* essentially those things but because the several *agree* with them. But if being predicated of several is the same as "agreeing" with several, then how do we say an individual is predicated "of one thing only" [(16)], since there is nothing that "agrees" with only one thing?

(57) Also, how is there any difference between a universal and a singular in virtue of being "predicated of several," since in entirely the same way as *man* agrees with several things, so too Socrates agrees with several things? Certainly *man* insofar as it is man and *Socrates* insofar as he is man agree with other things. But neither *man* insofar as it is Socrates nor *Socrates* insofar as he is Socrates agrees with other things. So whatever *man* has *Socrates* has, and in exactly the same way.

(58) Furthermore, since the things are granted to be entirely the same— that is, the *man* that is in Socrates and Socrates himself—there is no difference between the one and the other. For no thing is diverse from itself at one and the same time, since whatever it has in itself, it has in entirely the same way. Thus Socrates, both white and literate, even though he has diverse things in himself,[18] nevertheless is not diverse *from himself* because of them, since he has them both and in exactly the same way. For he is not literate in any other way than from himself, or white in any other way than from himself. So too, as white he is not something other than himself, or as literate something other than himself.

(59) Also how can their claim that Socrates and Plato "agree *in man*" be

---

18. Namely, whiteness and literacy.

taken, since it is plain that all men differ from one another both in matter and in form? For if Socrates agrees with Plato in the *thing* that is man, but no other *thing* is man but Socrates or someone else, then Socrates has to agree with Plato either in himself or in someone else. But *in himself* he is instead *diverse* from Plato; the case with someone else is also plain, since Socrates is *not* someone else.

(60) On the other hand, there are those who take '*agreeing in man*' negatively, as if to say: Socrates does *not* differ from Plato *in man*.

(61) But in this sense it can also be said that he does not differ from Plato *in rock*, since neither one is a rock. Thus there is no greater agreement between them to be noted *in man* than *in rock*, unless perhaps some premise is added in advance, as if to say "They are men because they do not differ *in man*."[19]

(62) But this cannot not work either, since it is completely false that they do not differ *in man*. For if Socrates does not differ from Plato in a thing that is *man*, then neither does he differ from Plato in himself. For if in himself Socrates differs from Plato, but Socrates is a thing that is *man*, then certainly Socrates also differs from him in a thing that is *man*.

[Abelard's own theory]

(63) But now that we have shown the reasons why *things* taken neither singly nor collectively can be called "universals" insofar as they are predicated of several, it remains to ascribe this kind of universality only to words.

(64) Thus just as some names are called "appellative"[20] by grammarians and some are called "proper," so too some simple expressions are called "universal" by dialecticians and some are called "particular"—that is, "singular."

(65) Now a universal word is one that on the basis of its invention* is apt to be predicated of several things one by one. For example the name 'man', which can be conjoined to particular names of men in accordance with the nature of the subject things it is imposed on. But a singular word is one that is predicable of one thing only. For example 'Socrates', when it is taken as the name of one person only. If you take it equivocally, you do not produce

19. *I. e.*, one might want to add a premise that allows that if *A* and *B* do not differ *in man* then they *agree in man*, but that does not allow this to work where certain other terms (like 'rock') are substituted for 'man'.

20. *I. e.*, "common names."

one word but *many* words in signification. For according to Priscian[21] [2. 145.9] many names can come together in one word.[22] Therefore, when a universal is described as being "*what* is predicated of several" [(16)], the 'what' at the beginning not only indicates the simplicity of the expression, to distinguish it from a complex phrase, but also indicates the unity of signification, to distinguish it from equivocal terms.[23]

(66) Now that we have shown what the term 'what' at the beginning of the definition of a universal involves, let us carefully consider the two other parts of the definition that follow it: 'predicated' and 'of several'.

(67) To be "predicated" is to be conjoinable to something truly by means of the expressive force of a present-tensed substantive verb.* For example 'man' can be truly conjoined to diverse things through a substantive verb. Verbs like 'runs' and 'walks', which are predicated of several things, also have the force of a substantive verb in its copulative function.[24]

(68) Thus Aristotle in *On Interpretation* II. [10, 20^{a}3–6],[25] says "In those propositions in which 'is' does not occur—for example in one where 'runs' or 'walks' occurs—the verbs produce the same effect occurring there as if 'is' were added."

(69) And again he says, [*ibid.* 12, 21^{b}9–10], "There is no difference between 'A man walks' and 'A man is walking'."

(70) His phrase 'of several' [(16)] groups names with respect to the diversity of what they name. Otherwise 'Socrates' would be predicated of several things when one says 'This man is Socrates', 'This animal is Socrates', 'This white thing is Socrates', 'This musician is Socrates'. Although these names are diverse in meaning, they have entirely the same subject thing.

(71) But note that *syntactical* conjoining, which grammarians are concerned with, is other than conjoining with respect to *predication*, which dialecticians consider. For according to the force of the syntactical construc-

---

21. A Latin grammarian, *fl.* 500 A.D. His work was frequently cited in the twelfth century.

22. 'Socrates' is a proper name even if there are many people named "Socrates." In that case it is a proper name of several people by *equivocation*, which is unlike the way a *common* name like 'man' names several people univocally.

23. A universal term signifies several things on the basis of *one* "institution" or "invention," whereas an equivocal term signifies several things on the basis of *several* institutions or inventions operating at once.

24. *I. e.*, 'runs' amounts to 'is running', and 'walks' to 'is walking'.

25. In the Middle Ages, the *On Interpretation* was divided into two parts or books. The division came between Chs. 9 and 10.

tion, 'man' and 'stone' (and any other noun in the nominative case) can be conjoined just as much as 'animal' and 'man' can with respect to making plain a certain understanding, but not with respect to showing the *status** of a thing.

(72) So a *syntactical* conjoining is a good one whenever it indicates a complete judgment, whether the judgment is so or not. But a conjoining with respect to *predication*, which we are concerned with here, pertains to the nature of things and to indicating the truth of their *status*. If someone says 'A man is a stone' he produces a well-formed syntactical construction of 'man' or 'stone' with respect to the sense he wanted to indicate. There was no grammatical mistake. With respect to the force of the statement, 'stone' is here predicated of 'man', with which it is grammatically construed as a predicate, insofar as false categorical propositions have a predicate term too. Nevertheless, 'stone' is *not* predicable of it in the nature of things. Here, when we are defining a "universal," we are concerned only with the latter kind of force of predication.

(73) Now it seems that a "universal" name is never quite the same as an "appellative" name, or a "singular" name as a "proper" name. Rather they are related to one another as broader and narrower. For appellative and proper names not only include nominative cases but also the oblique cases, which are not predicated and so are excluded by the expression 'to be predicated' in the definition of a universal.

(74) Because oblique forms are less necessary [than nominative forms] for making a statement—which according to Aristotle, [*On interpretation* 4, 17ᵃ6–7], is the only present topic of speculation (that is, of dialectical consideration)—and because only the statement makes up arguments, therefore oblique forms are in a way not counted by Aristotle himself as names. He does not call them "names" but "*cases* of names" [*ibid.* 2, 16ᵃ32–ᵇ1].

(75) On the other hand, just as not all appellative or proper names have to be called universal or singular respectively, so too the other way around. For "universal" not only includes names, but also verbs and infinite names, to which infinite names the definition of an appellative Priscian gives does not seem to apply.[26]

(76) Now that the definition of 'universal' and 'singular' has been applied to *words* [rather than to *things*], let us carefully investigate the characteristic of *universal* words especially.

---

26. Priscian, 1.58.14–16: "Now this is the difference between a proper name and an appellative: the appellative is naturally common to many things that the same general or specific substance or quality or quantity joins together."

(77) Questions have been raised about these universals. For there is a doubt about their signification [**K** Ch. 9] most of all, since they do not appear to have any [universal] subject thing [of which they can be predicated], or to establish a firm understanding of anything.

(78) Universal names did not seem to be imposed on any *things*, since all things subsisted discretely in themselves and did not agree in any *thing* (as was shown [(59)–(62)]) in such a way that universal names could be imposed in accordance with their agreement in this thing.

(79) So, since universal names are certainly not imposed on things according to the difference in their discreteness (for then they would not be common but singular names), and again since universal names cannot name things as agreeing in any *thing* (for there *is* no thing they agree in), therefore universal names seem to bring about no signification of things—especially since in addition they establish no understanding of any thing [**K** Ch. 9].

(80) Thus Boethius in his *On Division*, [889A–B], says the word 'man' produces a doubt in the understanding. When the term is heard, he says, "the hearer's intelligence is carried away by many disturbances and is drawn into errors. For unless someone delimits the term by saying '*Every* man walks', or at least '*Some* man walks', and indicates *this* man (if he happens to be walking), the hearer's understanding has nothing it can reasonably understand."

(81) Because 'man' is imposed on all single men from the same cause— namely because they are a rational, mortal animal—that very community of imposition prevents any one person from being understood in the term 'man', as on the contrary in the name 'Socrates' there *is* understood one man's own person. This is why 'Socrates' is called a "singular" name. In the common name 'man', neither Socrates himself nor anyone else nor the whole collection of men is reasonably understood on the basis of the word.

(82) Neither, as some people say, is Socrates himself "*insofar as he is a man*" picked out by the name 'man'. For even if only Socrates is sitting in this house, and even if the proposition 'A man is sitting in this house'[27] is true about him alone, nevertheless this is in no way imputed to Socrates by means of the name 'man' in subject position—not even "insofar as he is a man." Otherwise it would reasonably be understood from the proposition

---

27. Because Latin has no indefinite article, the sentence 'A man is sitting in this house' looks exactly the same in Latin as the sentence 'Man is sitting in this house'. I included the article for the sake of a smooth reading, but it should not be read as an existential quantifier.

itself that sitting inhered in Socrates, so that from the fact that a man is sitting in this house it could be inferred that *Socrates* is sitting in it.

(83) Likewise, no one else can be understood in the name 'man'. But neither is the whole collection of men understood in that term, since the proposition can be true on the basis of just one man.

(84) So neither 'man' nor any other universal word appears to signify anything. For it does not establish an understanding of any thing. But it seems there can be no understanding that does not have a subject thing it conceives. Thus Boethius in his *Commentary* [B (20)] says "Every understanding arises from a subject thing either as that thing is disposed or as it is not disposed (for no understanding can arise from *no* subject)."

(85) For these reasons universals seem wholly unsuited to signification.

(86) But this is not so. For they in a way "signify" diverse things by naming them, not by establishing an understanding that *arises* from them but one that *pertains* to each of them.

(87) For example, the word 'man' *names* single men on the basis of a common cause: that they are men. (It is called a "universal" on account of this cause.) It also *constitutes a certain understanding*, a common one, not a proper one—that is, a common understanding that pertains to the single men whose common likeness it conceives.

(88) But now let us carefully examine what we just touched on briefly: (i) what is the *common cause* in accordance with which a universal name is imposed, (ii) what is the understanding's *common conception* of the likeness of things, and (iii) whether a word is called "common" on account of the common cause things agree in, or on account of the common conception, or on account of both together.

(89) First let us consider the *common cause*. Single men, who are discrete from one another since they differ both in their own essences and in their own forms (as we mentioned above while investigating the physics of the matter [(28)–(40)]), nevertheless agree in *that they are men*. I do not say they agree in *man*, since no thing is a man[28] unless it is discrete. Rather they agree in *being a man*.

(90) Now *being a man* is not a man or any other *thing*, if we consider the matter carefully, any more than *not being in a subject* is any thing, or *not admitting contraries*, or *not admitting of greater and less*. Yet Aristotle says [*Categories* 5, 2ᵃ12–4ᵇ19] all substances agree in these respects. For since (as was shown above [(59)–(62)]) there can be no agreement in a *thing*, if

28. See n. 27 above.

nevertheless there is an agreement among some things, it must be taken according to what is *not* any thing. Thus Socrates and Plato are alike in *being a man*, as a horse and an ass are alike in *not being a man*, for which reason each of them is called a "nonman." So for things to agree with one another is for each one of them *to be the same* _____ or *not to be the same* _____[29]—for example, *to be a man* or *to be white*, or *not to be a man* or *not to be white*.

(91) But it seems we should balk at taking the agreement of things according to what is *not* any thing, as if we are uniting in *nothing* things that exist when we say this man and that man agree in the *status* of man—that is, *in that they are men*. But we mean only that they *are men* and in this respect do not differ at all—I mean in the respect *that they are men*, even though we appeal to no *essence* here.

(92) Now someone's *being a man*, which is not a thing, we call the *status* of man. We also called it [(88)–(89)] the "common cause" of the imposition of a name on single men insofar as they agree with one another. We often call by the name 'cause' what are not any *thing*. For example, when we say "He was flogged *because* he does not want to go to the forum." 'He does not want to go to the forum', which occurs as a "cause" here, is no essence. We can likewise call the *status* of man the things[30] themselves established in the nature of man, the common likeness of which he who imposed the word conceived.

(93) Now that the *signification* of universals has been shown (they signify *things* by naming them) and the *common cause* of their imposition has been pointed out, let us show what the *understandings* are that they constitute.

(94) First let us distinguish in general the nature of all understandings.

(95) Since both sensation and understanding belong to the soul, the difference between them is this: The senses are engaged only through bodily organs and perceive only bodies or what are *in* bodies. For example, vision perceives a tower or the tower's visible qualities. But the understanding, just as it needs no bodily organ, so neither does it have to have a subject body to which it is directed. Instead it is satisfied with a thing's likeness the mind itself makes up for itself, to which it directs the action of its intelligence. So

---

29. '*Idem esse vel non esse*'. I do not translate this as 'to be the same thing or not to be the same thing', since the point of the passage is that we are not talking about *things*. I think the '*idem*' here is simply a place-holder. The idea is that for things to "agree" is for each of them to be _____, where the blank is filled with *the same* term in each case. The examples immediately following bear out this interpretation.

30. The whole sentence is puzzling, but the word 'things' especially so. Abelard has been at pains to emphasize that the *status* is *not* a thing.

when the tower is destroyed or removed from sight, the sensation that dealt with it is lost, but the understanding of it remains since the thing's likeness is retained in the mind.

(96) Now just as the sense is not the thing sensed, to which it is directed, so the understanding is not the form of the thing it conceives. Instead an "understanding" is a certain *action* of the soul on the basis of which the soul is said to be in a state of understanding. But the form to which it is directed is a kind of imaginary and made-up thing, which the mind contrives for itself whenever it wants and however it wants. The imaginary cities seen in a dream are like this, or the form of a building that will be made, which the architect conceives as a model and exemplar of the thing to be formed. We cannot call this either a substance or an accident.

(97) Yet some people call this made-up thing the same as the "understanding." Thus the building (the tower) I conceive when the tower is absent, and observe as tall and square and in an open field, they call the same as the "understanding" of the tower. Aristotle seems to agree with them; in *On Interpretation* [1, 16^{a}7] he calls "likenesses of things" the passions of the soul they call "understandings."

(98) On the other hand, we call the *image* the "likeness of the thing." But there is no objection if the understanding too is called a "likeness" in a way—that is, because it *conceives* what is *properly* called the "likeness of the thing." We have said, and rightly so, that what is properly called the "likeness" is different from the understanding. For I ask: Is the squareness and the tallness a true form of the understanding that is led to the likeness of the tower's quantity and of its structure? But surely true squareness and true tallness inhere only in bodies. Also, neither an understanding nor any true essence can be formed by a *made-up* quality. Thus all that remains is that, just as the quality is a made-up one, so too a made-up substance is the subject of that quality.

(99) Perhaps an image in a mirror, which seems to appear to sight as being a subject,* can truly be said to be "nothing," because in the white surface of the mirror the quality of the contrary color [black] often appears.

(100) When the soul both senses and understands the same thing at once—as when it discerns a stone—it can be asked whether then too the understanding is dealing with the *image* of the stone, or whether the understanding and the sense together are both dealing with the stone itself. But it seems more reasonable that the understanding does not need an image in that case, since the truth of the substance itself is present to it.

(101) But if someone says that where sensation occurs there is no understanding, we do not grant that. For it often happens that the soul perceives

one thing and understands another, as is quite apparent with people who are studying. Although with their eyes open they perceive things present to them, yet they are thinking of the other things they are writing about.

(102) Now that we have seen the nature of understandings in general, let us distinguish the understandings of universals and singulars. They are divided from one another insofar as the understanding that goes with a universal name conceives a common and confused image of many things. But the understanding a singular word generates comprises the proper and so to speak "singular" form of one thing—that is, a form related to one "person"* only.

(103) Thus when I hear 'man', a kind of model rises up in my mind that is related to single men in such a way that it is common to all of them and proper to none. But when I hear 'Socrates', a certain form rises up in my mind that expresses the likeness of a certain person. Hence by the word 'Socrates', which produces in the mind the proper form of one person, a certain thing is picked out and determined. But with the word 'man', the understanding of which depends on the common form of all men, that very community produces a "confusion" so that we do not understand any one form from among them all.

(104) So 'man' is correctly said to signify neither Socrates nor anyone else, since no one man is picked out by the force of the name, even though it *names* singular men. But 'Socrates' or any other singular term, is not only able to *name* a singular but also to determine a subject thing.

(105) But because, following Boethius, we said above [(84)] that every understanding has a subject thing, how does this claim fit the understandings of universals?

(106) Certainly it should be noted that Boethius introduces this claim in the sophistical argument where he shows the understanding of universals is an empty one [B (20)]. So there is no problem if he does not proceed on this basis in stating the truth of the matter. Thus when he is avoiding falsehood [B (23)–(37)] he endorses other people's reasoning.

(107) Also, we can call the understanding's "subject thing" either (a) the true substance of the thing, as when understanding occurs together with sensation, or (b) the conceived form of any thing when the thing is absent, whether that form is common, as we said [happens in the case of a universal (102)], or proper. I mean "common" with respect to the likeness it preserves of many things, even though in itself it is regarded as *one* thing.

(108) In this way, to indicate the nature of all lions one picture can be made that is proper to none of the lions it represents. Again, another picture

can be applied to distinguish any one of them, a picture that denotes something proper to it. For example, if the lion is painted as limping, maimed or wounded by Hercules's spear.

(109) Therefore, just as one kind of figure of things is painted common and another is painted singular, so too one kind is conceived common and another is conceived proper.

(110) Now it is not absurd to doubt whether the name also signifies this form the understanding is directed to. That it does appears to be confirmed both by authority and by reason.

(111) For Priscian in the first part of his *Constructions* [2.135.7–10],[31] although he had already pointed out the common imposition of universals on individuals, seemed to add another kind of signification for them as well: signifying a common form. He says, "The terms by which the genera or species of the things in nature are indicated can also be proper to the general and special forms of things constructed intelligibly in the divine mind before they go forth into bodies." In this passage God is treated as a builder about to put something together, who conceives beforehand in his soul an exemplary form of the thing to be put together, and operates in accordance with the likeness of this form. The form is said to "proceed into a body" when a true thing is put together according to the likeness of this form.

(112) Now this common conception is rightly attributed to God, not to man. For those works—the general or special *status* in a nature—are God's[32] work, not a builder's. For instance *man, soul, stone* are God's work, but a house or a sword are man's. So the latter—the house and the sword—are not works of nature as the former are. The words for them do not fall under substance but rather accident, and so they are neither genera nor most specific species.

(113) Thus also such conceptions by abstraction are correctly attributed to the divine mind, not to the human mind. For men, who know things only through the senses, scarcely ever—or perhaps *never*—rise to this kind of simple intelligence. The external sensuousness of accidents prevents men from conceiving the natures of things purely. But God, to whom all the things he created are plain through themselves and who knew them before they existed, distinguishes the single *status* in themselves. Sensation is not an obstacle for him who alone has true intelligence.

31. Books 17–18 of Priscian's *Institutiones grammaticae* are on "construction—that is, the ordering of the parts of speech among themselves." (Priscian, 1.4.9–10).
32. Restoring 'dei' where the edition deleted it.

(114) Hence for things they do not touch[33] by sense, men succeed in having only *opinion* rather than *intelligence*. Experience itself teaches us this. For thinking of some city we have not seen, when we arrive there we find we thought of it otherwise than it is.

(115) So too, I believe, we have opinion rather than real intelligence of the internal forms that do not reach the senses, such as rationality, mortality, fatherhood, sitting.

(116) Yet any names of any existing things, insofar as is in their power, generate understanding rather than opinion, since their inventor* meant to impose them in accordance with certain natures or characteristics of things, even if he did not know how to think out the nature or characteristic of the thing.

(117) Priscian [(111)] calls these common conceptions "general" or "specific" because in one way or another they suggest general or specific names to us. He says universal terms are themselves, so to speak, proper names for these conceptions. Even though they are of confused signification as far as the named essences are concerned, they do immediately direct the listener's mind to the common conception, just as proper names do to the one thing they signify.

(118) Porphyry himself, when he says certain things are constituted out of matter and form and certain others after a *likeness* of matter and form, seems to have understood this kind of conception in the phrase 'after a likeness of matter and form' [**P** (51)]. This will be discussed more fully in the appropriate place.[34]

(119) Boethius too appears to have understood this same common conception when he says [**B** (31)] the thought gathered together from the likeness of many things is a genus or species.

(120) Some people also assert Plato was of the same view, insofar as he called the common Ideas he put in *nous* "genera" or "species."

(121) Perhaps it is in this respect that Boethius mentions Plato disagreed with Aristotle, where Boethius [**B** (36)] says Plato meant genera and species and the rest not only to be *understood* as universal but also *to be* universal and to subsist outside bodies—as if he had said Plato was understanding by "universals" the common conceptions he set up in *nous* as separated from bodies, perhaps not taking 'universal' according to common predication, as Aristotle does, but according to a common likeness of many things. For that

---

33. I conjecture '*attrectaverunt*' for the edition's '*attractaverunt*', and am translating accordingly.

34. Peter Abelard, 1.79.31–81.34 (not translated here).

common conception does not seem to be predicated of several things at all, like a name that is applied to several things one by one.

(122) The fact that Boethius says Plato thought universals subsist outside sensibles can be explained in another way too, so that there is no dispute between the two philosophers' views. For what Aristotle said, that universals always subsist in sensible things, he said insofar as their *act* is concerned. The nature *animal*, which is indicated by the universal name ['animal'] (and in this respect is called a kind of "universal" by a transfer of meaning), is never actually found except in a sensible thing. Yet Plato thinks this nature subsists naturally in itself in such a way that it would retain its being even if not subjected to sense, and according to this "natural" being is called by the name 'universal'. And so what Aristotle denies with respect to the *act* Plato, the investigator of physics, assigns to a natural *aptitude*. So there is no disagreement between them.

(123) Reason too seems to agree with the authorities we have listed who seem to maintain that common forms are designated by universal names. What is it to *conceive* these common forms by means of names, other than for them to be *signified* by the names? But surely in that sense, when we make these common forms to be *different* from understandings, there emerges a third signification of names besides the *thing* and the *understanding*. Although authority does not maintain this, yet reason is not opposed to it.

(124) Now let us settle what we promised above [(88)] to decide, whether the community of universal names is judged by the common cause of imposition or by the common conception, or by both. There is no objection if it is by both. But the common cause, which is taken in accordance with the nature of things, seems to have the greater force.

(125) What we mentioned above [(103)?] must also be decided, how the understandings of universals comes about by abstraction, and also how we call them "alone," "bare," and "pure"—but not "empty."

(126) First about abstraction. You need to know that matter and form always exist thoroughly mixed together. But the mind's reason has the power now to gaze on the matter by itself, now to attend to the form alone, now to conceive both mixed together. The first two understandings are by abstraction; they abstract something from conjoined things, to consider its very nature. But the third one is by conjunction.

(127) For example, the substance of this man is *body* and *animal* and *man*, and is covered with an infinity of forms. When I attend to it in the material essence *substance*, setting aside all its additional forms, I have an understanding "by abstraction." Again, when I pay attention to the corporeality alone in it, which I conjoin to *substance*, here too even though the understanding

is "by conjunction" with respect the first one (which only attended to the nature *substance*), nevertheless the same understanding also comes about "by abstraction" with respect to the forms other than corporeality, none of which I am paying attention to—for example being animate, having sensation, rationality, whiteness.

(128) Such understandings "by abstraction" perhaps seemed to be "false" or "empty" because they perceive the thing otherwise than as it subsists. For since such understandings attend to the matter by itself or the form separately, but neither of these subsists separately, those understandings certainly seem to conceive the thing otherwise than as it is, and so to be "empty."

(129) But that is not so. If someone understands a thing otherwise than as it is in the sense that he attends to it in terms of a nature or characteristic it does not have, *that* understanding is surely empty. But this does not happen with abstraction. For when I attend to this man only in terms of the nature *substance* or *body*, but not also in terms of the nature *animal* or *man* or *literate*, surely I understand nothing but what is in the nature. But I do not pay attention to *all* the features it has. And when I say that I attend to the nature "only" insofar as it has this or that feature, the term 'only' refers to the *attention*, not to the mode of subsisting. Otherwise the understanding *would* be empty. For the thing does not *have* only this, but it is only *attended to* as having this.

(130) Yet in another sense a thing *is* said to be understood in a certain way otherwise than as it is—not in another *status* than it is, as was said above [(91)?], but "otherwise" insofar as the mode of understanding is other than the mode of subsisting. For *this* thing is understood *separately*—not as *separated*—from *that* other one, although it does *exist* separately. The matter is perceived purely, and the form simply, although the former does not *exist* purely or the latter simply. Thus the purity or the simplicity is reduced to the *understanding*, not to the *subsistence* of the thing, so that they are a mode of understanding, not of subsisting.

(131) The senses too often deal with composites differently. For example if a statue is half gold and half silver, I can perceive the conjoined gold and silver separately, looking now at the gold by itself, now at the silver by itself, perceiving the conjoined metals *dividedly*, not as *divided*. Indeed they are *not* divided.

(132) So too the understanding attends by abstraction "dividedly," not as "divided." Otherwise it would be empty.

(133) Yet perhaps there could be a sound understanding that considers what are conjoined as *divided* in one sense and *conjoined* in another, and conversely. For again, both the conjunction and division of things can be

taken in two senses. We call certain things "conjoined" to one another through some likeness—for example these two men insofar as they are men, or insofar as they are literate. But certain other things we call "conjoined" through a putting together or a kind of aggregation—for example matter and form, or wine and water. Things adjoined to one another in the latter way are conceived in one way as divided and in another way as conjoined.

(134) Thus Boethius [B (27)] ascribes to the mind the power of being able, by means of its reason, to put together disjoint things and to resolve composite ones. Yet in neither operation does it go beyond the nature of the thing, but perceives only what is in the nature of the thing. Otherwise it would not be reason but opinion—that is, if the intelligence were to depart from the *status* of the thing.

(135) But a question arises here about the builder's plan:[35] Is it "empty" while he *now* holds in his mind the form of the *future* work, when the thing is not that way yet? If we grant this, we are forced to call God's plan "empty" too, which he had before his works were established. But if one says "empty" with respect to the effect—that is, in the sense that God would not by his labor complete what he foresees—then it is false that his providence was "empty." On the other hand, if someone calls it "empty" on the grounds that it would not yet be in harmony with the *status* of the future thing, we shudder at the awful words but do not reject the judgment. For it is true that the future *status* of the world did not materially exist while God was intelligibly arranging what was still future.

(136) But we do not usually call someone's thought or plan "empty" unless it lacks an effect, [so that it is not fulfilled]. Neither do we say we think "in vain" unless we think of things we do not finish by working them out. And so, changing the words back to their usual sense, we do not call a plan "empty" that does not think "in vain" but only conceives things that do not yet exist materially as if they subsisted. That is natural to all plans.

(137) Thinking about future matters is called "planning," about past ones is called "memory," and about present ones is called properly "intelligence."

(138) Now if someone calls a person "deceived" who in his planning thinks about a future *status* as if about what already exists, rather he himself is deceived who thinks such a person should be called "deceived." For one who plans the future is not deceived unless he believes the situation to be already as he plans. Neither does the *conception* of a nonexistent thing make one

---

35. '*Providentia*'. The term may also be translated 'providence' or 'foresight' depending on the context. Some of the following discussion may be clearer if the reader keeps these alternatives in mind.

"deceived," but rather the *belief* added to it. For even if I think of a rational crow, yet if I do not believe in it I am not deceived. So too neither is the planner deceived. For what he thinks of *as if* already existing he does not regard as really existing so. Rather he thinks of it as "present" in the sense that he posits it as present *in the future.*

(139) Surely *every* conception of the mind is so to speak about what is present. For example, if I consider Socrates either insofar as he *was* a boy or insofar as he *will be* an old man, I join childhood or old age to him *as if* at present. For I attend to him at present *in* a past or future characteristic. But no one calls this kind of memory "empty," because what it conceives as present it attends to in the past. We will discuss this more fully in our treatment of the *On Interpretation.*[36]

(140) The problem in the case of God—that his substance, which alone is immutable and simple, is not varied by any conceptions of things or by any other forms, [and so the above account of planning cannot be applied to him]—is solved rather satisfactorily. For although the custom of human speech presumes to speak about the creator as if about creatures, since it calls him "provident" or "understanding," yet nothing should be understood or can exist in him distinct from him—neither understanding nor any other form. So every question about the understanding is superfluous as applied to God. But if we speak the truth more plainly, for him to plan the future is nothing other than for future things not be to hidden from him who in himself is true reason.

(141) Now that we have pointed out many facts about the nature of abstraction, let us return to the understandings of universals, which must always come about by abstraction. For when I hear the term 'man' or 'whiteness' or 'white', I am not by the force of the name itself reminded of all the natures or characteristics in the subject things. Rather by 'man' I have a conception only of *animal, rational, mortal*, not of later accidents as well. Yet this is a *confused* conception, not a discrete one. For the understandings of singulars too come about by abstraction, as when we say 'this substance', 'this body', 'this animal', 'this man', 'this white thing'. By the phrase 'this man' I attend only to the nature *man*, but as regards a certain subject thing. But by the word 'man' I attend to the same nature simply in itself, not as regards any one man.

(142) Thus the understanding of universals is deservedly called "alone" and "bare" and "pure." "Alone," apart from sensation, because it does not perceive the thing as sensible. "Bare," with respect to the abstraction of

36. Peter Abelard, 1.325.12–334.17 (not translated here).

forms, either all or some of them. "Pure" of everything, as far as being discrete is concerned, because no thing, whether matter or form, is picked out in it. In this last respect we called this kind of conception "confused," above [(102)].

(143) Now that we have examined these points, let us proceed to solve the questions about genera and species posed by Porphyry. We can do this easily now that the nature of all universals has been clarified.

(144) Thus the first of these questions [(4)] was whether genera and species subsist—that is, signify any truly existing things—or are posited in the intellect alone, etc.—that is, are posited in empty opinion without any thing, such as the names 'chimera' and 'goat-stag', which do not generate a correct understanding.

(145) To this it must be replied that they really do signify truly existing things by *naming* them, the same things singular names signify. They are not posited in empty opinion at all. Yet in a certain sense they are established by an intellect that is "alone" and "bare" and "pure," in the sense given above [(142)]. Now there is no objection if one who proposes a question takes certain words in one sense in asking it, and one who answers the question takes them in another sense in answering it.[37] It is as if the one who answers it were to say: "You are asking whether they are posited in the intellect alone," etc. You can take this so that it is true, as we have already explained above.

(146) The words can also be taken in exactly the same sense on both sides, both by the answerer and by the asker. In that case there will be *one* question, not made up of opposites, about the first members of *two* dialectical questions, namely: "Do they exist or not?" and again "Are they posited in intellects alone, bare, and pure, or are they not?"

(147) The same thing can be said in the case of the second question [(5)], which is whether, as subsisting, they are corporeal or incorporeal. That is, since it is granted that they signify subsistents, do they signify subsistents[38] that are corporeal or that are incorporeal?

(148) Surely as Boethius says [B (5)] everything that exists is either

---

37. As Abelard is doing here. In the original question, the two alternatives were intended to be *exclusive*, so that the question meant: "Are universals to be regarded in the one way *and not the other*, or in the other way *and not the one*?" Abelard is answering the question as though the alternatives were *not* intended to be exclusive, so that he can say "They are to be regarded in *both* ways."

38. Conjecturing 'aliqua' for the edition's 'alia'. I have left the word untranslated, as implied in the word 'subsistents', which I have supplied.

corporeal or incorporeal, whether we take the names 'corporeal' and 'incorporeal' for a substantial body and for a nonbody, respectively, or for what can be perceived by a bodily sense (like man, stone, whiteness) and[39] for what cannot, (like the soul, justice).

(149) The term 'corporeal' can also be taken for what is discrete, as if the question is: "Since they signify subsistents, do they signify them as discrete or as nondiscrete?" For whoever investigates the truth of a matter well not only pays attention to what can be said truly but also to whatever can be maintained in an opinion. So even if it is certain to someone that no things besides discrete ones subsist, nevertheless because there could be an opinion to the effect that there were other things too, it is not out of place to ask about them as well. This last way of taking the term 'corporeal', so that the question asks about the discrete and the nondiscrete, seems to approximate the sense of the question more.

(150) But in that case, when Boethius says everything that exists is either corporeal or incorporeal, the alternative 'incorporeal' perhaps seems superfluous, since nothing that exists is "incorporeal"—that is, nondiscrete.

(151) Likewise, in that case, neither does the point about the order of the questions seem important at all,[40] except perhaps insofar as, just as 'corporeal' and 'incorporeal' divide subsistents in another signification of the terms, so it seems they divide subsistents in this signification too, as if the one asking the question said: "I see that some existents are called corporeal and others incorporeal. Which of these shall we say are the things signified by universals?"[41]

(152) The reply to this is: Corporeal things, in a sense. That is, things discrete in their essence and yet incorporeal with respect to being designated by a universal name—since universal names do not name them discretely and determinately but confusedly, as we explained well enough above [(102)].

(153) Thus universal names are called "corporeal" with respect to the nature of the things, and "incorporeal" with respect to the mode of signification. For although they name what are discrete, yet they do not do so discretely and determinately.

(154) Now the third question [(6)], whether universals are posited in sensibles, etc., is derived from their being granted as being incorporeal. For

39. Conjecturing '*et*' for the edition's '*vel*'.

40. *I. e.*, the words "*as subsisting*" at the beginning of question 2 (147), which presuppose the answer to question 1.

41. The sense of the paragraph is very obscure.

taken in a certain sense, 'incorporeal' is divided by being in a sensible and not being in a sensible, as we also remarked above [(6)].

(155) Universals are said to subsist in sensibles—that is, to signify an intrinsic substance existing in a sensible thing on the basis of the thing's exterior forms. And although they signify the substance that actually subsists in a sensible thing, nevertheless they naturally indicate the same substance as separated from a sensible thing, as we explained above in accordance with Plato [(122)].

(156) Thus Boethius says [B (35)] that genera and species are *understood* (he does not say *exist*) beyond sensibles—that is, insofar as the realities of genera and species are rationally attended to in themselves with respect to their nature, beyond all sensibility. For they could truly subsist in themselves if the exterior forms through which they come to the senses were removed. For we grant that all genera or species inhere in sensible things. But because the understanding of them was always said to be apart from sensation [(142)], they seemed to be in no way in sensible things. Hence it was worth asking whether they could ever be in sensibles. For some of them, the answer is that they do exist in sensibles, but in such a way that they naturally persist beyond sensibility, as has been said [(122)].[42]

(157) On the other hand, we can also take 'corporeal' and 'incorporeal' in the second question for "sensible" and "insensible" [(148)], so that the order of the questions is more appropriate. Because the understanding of universals was said to be "alone apart from sensation," as was said [(142)], it was right to ask [in question 2] whether they were sensible or insensible. The answer was that some of them are sensible with respect to the nature of the things, and that the same ones are insensible with respect to the mode of signifying [(153)]. For they do not designate the sensible things they name in the same way they are sensed (that is, as discrete), and sensation does not find them by their being pointed out to it. Hence the question remained whether universals appellated only the sensibles themselves or also signified something else.

(158) The reply to this is that they signify the sensibles themselves and at the same time the common conception that Priscian ascribes especially to the divine mind [(111)].

(159) "And agree with them" [P (2), B (1)]. According to what we here understand as the fourth question, as we mentioned above [(10)], this is the answer: We say names are not universal at all when, with their subject things destroyed, they are no longer predicable of several things. Indeed they are

42. The paragraph is remarkably obscure.

not then common to *any* things. For example, the name 'rose' when roses no longer exist. But even then the name is significative in virtue of the understanding, although it lacks naming. Otherwise the proposition 'There is no rose' would not exist.

(160) Questions rightly arose about universal but not about singular words, because there was no such doubt about the signification of singular words. Their mode of signifying was surely quite in accordance with the *status* of things. Just as the things are discrete in themselves, so too they are signified discretely by singular terms. The understanding of singular terms grasps a fixed thing, which is not so for universal terms.

(161) Furthermore, while universal terms do not signify things as discrete, they do not seem to signify them as agreeing either. For there is no *thing* in which they agree, as we also explained above [(59)–(62)].

(162) So because there was such a great doubt about universals, Porphyry chose to treat universals only, and excluded singulars from his purpose as if they were plain enough by themselves, even though he sometimes treats them in passing in the course of discussing other matters.

(163) But note that even though the definition of a universal or a genus or species includes only words, nevertheless these names are often used figuratively for the corresponding *things*. For example, when someone says a species consists of genus and difference—that is, a thing in a species consists of a thing in a genus. For where the nature of words is being explained with respect to their signification, at one time the words are discussed and at another time the things, and the names of the former are often applied figuratively to the latter, and conversely.

(164) Thus because the treatment both of logic and of grammar was made extremely ambiguous because of such a figurative use of names, this led many people into error. They were not rightly distinguishing between the correct imposition of names and their figurative misuse.

(165) More than anyone else, Boethius in his *Commentaries* produces this confusion by figurative usages, especially in his investigation of the above questions. So it seems right to ignore the question what *he* calls genera or species. Nevertheless, let us quickly run through his questions and apply them as needed to the above theory.

(166) Here then in his investigation of these questions, in order to resolve the matter better, he first confuses the issue by means of sophistical questions and arguments so that afterwards he may teach us how to escape from them.

(167) He sets out [B (22)] such a great problem that all concern for and investigation of genera and species has to be postponed because of it. It is as if he says that the words 'genera' and 'species' cannot be said to be what

they seem, either with respect to the signification of things or with respect to the understanding.

(168) He shows this for the signification of things, insofar as a universal *thing*, whether one thing or a multiple thing, is never found—that is, a thing predicable of several, as he carefully explains and as we proved above.

(169) First he proves that *one* thing is not a universal, and so is neither a genus nor a species. He says [**B (12)**] everything that is one is *numerically* one—that is, discrete in its own essence. But genera and species, which have to be common to several things, cannot be numerically one, and so not one at all.

(170) But because someone could say, contrary to the assumption, that genera and species are numerically "one" in such a way that the "one" is nevertheless common, Boethius takes that means of escape away from him when he says [**B (14)–(18)**] that everything numerically one but common is common either *by parts*, or as a whole *by a succession in time*, or else as a whole at the same time but in such a way that *it does not constitute the substances of what it is common to*. He immediately distinguishes all these ways of being common from genus and species when he says the latter are common in such a way that they are as a whole and at the same time in singular things and constitute their substance. Surely universal names are not participated part by part by the different things they name. Rather they are, as wholes, in their entireties and at the same time, names of singulars. They can also be said to constitute the substances of what they are common to, insofar as they signify by a figurative usage things that constitute other things. For example 'animal' names a certain something in a horse and in a man that is their matter, or even the matter of the men who are inferior to the term 'animal'.[43] Or else universal names are said to make up their substance insofar as they enter into a judgment about such things.[44] Thus they are said to be "substantial" to them. Certainly 'man' denotes the whole that is an animal and rational and mortal.[45]

(171) After Boethius has shown that *one* thing is not universal, he proves this also about a multiple thing, showing that neither is a multitude of discrete things a species or a genus [**B (13)**]. He demolishes the theory according to which someone could say all substances collected together are the genus

43. I do not know what this clause adds. Men have already been accounted for earlier in the sentence.

44. The only plausible antecedents here are 'horse' and 'man' a few lines above.

45. The overall sense of the paragraph is perhaps not totally missing, but there are lots of obscurities in it.

substance, and all men the species *man*, as if to say: If we maintain every genus is a multitude of things that substantially agree, then on the other hand every such multitude will naturally have another one above it, and that one again will have another, and so on to infinity—which is inconsistent.

(172) So it has been shown that universal names do not appear to be universals with respect to their signification of things—whether that signification is of one thing or of a multiple thing. For they signify no universal thing—that is, one predicable of several.

(173) He goes on to argue that they should not be called "universals" with respect to the signification of the understanding either. He shows (sophistically) that this understanding is empty [**B (21)**], because it regards the thing otherwise than it is, since this understanding is by way of abstraction. Both he and we have carefully untied the knot of that sophism well enough above [(128)–(129)].

(174) But the other part of the argument [**B (11)–(19)**], by which he showed that no thing is a universal, he did not think needed to be decided, because it was *not* sophistical. There he takes 'thing' in the sense of "*thing*," not in the sense of "*word*." For a common word, although it is so to speak essentially one thing in itself, nevertheless is "common" by naming in virtue of its appellating many things. It is predicable of several things according to this appellation, not according to its essence.

(175) Yet the multitude of the things themselves is the cause of the universality of the name. For as we remarked above [(159)], there is no universal that does not contain many things. But the universality a thing confers on a word the thing does not have in itself. For surely the word does not have signification by virtue of the thing. And a name is judged to be appellative *in accordance with* the multitude of things, even though we do not say *things* signify or are appellative.

John Duns Scotus

Six Questions on Individuation
from His *Ordinatio* II. d. 3, part 1, qq. 1–6

[Question 1

Is a material substance individual or
singular from itself—that is, from its nature?]

(1) With Distinction 3, we must ask about the personal distinction* among angels.[1] But to see this distinction among them, we must first ask about the individual distinction among material substances. For just as different people say different things about the latter topic, so consequently they say different things about the plurality of individuals in the same angelic species. In order for the various views concerning the distinction or nondistinction of material substance to be seen distinctly, I ask one by one about the various ways of setting up that distinction. First: Is a material substance individual or singular from itself—that is, from its nature?

[Argument for the affirmative]

(2) Yes: In *Metaphysics* VII. [13, 1038^{b}10–11], the Philosopher argues against Plato that "the substance of anything whatever is proper to what it belongs to, and is not in anything else"; therefore, etc.[2] Therefore, a material substance from its nature, disregarding everything else, is proper to what it is in, so that from its nature it is unable to be in anything else; therefore, from its nature it is individual.

---

1. Scotus returns to the topic of the personal distinction among angels in q. 7 (not translated here).

2. Scholastic authors very often truncated their arguments like this when it was obvious what the conclusion was. Here the practice seems idle, since Scotus goes on in the rest of the paragraph to spell out the conclusion anyway in some detail.

[Arguments for the negative]

(3) To the contrary: Whatever from its own notion is in something *per se* is in it in every instance; therefore, if the nature of stone were of itself a "this," then whatever the nature of stone were in, that nature would be "this stone." The consequent is nonsense if we are speaking about a determinate singularity,[3] which is what the question is about.

(4) Furthermore what one opposite belongs to of itself, the other opposite is of itself incompatible with it. Therefore, if a nature is of itself numerically one, then numerical multitude is incompatible with it.

[Statement of a previous theory]

(5) Here it is said that just as a nature is formally a nature from itself, so too it is singular from itself. Thus one does not have to look for any other cause of singularity than the cause of the nature, as if a nature is a nature before (temporally or naturally) it is singular, and only then is contracted by something added on to it so that it becomes singular.

(6) This is proved by a simile. For of itself a nature has true being outside the soul. But it does not have being *in* the soul except from something else—that is, from the soul itself. The reason is that true being belongs to it absolutely, whereas being in the soul is its being only in a certain respect. So too likewise, universality does not belong to a thing except according to its being in a certain respect—namely, in the soul—whereas singularity belongs to a thing according to its true being, and so belongs to it from itself and absolutely. Therefore, one should look for a cause why the nature is universal (the intellect is to be assigned as the cause of that), but one should not look for any cause why the nature is singular—a cause that would be other than the thing's own nature and mediating between the thing and its singularity. Rather the same causes that are the causes of the unity of a thing are also the causes of its singularity. Therefore, etc.

[Arguments against the previous theory]

(7) Against this view, one argues like this: An object,* insofar as it is an object, is naturally prior to the act itself. And in that prior state, according

---

3. That is, such that every stone would be identical with the *same* stone. Scotus means to be contrasting this with the innocuous claim that every stone is a "this" in the sense of there being a *different* "this" for each stone.

to you,[4] the object is of itself singular. For this always belongs to a nature not taken in only a certain respect or according to the being it has in the soul. Therefore, the intellect, understanding that object under the aspect of a universal, understands it under an aspect *opposite* to the object's very notion. For insofar as the object precedes the act, it is determined of itself to the opposite of that aspect—namely, to the opposite of the aspect of a universal.

(8) Furthermore, anything with a real, proper, and sufficient unity less than numerical unity is not of itself one by numerical unity—that is, it is not of itself a "this." But the proper, real or sufficient unity of the nature existing in this stone is less than numerical unity. Therefore, etc.

(9) The major premise is plain in itself, because nothing is one of itself by a unity greater than the unity sufficient for it. Now if the proper unity, which belongs to something of itself, is less than numerical unity, then numerical unity does not belong to that something from its own nature and according to itself. Otherwise precisely from its nature it would have both the greater and the lesser unity, which are opposites when applied to the same item and with respect to the same item. For the multitude opposed to the greater unity can go together with the lesser unity without contradiction. But this multitude cannot go together with the greater unity, because it is incompatible with it. Therefore, etc.

(10) Proof of the minor premise [in (8)]: If there is no real unity of a nature less than singularity, and every unity other than the unity of singularity and the unity of the specific nature is less than a real unity, therefore there will be no real unity less than numerical unity. The consequent is false, as I shall now prove in five or six ways.[5] Therefore, etc.

[Seven arguments in favor of a real less than numerical unity]

(11) The first way is this: According to the Philosopher, *Metaphysics* X. [1, 1052^{b}18], "In every genus there is something one and primary that is the metric and measure of all that are in that genus."

(12) This unity of what first measures is a real unity, because the Philosopher proves [*ibid.*, 19–24], that the primary notion of measuring belongs to "one." He explains in sequence how in every genus, that to which the notion of measuring belongs is one. Now this unity belongs to something insofar as it is first in the genus. Therefore, it is real, because what are measured

---

4. That is, the proponent of the theory under consideration.

5. In fact, Scotus gives seven arguments. See (11), (16), (18)–(20), (23), (28).

are real and are really measured. But a real being cannot be really measured by a being of reason. Therefore, this unity is real.

(13) But this real unity is not numerical, because in a genus there is no singular that is the measure of all that are in that genus. For according to the Philosopher, *Metaphysics* III. [3, 999ᵃ12–13], "Among individuals of the same species, this one is not prior and that one posterior."

(14) Even though the Commentator, [*Metaphysics* III. comm. 11, 50H], explains the term 'prior' here in the sense of the prior that *constitutes* a posterior, that is irrelevant to *b*.[6] For the Philosopher there means to give the reason why Plato posited the notion of a species as separated, and did not do so for genus. For among species there is an essential order on the basis of which a posterior species can be reduced to a prior one. (And therefore, according to Plato, one need not posit an Idea for the genus, through participation in which the species are what they are. But one does need to posit the Idea of a species to which all other species in the genus are reduced.) But among individuals, according to Plato and according to the Philosopher, who is reporting him, there is no such order, whether the one constitutes the other or not. Therefore, etc.

(15) Therefore, the Philosopher's purpose in that passage is to agree with Plato that among individuals of the same species there is no essential order. Therefore, no individual is by itself the measure of what are in its species. Therefore, neither is numerical or individual unity such a measure.

(16) Moreover second, I prove that the same consequent [(10)] is false, because according to the Philosopher, *Physics* VII. [4, 249ᵃ3–8], in an indivisible species comparison occurs, because it is one nature. But in a genus it does not, because a genus does not have such a unity.

(17) This difference is not a difference in unity according to reason alone, because the concept of a genus is just as numerically one for the intellect as the concept of a species is. Otherwise no one concept would be said *in quid* of many species, and so no one concept would be a genus. Rather there would be as many concepts said of the various species as there are concepts of those species. In that case, in each of the predications the same item would be predicated of itself. Likewise, the unity of a concept or of a non-concept is irrelevant to the Philosopher's meaning in that passage—that is, it is

6. The critical edition suggests that this simply means "the minor premise," a not uncommon reading for the notation '*b*' in manuscripts of this period. The "minor premise" is then "Now a real being cannot be really measured by a being of reason" in (12) above. But that passage seems irrelevant here. Another possibility comes from **W** 6. 335, which marks the beginning of (5) above with the sign '*b*'.

irrelevant to whether there is a comparison or not. Therefore, the Philosopher means there that the specific nature is one by the unity of a specific nature. But he does not mean that it is one like this by a numerical unity. For in numerical unity there is no comparison. Therefore, etc.

(18) Moreover third: According to the Philosopher, *Metaphysics* V. [15, 1021ª9–12], (the chapter on relation), the same, the similar, and the equal are all based on the notion of one, so that even though a similarity has for its foundation a thing in the genus of quality, nevertheless such[7] a relation is not real unless it has a real foundation and a real proximate basis for the founding. Therefore, the unity required in the foundation of the relation of similarity is a real one. But it is not numerical unity, since nothing one and the same is similar or equal to itself.[8]

(19) Moreover fourth: For one real opposition there are two primary real extremes. But contrariety is a real opposition. This is clear, because one contrary really destroys the other, even disregarding any operation of the intellect. And this happens only because they are contraries. Therefore, each primary extreme of this opposition is real and one by some real unity. But not a numerical unity, because in that case precisely this white thing or precisely that white thing would be the primary contrary of this black thing, which is nonsense. For then there would be as many primary contrarieties as there are individuals. Therefore, etc.

(20) Moreover fifth: For one action of a sense power there is one object, according to some real unity. But not numerical unity. Therefore, there is some other real unity than numerical unity.

(21) Proof of the minor: The power that cognizes the object in this way—that is, insofar as the object is one by this unity—cognizes it insofar as it is distinct from whatever is not one by that unity. But sense does not cognize the object insofar as it is distinct from whatever is not one by that *numerical* unity. This is apparent because no sense distinguishes this ray of the sun as differing numerically from that ray, even though they *are* nevertheless [numerically] diverse because of the motion of the sun. If all the

---

7. Repunctuating the Latin edition (398.14–15) to read 'talis' with 'relatio', not with 'qualitatis'.

8. This is a terminological matter. For mediaeval authors, similarity, equality, and identity are irreflexive relations. A thing *x* is not (qualitatively) similar *to itself* (a dyadic relation), but just has a quality. Similarly, *x* is not (quantitatively) equal *to itself*, but just has a quantity. So too, *x* is not numerically identical *with itself*, but is just "numerically one." In each case the dyadic way of expressing the situation is replaced by a monadic one.

common sensibles*—for example, diversity of place and orientation—are disregarded, and if two quanta* were posited as existing simultaneously by divine power, and they were entirely similar and equal in whiteness, then vision would not distinguish that there were two white things there. But if it cognized one of them insofar as it is one by *numerical* unity, it would cognize it insofar as it is a *distinct* one by numerical unity.

(22) One could also argue the point for the primary object of a sense power, namely that it is one in itself by some real unity, because just as the object of this power, insofar as it is an object, precedes the intellect, so too in accordance with its real unity it precedes every action of the intellect.

But this reasoning is not so conclusive as the preceding one. For it could be maintained that a primary object, insofar as it fits the scope of the power, is something common abstracted from all particular objects, and so does not have any unity except the unity of being common to the several particular objects. But for *one* object, of *one* act of sensing, this counterargument does not seem to deny that the object necessarily has a real and lesser unity than numerical unity.

(23) Moreover sixth: If every real unity is numerical unity, therefore every real diversity is numerical diversity. The consequent is false. For every numerical diversity, insofar as it is numerical, is equal. And so all things would be equally distinct. In that case, it follows that the intellect could not abstract something common from Socrates and Plato any more than it can from Socrates and a line. Every universal would be a pure figment of the intellect.

(24) The first conditional [(23)] is proved in two ways. First because one and many, same and diverse, are opposites, from *Metaphysics* X. Ch. 5 [= 3, 1054ª20–21]. But one of a pair of opposites is said in as many ways as the other one is said, from *Topics* I. [15, 106ᵇ14–15]. Therefore, to each kind of unity there corresponds its own diversity.

(25) Second, it is proved because each extreme of any diversity is one in itself. And in the same way that it is one in itself it seems to be diverse from the other extreme, so that the unity of one extreme seems to be by itself the reason for the diversity of the other extreme.

(26) This is also confirmed in another way. For if there is only a real numerical unity in this thing, then whatever unity is in the thing is of itself numerically one. Therefore, this thing and that one are primally diverse according to *every* kind of entity* there is in them. For they are diverse and agree in *nothing* in any way one. [Hence they are numerically diverse.]

(27) It is also confirmed by the fact that numerical diversity is for this

singular not to be that singular, assuming the being of each extreme. But such a unity necessarily belongs to the other extreme.[9]

(28) Moreover, even if no intellect existed, fire would still generate fire and destroy water. And there would be some real unity of form between generator and generated, according to which unity univocal generation would occur. For the intellect that considers a case of generation does not *make* the generation be univocal, but *recognizes* it to be univocal.

[Reply to the main question]

(29) Therefore, I reply to the question [(1)]: Granting the conclusions of the two arguments [(7)–(8)], I say that a material substance from its nature is *not* of itself a "this." For in that case, as the first argument [(7)] deduces, the intellect could not understand it under the opposite aspect unless it understood its object under an intelligible aspect incompatible with the notion of such an object.

(30) Also, as the second argument [(8)] deduces together with its proofs [(9)–(28)], even without any operation of the intellect there is some real unity in a thing, less than numerical unity—that is, less than the proper unity of a singular. This lesser unity belongs to the nature by itself. In accordance with this unity, which is proper to the nature insofar as it is a nature, the nature is indifferent to the unity of singularity. Therefore, it is not of itself one by that unity—that is, by the unity of singularity.

(31) In a way, one can see how this should be understood from Avicenna, *Metaphysics* V. [1, 86va], where he says "Equinity is only equinity. Of itself it is neither one nor several, neither universal nor particular." I understand: It is not from itself one by numerical unity, or several by the plurality opposite to that unity. It is neither actually universal—that is, in the way something is universal insofar as it is an object of the intellect—nor is it particular of itself.

(32) For although it is never really *without* some one of these features, yet it is not any of them *of itself*, but is naturally prior to all of them. In accordance with this natural priority, the [quiddity or] what-the-thing-is is the *per se* object of the intellect and is *per se*, as such, considered by the metaphysician and expressed by the definition. Propositions true [*per se*] in the first mode* are true by reason of the quiddity so taken. For nothing is said of a quiddity

---

9. The sentence is puzzling and does not seem to bear on the argument.

per se in the first mode unless it is included in it essentially, insofar as the quiddity is abstracted from all features naturally posterior to it.

(33) But not only is the nature itself indifferent of itself to being in the intellect and to being in a particular—and therefore also to being universal and to being particular or singular. It does not primarily of itself have universality even when it does have being in the intellect. For even though it is understood under universality (as under the mode of understanding it), nevertheless universality is not a part of its primary concept, since it is not a part of the metaphysical concept, but of the logical concept. For the logician considers second intentions applied to first ones [**K** Ch. 23], according to him.[10] Therefore, the first intellection is an intellection of the nature without there being any co-understood mode, either the mode it has in the intellect or the one it has outside the intellect. Although universality is the mode of understanding what is understood, that mode is not itself understood.

(34) Just as a nature, according to its being, is not *of itself* universal but rather universality is *accidental* to the nature according to its primary aspect according to which it is an object, so too in the external thing where the nature is together with singularity, the nature is not *of itself* determined to singularity but is naturally prior to the aspect that contracts it to that singularity. And insofar as it is naturally prior to that contracting aspect, it is not incompatible with it to be without that contracting aspect.

Just as, according to its abovementioned primacy,[11] the object in the intellect had truly intelligible being, so too in the thing the nature according to that entity has true real being outside the soul. And according to that entity, it has a unity proportional to it. That unity is indifferent to singularity, so that it is not incompatible with that unity of itself that it be found together with some unity of singularity. In this way, then, I understand a nature to have a *real unity less than numerical unity*. Granted, it does not have this lesser unity of itself in such a way that the unity is contained within the notion of the nature. For "Equinity is only equinity," according to Avicenna, *Metaphysics* V. [1, 86va]. Nevertheless that unity is a proper attribute of the nature according to its primary entity. Consequently, the nature is intrinsically

10. It is not known who is being referred to here. One manuscript has 'the Philosopher' for 'him'.

11. This appears to refer to the "primary aspect" mentioned in the preceding paragraph. The edition (404.11–12) adds 'and universality' here, which does not seem to fit the argument. I have omitted it in agreement with certain variant readings in the manuscripts.

"this" neither from itself nor according to its proper unity,[12] which is necessarily included in the nature according to its primary entity.

[Two objections to this reply]

(35) But there appear to be two objections against this. First, because it seems to claim the universal is something real in the thing. (This is contrary to the Commentator, *On the Soul* I. comm. 8. [25–28 (on 402^{b}5–9)], who says "the intellect makes universality in things, so that universality does not exist except through the intellect." So universality is only a being of reason.) For this nature, insofar as it is in this stone and yet naturally prior to the singularity of the stone, is indifferent to this singular and that one, from what has been said [(34)].

(36) Moreover [John] Damascene, [*On the Orthodox Faith*] Ch. 8, [42], "One must know that it is one thing to be considered in reality, and another to be considered in reason and thought. Therefore and more especially, in all creatures the division of hypostases is considered in reality. For in reality Peter is considered as separate from Paul. But their community and connection is considered only in the intellect, reason, and thought. For we understand by the intellect that Peter and Paul are of one nature and have one common nature." Again [*ibid.*, 43], "For these hypostases are not in one another. Rather each one is partitioned off separately—that is, separated according to reality." And later on, [*ibid.*]: "But in the holy and supersubstantial Trinity it is the other way around. For there the common is considered as one in reality." Again, [*ibid.*, 44]: "but afterwards divided in thought."

(37) To the first argument [(35)], I say that the universal in act is what has some indifferent unity according to which it itself, the very same, is in proximate potency to being *said of* each *suppositum*.* For according to the Philosopher, *Posterior Analytics* I. [4, 73^{b}26–33], the universal is what is one in many and said of many.

Nothing in reality, according to any unity at all, is such that according to that precise unity it is in proximate potency to each *suppositum* by a predication that says "This is this." For although it is not incompatible with something existing in reality for it to *be* in another singularity than the one it is in, nevertheless it cannot be truly *said* of each of its inferiors that each one

12. The edition (405.1) has 'entity' and shows no variants. But the sense of the paragraph, especially the occurrence of 'proper entity' at the end of the sentence, strongly suggests the emendation to 'unity' here. I am translating accordingly.

is it. This is possible only for an object, the same in number, actually considered by the intellect. This object as understood has also the numerical unity of an object, according to which it itself, the very same, is predicable of every singular by saying "this is this."

(38) The disproof of the statement that "the agent intellect* makes universality in things" [(35)] is apparent from this, both from the fact (a) that it can be said of every what-the-thing-is existing in the phantasm [K Ch. 30] that it is such that it is not incompatible with it to be in something else, and also from the fact (b) that the agent intellect strips[13] the what-the-thing-is existing in the phantasm. For wherever it is before it has objective being* in the possible intellect,* whether in reality or in the phantasm, whether it has certain being or being that is derived by reasoning (and so not by any [divine] light),[14] it is always such a nature of itself that it is not incompatible with it to *be* in something else. Nevertheless it is not such that it pertains to it by a proximate potency to be *said* of every individual. Rather it is in that proximate potency only in the possible intellect.

Therefore, there is in reality something common that is not of itself a "this." Consequently it is not incompatible with it of itself to be "not-this." But that common something is not a universal in act, because it lacks that indifference according to which the universal is completely universal—that is, the indifference according to which it itself, the very same, is predicable by some identity of each individual in such a way that each is it.

(39) To the second objection [(36)], about Damascene, I say that what is common in creatures is not really one in the way in which what is common is really one in the divine. For there the common is singular and individual because the divine nature itself is of itself a "this." And it is plain that with creatures no universal is really one in that way. For to maintain this would be to maintain that some created, undivided nature would be predicated of many individuals by a predication that says "this is this," just as it is said that the Father is God and the Son is the same God.

Yet in creatures there is something common that is one by a real unity less than numerical unity. This common something is not common in such a way that it is predicable of many, although it is common in such a way that it is not incompatible with it to be in something other than in what it is in.

---

13. *I. e.*, separates it from its particular and material conditions.

14. A reference to the Augustinian theory of "illumination," which Scotus rejected. See John Duns Scotus, *Philosophical Writings*, 96–132. The term 'certain' earlier in the sentence was a characteristic term used for knowledge by illumination. (I am repositioning the edition's parentheses in this sentence.)

(40) Therefore, it is clear in two ways how Damascene's text does not count against me. First, because he is speaking about the unity of singularity in the divine. And in this sense, not only is a created *universal* not one, but what is *common* in creatures is not one either.

Second, because he is speaking about what is common and predicable, not precisely about the common that is determinate in fact even though it is not incompatible with it to be in something else. What is common in the latter sense can be really posited precisely in creatures.

[Reply to the main argument for the affirmative]

(41) From what has been said [**(29)**–**(40)**], the reply to the main argument [**(2)**] is clear. For the Philosopher refutes the fiction he attributes to Plato. That is, he shows that "this man" existing by himself, which is maintained as an "Idea" [by Plato], cannot by itself be universal to every man. For "every substance existing by itself is proper to what it belongs to" [**(2)**]. That is, it is either proper from itself or else *made* proper by something contracting it. Once this contracting principle is posited, the substance cannot be in anything else, even though it is not incompatible with it *of itself* to be in something else.

This gloss is true even speaking about substance insofar as the term is taken for "nature." In that case it follows that the Idea will not be the substance of Socrates, because it is not the nature of Socrates. For it is neither of itself proper nor made proper to Socrates so that it is in him only. Rather it is also in someone else, according to Plato.

But if 'substance' is taken for first substance, then it is true that every substance is of itself proper to what it belongs to. And in that case it follows all the more that the Idea, which is posited as a substance existing by itself, cannot in that sense be the substance of Socrates or Plato. But the first alternative, [in the preceding paragraph], suffices for the point.

(42) To the confirmation of the opposing view [**(6)**], it is clear that community and singularity are not related to the nature like being in the intellect and true being outside the soul. For community belongs to the nature outside the intellect, and so does singularity. Community belongs to the nature from itself, while singularity belongs to the nature through something in the thing that contracts the nature. But universality does not belong to the thing from itself.

Therefore, I grant that one must look for a cause of universality, but one need not look for a cause of community other than the nature itself. Once community has been established in the nature itself according to its own entity and unity, one must necessarily look for the cause of singularity, which adds something over and above the nature it belongs to.

[Question 2

Is a material substance of itself individual through something positive intrinsic to it?]

(43) Second, I ask whether a material substance is of itself individual through something positive intrinsic to it.

[Argument for the negative]

(44) No. For 'one' only indicates the privation of division in itself and the privation of identity with something else. Therefore, since 'singularity' or 'individuation' only indicates a twofold negation,[15] one does not have to look for its cause in anything positive. Rather negation is enough.

(45) The first premise is proved because if 'one' did indicate a positive aspect, it would not be the same that 'being' indicates. For in that case it would be unnecessary repetition* to say 'one being'. Neither does it indicate any other positive aspect. For in that case in every being there would be entity added to entity, which seems nonsense.

[Argument for the affirmative]

(46) To the contrary: First substance is generated *per se* (from *Metaphysics* VII. [8, 1033ª24–ᵇ19],) and operates *per se* (from *Metaphysics* I. [1, 981ª16–20]). In this respect it is distinguished from second substance, to which neither of these belongs *per se*. Therefore, they belong to first substance through what first substance adds over and above second substance. But they do not belong formally to anything through a negation. Therefore, first substance does not add only a negation to second substance.

---

15. Namely the two kinds of "privation" mentioned in the preceding sentence. Something is "singular," or an "individual," if it is (a) internally undivided in itself and (b) nonidentical with anything else.

[Henry of Ghent's Theory]

(47) Here it is said that individuation in created things comes about through a twofold negation [**(44)**]. Look up this theory in [Henry of Ghent's] *Quodlibet* V. q. 8, [166M].[16]

[Arguments against Henry of Ghent's Theory]

(48) But against this theory, I first explain how the questions raised on this topic are understood. I am not looking for that by which the nature is singular or individual, if 'singular' and 'individual' signify a second intention. For in that case the nature would be singular by a second intention, and would be efficiently caused by the intellect that causes the second intention—that is, that compares "this nature" to "nature" as what can serve as a subject is compared to what can serve as its predicate. Neither am I asking about the real numerical unity by which a nature is formally one in this way. For by numerical unity a thing is formally one, whether that unity is converted with being or belongs to the genus quantity, or whether it indicates a privation or a positing.

Instead, because there is among beings something indivisible into subjective parts*—that is, such that it is formally incompatible for it to be divided into several parts each of which is it—the question is not what it is by which such a division is formally incompatible with it (because it is formally incompatible by incompatibility), but rather what it is by which, as by a proximate and intrinsic foundation, this incompatibility is in it.

Therefore, the sense of the questions on this topic is: What is it in this stone, by which as by a proximate foundation it is absolutely incompatible with the stone for it to be divided into several parts each of which is this stone, the kind of division that is proper to a universal whole* as divided into its subjective parts?

(49) Understanding the question in this sense, I prove there is nothing formally individual in the way this theory seems to hold [**(47)**].

First, because nothing is absolutely incompatible with any being through only a privation in that being, but rather through something positive in it. Therefore, to be divided into subjective parts is not incompatible with the stone, insofar as it is a certain being, through any negations.

16. See also Henry of Ghent, *Summae* a. 39, q. 3, (1. 246Q–S); q. 4, ad 5 (1. 248L), and a. 53, q. 3 (2. 62S–63S).

(50) Proof of the antecedent: No matter how much a negation takes away the proximate potency to acting and being acted on, so that for this reason the being the negation is in is not in proximate potency to anything, nevertheless it does not establish a formal *incompatibility* of that being with anything. For although they are unreal, nevertheless setting those negations aside (whether that is possible or impossible),[17] such a being would be compatible with the opposite of those negations and so with what it is said to be incompatible with *per se*. That is impossible.

Here is an example: If substance is understood as non-quantified, it is not divisible. That is, it cannot be divided by a proximate potency. Yet it is not *incompatible* with it that it be divided, because then it would be incompatible with it to receive a quantity through which it would be formally able to be divided. Therefore, while staying the nature of the same incorporeal[18] substance, it is not incompatible with it to be divisible.

Likewise, if not having a seen object takes the proximate potency to seeing away [from the sense of sight], nevertheless it does not produce an *incompatibility* with seeing. For the sense of sight can stay the same positive nature in which there was this negation, and yet the opposite of that negation can be in it without any incompatibility on the part of the nature.

(51) So too it could be argued in the present case. Although Henry posits a nature one and individual from itself, nevertheless to be divided will never be formally incompatible with it through a negation posited in the nature. And so among things there will never be any positive being that will be completely individual.

(52) If somehow there should be an objection to the first premise of this reasoning [(49)], then I assume at least the proposition 'No *imperfection* is formally incompatible with something except on account of some perfection'. This perfection is something positive and a positive entity. But to be divided is a kind of imperfection (and therefore cannot belong to the divine nature). Therefore, etc.

(53) Again, by a negation there is not constituted in an entity anything more perfect than is the entity presupposed by the negation. Otherwise the negation would be formally a certain positive entity. But first substance, according to the Philosopher in *Categories* [5, 2ᵃ11–15], is substance most of all, and also is more substance than second substance is. Therefore, it is

17. The syntax is awkward, but the sense is that we are to perform a kind of thought experiment and remove the negations, even though—since they are negative—there is really nothing to remove.

18. Reading 'incorporeae', with some of the manuscripts, instead of the edition's 'corporeae'.

not constituted in being first substance (insofar as that is distinguished from second substance) through a negation.

(54) Again, of a singular there is predicated *per se* in the first mode what it is a singular of. But of a being taken under a negation there is not any entity predicated *per se* by reason of the whole subject, because the whole is not *per se* one. If it is predicated by reason of a part, then a superior is not being predicated of an inferior but the same thing is being predicated of itself.

(55) Furthermore even though Henry's theory, if he understands the individual to be constituted in the entity and unity of singularity through a negation, seems to be false in itself because of the arguments already given [(49)–(54)], nevertheless it also seems entirely superfluous and seems not to answer the question. Even maintaining this theory, the same question still remains.

For about the twofold negation Henry posits, I ask: What is the reason why this negation belongs to this individual? If he says this twofold negation is the cause by itself, he is not answering the question. For we are asking about that through which the opposites of these negations are incompatible with this individual, and consequently about that through which these negations are in it.

(56) Likewise, I ask how it comes about that the negation is a "this," since it is of the same kind in this and that case. For just as in Socrates there is a twofold negation, so in Plato there is negation of two kinds. How does it come about therefore that Socrates is a singular by *this* proper and determinate singularity and not by Plato's singularity? There is nothing that can be said unless one finds out how it comes about that negation is *this* negation. And that cannot be except through something positive.

[Reply to the question]

(57) Therefore, I grant the conclusions of these arguments [(49)–(56)], that it is necessary through something positive intrinsic to this stone, as through a proper reason, that it be incompatible with the stone for it to be divided into subjective parts. That positive feature will be what will be said to be by itself the cause of individuation. For by 'individuation' I understand that indivisibility—that is, incompatibility with divisibility.

[Reply to the argument for the negative]

(58) To the argument for the opposite [(44)]: Although the premise is perhaps false (more on that elsewhere),[19] nevertheless even if it were true

19. Scotus does not return to this topic elsewhere in his *Ordinatio*.

that 'one' formally signified that twofold negation, it does not follow that an individual does not have any positive cause through which that twofold negation is in it. For by the same reasoning specific unity too would signify a twofold negation. Yet no one denies there is a positive entity in a specific entity's notion, from which positive entity the notion of the specific difference is taken.

This is a good argument for solving the question [(43)] and for responding to the theory [(47)]. For since in each unity less than numerical unity there is found a positive entity that is by itself the reason for that unity and for that incompatibility with the opposite multitude, this will be found most of all—or at least equally—in the case of the most perfect unity, which is numerical unity.

[Question 3

Is a material substance individual, or the reason for individuating something else, through actual existence?]

(59) Third, I ask—without preliminary arguments—whether a material substance is individual, or the reason for individuating something else, through actual existence.

[One previous theory]

(60) It is said that it is.[20] For from *Metaphysics* VII. [13, 1039ᵃ3–7], "act determines and distinguishes." Therefore, the ultimate distinction occurs through the ultimate act. But the ultimate act of individuals is according to their being of existence, because everything other than that is understood in potency to that.

[Arguments against this theory]

(61) Against this: First, because what is not of itself distinct or determinate cannot be what first distinguishes or determines something else. But the being of existence, in the sense in which it is distinguished from the being of essence, is not of itself distinct or determinate. For the being of existence

---

20. Scotus's editors (418) were unable to associate this view with any particular author.

does not have its own differences other than the differences of the being of essence, because in that case one would have to posit a proper hierarchy of existences other than the hierarchy of essences. Rather the being of existence is precisely determined from something else's determination. Therefore, it does not determine anything else.

(62) From this one could argue another way: What presupposes the determination and distinction of another is not the reason for distinguishing or determining that other. But existence, as determined and distinct, presupposes the hierarchy and distinction of essences. Therefore, etc.

(63) If it is said that it presupposes every other distinction than the distinction into individuals, but it causes the distinction that so to speak results in the individual, then to the contrary: In a categorial hierarchy, there are contained all the things that pertain by themselves to that hierarchy, disregarding whatever is irrelevant to that hierarchy. For according to the Philosopher, *Posterior Analytics* I. [20, 82^{a}21–24], "there is an end-point in each category, at the high end and at the low end." Therefore, just as there is found a highest in a genus, considering it precisely under the aspect of essence, so there are found intermediate genera, and species and differences. There is also found there a lowest, namely, the singular—actual existence being disregarded altogether. This is plainly evident because "this man" does not formally include actual existence any more than "man" in general does.

(64) Furthermore, there is the same question about existence as there is about the nature: By what and from where is it contracted, so that it is 'this'? If the specific nature is the same in several individuals, it has the same kind of existence in them. Just as it is proved in the solution to the first question [(29)–(30)] that the nature is not of itself a "this," so too it can be asked what it is through which existence is a "this," because it is not "this" of itself. So it is not enough to give existence as that by which the nature is a "this."

[Reply to the argument for this theory]

(65) On this basis I say to the argument in favor of this theory [(60)] that an act distinguishes in the same way it is an act. But an accidental act distinguishes accidentally, just as an essential act distinguishes essentially. So I say the ultimate distinction in a categorial hierarchy is the individual distinction, and it occurs through the ultimate act that pertains by itself to the categorial hierarchy. But actual existence does not by itself pertain to this hierarchy. Actual existence *is* the ultimate act, but it is posterior to the whole categorial hierarchy. Therefore, I grant that it distinguishes ultimately, but by a distinction outside the whole *per se* categorial hierarchy. This distinction is so to speak "accidental" in a certain sense. Granted, it is not truly accidental. Yet it does follow the whole hierarchy of quidditative being. Therefore, it distinguishes in the way it is an act. And it ultimately distinguishes in the way it is the ultimate act.

[Question 4

Is a material substance individual or singular through quantity?]

(66) Fourth, I ask whether a material substance is individual or singular through quantity.

[Arguments for the affirmative]

(67) Yes. Boethius in *On the Trinity* [1. 24–31]: "The variety of accidents is what makes difference in number. For three men differ neither by species nor by genus, but by their accidents. If in the mind we separate out all the accidents, nevertheless place is diverse for each of them. We can in no way suppose that it is one for two men. For two bodies will not occupy the same place, which is an accident. Therefore, they are numerically as several as their accidents are several." Among all accidents, the first accident is quantity, which seems to be implied in a special sense even in the notion of "place" (in saying "we cannot suppose it is the same place"). Place pertains to bodies insofar as they are quantified.

(68) Furthermore, [John] Damascene in the *Elementarium*, Ch. 5 (not counting the prologue) [= Ch. 4, col. 103]: "Every thing by which a hypostasis differs from another hypostasis of the same species is called an adventitious difference, and a characteristic peculiarity, and a hypostatic quality. Now this is an accident. For example, a man differs from another man because this one is tall while that one is short."

(69) Furthermore, Avicenna in *Metaphysics* V. 2, [87ᵛᵃ]: "A nature that needs matter is such that for its being there come together accidents and dispositions from outside, by which it is individuated."

[Argument for the negative]

(70) To the contrary: As was argued in the second question [(46)], first substance is *per se* generated and *per se* operates, and this insofar as it is distinguished from second substance, to which these features do not belong

per se. Now they do not belong by accident to a being. This is clear for being generated, from *Metaphysics* VI. [2, 1026^{b}22–24]; it is also clear for operating, because one *per se* agent is one being *per se*, [not one being accidentally]. This holds within one order of cause.

[The theory of Giles of Rome and Godfrey of Fontaines]

(71) Here it is said[21] that yes, a material substance is singular and individual through quantity.

(72) The following reason is offered for this [Godfrey VII. 5, 333]: What primarily and *per se* belongs to something belongs to anything else by reason of that something. Now substance and accident do not make up something one *per se*, but only one by accident. Therefore, to whichever of these it is that divisibility into parts of the same kind belongs primarily and *per se*, singularity will belong to that. Quantity is like this, because of itself it is able to be divided to infinity (*Metaphysics* V. [13, 1020^{a}7–8]). Therefore, what belongs to quantity primarily and *per se* does not belong to anything else except by reason of quantity. For example, the division of a species into its individuals, because these dividing individuals are not formally of another kind, as the species that divide a genus are.

From this it is argued further [Godfrey VII. 5, 328]: To be divisible into parts of the same kind belongs to something by reason of quantity (from *Metaphysics* V. [13, 1020^{a}7–8]). And the principle of division in any nature is the same as the principle of distinction in what are divided. Therefore, individuals are distinguished individually from one another by quantity. From this it is concluded that it is through quantity that division into individuals belongs to whatever thing such a distinction belongs to. Therefore, an individual is individual through quantity.

(73) Furthermore, this fire does not differ from that fire except because the one form differs from the other form. And the one form does not differ from the other form except because it is received in one or another part of matter. Neither does a part of matter differ from another part except because it is under another part of quantity. Therefore, the whole distinction of this fire from that fire is reduced to quantity as to what primarily distinguishes.

(74) This reasoning is confirmed. The generator does not generate any-

---

21. Here and throughout the question, the critical edition cites several passages from Aquinas, but also especially the *Quodlibets* by Giles of Rome and Godfrey of Fontaines. Scotus seems to be thinking mainly of the latter two.

thing else except on account of a distinction of matter [Aristotle, *Metaphysics* VII. 8, 1034ª4–8—see **(132)**]. Now the matter of the generated is necessarily presupposed as quantified and under a quantity distinct from the generator's quantity. That it has to be quantified is clear, because a natural agent cannot act on what is not quantified. It is also clear that it has to be quantified by another quantity, because it cannot be quantified by the generator's quantity. But this quantity [of the generated] naturally precedes the being of the generated, and therefore precedes the distinction between the generator and the generated. Now it would not naturally precede if it were not naturally and *per se* required as what distinguishes the generated from the generator. Therefore, etc.

[Against Giles's and Godfrey's theory]

(75) I argue against the conclusion [**(71)**] in four ways. First, from the identity of the numerical aspect—that is, of individuation or singularity; second, from the ordering of substance to accident; third, from the notion of a categorical hierarchy. These three ways will prove in general that no accident can by itself be the reason by which a material substance is individuated. The fourth way will be against quantity in particular, with respect to the conclusion of the theory [**(71)**].[22]

Fifth, it will be argued in particular against the reasons for that theory [**(72)**–**(73)**].

(76) As for the first way, first I explain what I understand by individuation or numerical unity or singularity: Certainly not the indeterminate unity by which anything in the species is said to be one in number. Instead I mean signate unity as a "this," so that just as it was said above [**(48)**] that an individual is incompossible with being divided into subjective parts and the reason for that incompossibility is asked there, so too I say here that an individual is incompossible with not being a designated "this" by *this* singularity and the cause is asked not of singularity in general but of *this* designated singularity in particular—that is, as it is determinately "this."

(77) Understanding singularity in this sense, I argue from the first way [**(75)**] in a twofold manner:

First: An actually existing substance, not changed by any substantial change, cannot from "this" become "not this." For this singularity, according to what was just said, cannot be one singularity and another in the same substance that remains the same and is not substantially changed. But an

22. For these four ways, see **(76)**–**(81)**, **(82)**–**(88)**, **(89)**–**(98)**, **(99)**–**(104)**.

actually existing substance, even if there is no substantial change made or changed in it, can be under one or another quantity without contradiction, and under any absolute accident* whatever. Therefore, by no such accident is this substance formally designated by this singularity.

(78) The minor premise is clear. For it is not a contradiction that God preserve the same substance, now quantified by this quantity, and inform it by another quantity. The actually existing substance will not for this reason be changed by a substantial change, because there will be no change except from one quantity into another quantity. Likewise, if it is changed from *any* accident it now has, the substance will not be changed by a substantial change. Whether this is possible or impossible,[23] the substance will not for this reason be formally "not this."

(79) If you say the described situation is a miracle and therefore does not argue against natural reason, to the contrary: A miracle does not occur with respect to contradictories; there is *no* power that can do that. But it is a contradiction for the same remaining substance to be two substances without a substantial change. It is impossible both successively and at once. Yet this follows if the substance were *this* substance through some accident. For in that case, when one accident follows another accident, the same substance, without being changed, would be two substances in succession.

(80) This is confirmed also by an analogy with specific unity. For it is incompossible for one substance, remaining substantially unchanged, to be this species and not this species, either together or successively. Therefore, by analogy in the present case too.

(81) Second: There cannot be the same primary end-point for two completed productions in substantial being. (*Proof:* For in that case each one would take on the perfect substantial being by which each is made complete. So the same product would be completely produced twice. Also, if those two productions were not simultaneous, then the same substance, which already exists *per se* and actually, would be produced when it already actually exists. Therefore, there cannot be the same end-point, at least for two successive productions.) But in the generation of bread, *this* bread was a primary end-point. The bread however is transubstantiated, while the same quantity remains. Therefore, let another bread be created, and let it be affected by this quantity that remains. It follows that the end-point of this creation will be this bread, the same as the bread that was the end-point of the earlier generation. For this bread will be a "this" by numerically the same singularity by which that bread was a "this."

23. The purpose of the clause is unclear.

It follows further that the same "this bread" is transubstantiated and not transubstantiated. Indeed it follows that no bread is transubstantiated. For it is not universal bread that is transubstantiated. Neither is it *this* singular bread, because this bread remains whenever the quantity by which it was formally "this" is not changed, from what was given above [(71)]. Therefore, nothing whatever is transubstantiated into the body of Christ, which is heretical to say.

(82) From the second way [(75)], I argue as follows: Substance is naturally prior to every accident, according to the Philosopher, *Metaphysics* VII. [1, 1028[a]10–[b]2]. His meaning for 'substance' in that passage is that it is one of the categories that divide being, so that to analyze 'substance' there as referring only to God, or to first substance, is irrelevant to his meaning.[24] For he proves that substance is primary among the categories in the same way he proves that substance is included at all in the number of categories that divide being: it is prior to every accident. So for fixing all the categories that divide being, it is enough to settle on substance as the first, since the cognition of accidents is had insofar as they are attributed to substance. But this is beside the point unless it is about substance according to its whole categorial hierarchy. Therefore,[25] nothing posterior to this entire hierarchy can be the formal reason by which something is in this hierarchy. Thus by reason of the priority of substance universally, insofar as it is common, fixing the order of first substance (to which there belongs this natural priority to every accident) is enough to establish the point. Therefore, it belongs to first substance, from its very notion, that it be a "this" naturally prior to being determined by any accident.

(83) This inference could be confirmed, because when something is prior to something else, the most primary of the former is prior to the latter. But the most primary in the case of substance in general is first substance. Therefore, it is absolutely prior to every accident, and so is a "this" prior to being determined in any way through something else.

(84) Here it is said that first substance, even though it is prior in being to quantity, nevertheless is not prior in dividing, just as second substance too is prior in entity, but not in divisibility.

(85) To the contrary: This reply is self-refuting. For if first substance is

24. Averroes gave such an interpretation of the passage. See his *Commentary on the Metaphysics* VII. comm. 2 (8. 153G–K).

25. This continues the argument begun in the second sentence of the paragraph. Everything in between has been directed to the interpretation of 'substance' in the passage from Aristotle.

naturally prior in being to quantity itself, and first substance cannot be understood in its being except insofar as it is a "this," therefore it is not prior in being unless it is prior insofar as it is a "this." Therefore, it is not a "this" through quantity.

(86) Furthermore, form is absolutely prior to the composite, according to the Philosopher's proof in *Metaphysics* VII. 2, [1029ª5–7]. Thus if quantity is the form of a first substance insofar as it is first substance, it will be absolutely prior to first substance in being. For if it is not a form prior in being, it is neither prior in dividing nor prior in the unity belonging to a first substance insofar as it is such a being. For from every entity there follows its own unity that does not have any other cause of itself than the cause of the entity.

(87) Furthermore, substance is naturally prior to every accident in the same way it is a subject for every accident. For insofar as it is a subject, it is proved to be prior by definition to every accident, because as a subject it is included as an addition in the course of giving the definition of any accident. But insofar as it is a subject, it is "this substance." For according to the Philosopher, *Physics* I [= II. 3, 195ª25–26], and *Metaphysics* II [= I. 1, 981ᵇ16–19], singulars are the causes of singulars in whatever genus of cause. Therefore, a singular subject is the cause of a singular accident.

This is confirmed especially in the case of an accidental accident,[26] because that is in the singular primarily, according to the Philosopher, *Metaphysics* V, the chapter on "same" [9, 1017ᵇ35–1018ª3].

(88) Furthermore, everything prior by nature to something else is also prior in duration in the sense that, insofar as it itself is concerned, it is not contradictorily incompatible with it to be able to be prior in duration to what is posterior to it. For in general a priority of nature includes in what is prior its being able without contradiction to be without what is posterior, from *Metaphysics* V, the chapter on "prior" [11, 1019ª2–4]. Therefore, without contradiction any substance, as far as it itself is concerned, could be prior in duration to every accident—and so to quantity.

(89) From the third way [(75)], I argue as follows: In every categorial hierarchy there are contained all that pertain to that hierarchy, disregarding everything else that is not something belonging essentially to that hierarchy. (This is proved because any two such hierarchies are primarily diverse, and so nothing belonging to the one does so through the other's hierarchy.) But just as there belongs to that hierarchy, insofar as it is limited at both the top and the bottom (according to the Philosopher, *Posterior Analytics* I. [20, 82ª21–24]), a first predicate, of which nothing else is predicated, so too

---

26. *de accidente per accidens.* I am not sure of the sense here.

there belongs to it a lowest subject, to which nothing else is made subject. Therefore, in every categorial hierarchy the singular or individual is not established through anything belonging to any other hierarchy.

(90) Furthermore second: In every categorial hierarchy, disregarding everything belonging to any other hierarchy, there is the notion of species. For no theory pretends that the species in some genus is established by reason of an accident (speaking about absolute accidents). But it belongs to the notion of a species that it be predicable of several items differing in number. Therefore, in every categorial hierarchy there can be found something intrinsically individual and singular of which the species is predicated—or at least there can be found something not predicable of many.[27] Otherwise, if nothing can serve as a subject like this, then nothing in this hierarchy will be a most specific species, to the very notion of which it belongs to be predicable.

(91) Furthermore third: What can and does serve as the lowest subject receives the *per se* predication of every predicable in the hierarchy, just as the first predicate is predicated *per se* of every predicate in the hierarchy. But a being by accident, insofar as it is by accident, receives no predication *per se*. Therefore, what can serve as the lowest subject cannot be a being by accident. But what attaches things of diverse genera to one another is a being by accident, according to the Philosopher, *Metaphysics* V, the chapter on "one" [6, 1015^{b}16–36].

(92) Furthermore fourth: When something is naturally apt to belong to something precisely according to some reason, then whatever it belongs to essentially according to that reason it belongs to it *absolutely* and essentially according to that reason. But universal[28] being in the hierarchy of the genus substance belongs to something precisely insofar as that something belongs to that hierarchy, disregarding everything that belongs to another hierarchy. Therefore, what community belongs to essentially insofar as it is in that hierarchy, it belongs to *absolutely* and essentially. Now no matter how much it is contracted by something in another genus, nothing is taken away from it that is relevant to its hierarchy. For no matter how much Socrates is determined by white or black (to which he is in potency), Socrates is no more determinately in the genus substance that he was before, because he was already a "this" before. Therefore, no matter how much a nature in the

27. The role of this clause is unclear. The critical edition (434 n. 2) suggests it is an allusion to the celestial bodies, which have only a single individual per species. But it is hard to see how that is relevant here.

28. Thus the edition (435.10). 'Common' would seem a more likely reading in virtue of the rest of the paragraph. The manuscripts show no relevant variants here.

genus substance is claimed to be contracted to individuals through something in another genus, that nature will remain formally common when it is contracted just as when it was not contracted. Therefore, to claim that the common becomes individual through something in another genus is to claim it is both common and individual or singular at once.

(93) Perhaps in order to avoid the arguments of these two ways [(82)–(88), (89)–(92)], the theory about quantity is also held in another version—namely, in the sense that just as the extension of matter itself is by nature other than the nature[29] of the quantity of the matter itself, and adds nothing to the essence of the matter, so too the designation of the matter itself, which it has causally through the quantity, is other than the designation of the quantity itself and naturally prior to the designation the matter has through the quantity. This designation of the matter is other than the one that belongs to the quantity, but it is not other than substance. Thus just as matter does not have parts through the nature of quantity, because a part of matter is matter, so designated substance is nothing but substance. For "designation" only indicates a mode of being.[30]

---

29. Thus the edition (436.7). 'Extension' would seem better. See n. 30 below. The edition shows no relevant variants.

30. The paragraph is virtually unintelligible as it stands. Scotus is apparently thinking of Giles of Rome's theory, as found in his *Quodlibeta* I. 11, 7[rb]:

> Matter is not extended of itself, but is extended through quantity. Nevertheless the extension of the matter is other than the extension of the quantity. So too, even though substance is individuated and designated by quantity, and the former designation comes from the latter, nevertheless the designation and individuation of the substance is other than the designation and individuation of the quantity. Therefore, just as matter does not have parts except through quantity, and the parts of the matter are other than the parts of the quantity (yet the parts of matter do not involve anything but matter, insofar as every part of matter is matter), so too even though the designation in the substance comes from the quantity, nevertheless the designation of the substance is other than the designation of the quantity. Substance together with its designation does not involve anything but substance, but only involves a certain mode of being the substance has under quantity, just as matter that has parts does not involve anything but matter, but only involves a certain mode of being the matter has from the fact that it is perfected by quantity. Therefore, it is clear how individuation comes about and how individuation does not remove things from their proper categories.

Giles's view is also discussed by Godfrey of Fontaines, *Quodlibet* VII. 5, 306–307.

(94) To the contrary: This position seems to include contradictories in two ways. First because it is impossible for something that depends on what is naturally posterior to be the same as what is naturally prior. For in that case it would be both prior and not prior. But substance is naturally prior to quantity, according to them. Therefore, nothing in any way presupposing the nature of quantity can be the same as substance. Therefore, the designation [described in **(93)**] is not both the designation of substance and yet also caused by quantity.

(95) Proof of the major premise: Wherever there is a true and real identity between this and that (even though it is not formal identity), it is impossible for this to be and that not to be. For in that case what is really the same would both be and not be. But it is possible for the naturally prior to be without the naturally posterior. Therefore, consequently it is all the more possible for the naturally prior to be without what is left behind[31] or caused by the naturally posterior.

(96) Furthermore, what is a necessary condition for a cause's causing cannot be had from the caused. For in that case the cause, insofar as it is sufficient for the causing, would be caused by the caused. And so the caused would be the cause of itself and to that extent could give to its cause the causing of the caused itself. But singularity—that is, designation—is a necessary condition in a substance for causing quantity because, as has been argued [**(87)**], a singular caused requires a singular cause. Therefore, it is impossible for this designation of a designated or singular substance to be from a singular quantity (or to be from the caused) and not from a substance insofar as it is singular.

(97) Furthermore, what is it for quantity to leave behind or cause such a mode in a substance? If there is nothing but what was there before the quantity, then in no way does the designation come about through the quantity. For in that case the substance's designation would naturally precede the quantity absolutely. But if there is something else, I ask how it is caused by the quantity and in what genus of cause? It does not seem that any genus can be assigned except the genus of efficient cause. But quantity is not an active form. Therefore, etc.

---

31. The metaphor here is one of "impressions," as from a seal-ring. Just as the ring leaves a shape impressed in the wax, even though the shape of the wax is numerically distinct from the shape of the ring, so too, the theory holds, the individuation (or "designation") of the quantity leaves behind a kind of impression in matter, even though the individuation of the matter is distinct from that of the quantity.

(98) Furthermore, why does quantity leave behind such a mode in the substance, really the same as the substance, any more than does a quality like whiteness? There seems to be no reason. For just as whiteness is by itself the form of a surface, and not by means of any other form left behind, so it seems that quantity is the form of a substance by which the substance is quantified, and never leaves behind another form.

(99) From the fourth way [(75)], I argue as follows: This quantity by which a substance is a "this," so designated, is either determinate quantity or indeterminate quantity.[32] It is not determinate quantity, because that follows on the form's being in matter, and consequently follows on the substances's singularity. For if substance is the cause of quantity as determinate, this substance is the cause of it as this determinate quantity.

If indeterminate quantity is the cause why this substance is a "this," then to the contrary: That quantity—that is, indeterminate quantity—stays the same in the generated and the corrupted. Therefore, it is not the cause of any determinate designation.

(100) If you say this does not follow, because quantity is not supposed to be the cause of singularity unless a specific unity is presupposed, but the generated and the corrupted do not belong to the same species, then to the contrary: I posit that first, from water there is generated fire, and then second, from fire there is generated water. In the first (the corrupted) water and in the second (the generated) water there is the same quantity—not only an indeterminate quantity but also a determinate one. For it can have the same determination from the form. Or at any rate, it is enough that there is the same indeterminate quantity. And according to you, that is the cause of singularity if specific unity is presupposed. Therefore, the first water and the second water are numerically the same "this water." This seems impossible, because numerically the same individual does not recur by any natural action, from *Physics* V. [4, 228ª4–6], and *On Generation* II. [11, 338ᵇ16–18].

(101) Furthermore if quantity is what primarily individuates substance, then it must be in itself primarily "this" and numerically distinct of itself from "that," just as this substance is distinct from that one. But in that case

---

32. On the theory of determinate or indeterminate quantity as the principle of individuation, see Roland-Gosselin, especially Chs. 3–4 on Avicenna and Averroes. See also Averroes, *On the Substance of the Sphere*, Juntas ed., 9. 3A–5L; Hyman tr., 39–73. The critical edition of Scotus also cites several passages in Aquinas, Giles of Rome, and Godfrey of Fontaines.

your proposition is not true—that is, that "every formal difference is specific" [Godfrey, VI. 16, 259, & VII. 5, 332]. For this quantity and that one are forms, and therefore differ specifically [if your proposition is true].

(102) If you make quantity an exception to this fundamental proposition of your ruined edifice,[33] how will it be proven that *any* formal difference is specific? For whatever aspect is added by form will have the same role here too, since quantity is a form just as the other categories are.

(103) If you say, "On the contrary, a quantity of itself has a determinate position, and in this respect is distinguished of itself from any other quantity," then to the contrary: What position are you talking about? Either you are talking about categorial position, which is a certain category and is naturally posterior to quantity. Or else you are talking about the kind of position that is a difference of quantity insofar as quantity is said to consist of parts having position. In that case, there is the same question as before: Why does this position of this quantity differ from that position of that quantity? This question amounts to "How does this quantity numerically differ from that one?" So it seems you are making this distinction the reason for itself. For it is no better known that the permanent and continuous parts in *this* whole are distinguished by themselves from the permanent and continuous parts in this *other* whole (position as a difference of quantity contains the two factors: continuation and permanence) than it is that this quantity differs by itself from that one.

(104) Furthermore, all the same arguments [(7)–(28)] given against the theory in the first question, to prove that flesh[34] is not of itself a "this," can be given here to prove that quantity is not of itself a "this." For it is plain that the notion of "line"[35] is of itself common to this line and that one. Neither is there any greater contradiction in understanding "line" under the aspect of a universal than in understanding flesh that way. "Line" too has a real unity less than numerical unity just as flesh has, by the same proofs that were given in the second reason [(9)–(28)] against the theory in the first question [(8)]. It is clear also that a line and a surface are of the same kind in this water and in that. Therefore, why is this water "this" water and singular? I am not talking about a vague and indeterminate singularity, but about a designated and determinate one.

---

33. *I. e.*, the theory of quantity as the principle of individuation. The "fundamental proposition" is 'Every formal difference is specific' **(101)**.

34. The argument in q. 1 is not put in terms of "flesh" but in terms of "stone." See **(8)**.

35. Lines are in the category of quantity (*Categories* 6, 4ᵇ23–24).

[Reply to the reasons in favor of this theory]

(105) I argue against the reasons [(72)–(73)] for this theory.[36]

First, against the first one [(72)], I argue that quantity is not the reason for divisibility into individuals. For whatever is the formal reason for any divisibility is formally in what is divisible by that division. But quantity is not formally in the species insofar as it is divisible into subjective parts. Therefore, it is not the formal reason for such a divisibility of the whole into such parts.

(106) This reasoning is confirmed.[37] For a universal whole, which is divided into individuals and into subjective parts, is predicated of each of those subjective parts in such a way that each subjective part is it. But the quantitative parts into which a continuous whole is divided never admit of the predication of the whole that is divided into them. And even though the division of a homogeneous whole into its quantitative parts might coincide with the division of a species or universal whole into its subjective parts (the latter parts are the individuals), nevertheless the two divisions are not of the same divided whole. For a quantitative whole is divided by a quantitative division and is not predicated of any dividing part, just as a heterogeneous quantum is not predicated of what divides it. For in general, no quantitative part is the whole of which it is a part. But coinciding with this there is the fact that there are several individuals having the same common being, which common being is divided into those individuals by another kind of division. That common being is not the quantum that was divided by the quantitative division. Therefore, the whole divided by the latter division is other than the whole divided by the former one. They are divided by accident into the same parts, but the parts are formally of different kinds with respect to the latter whole and the former one. For with respect to the latter whole, it is divided into integral parts, and with respect to the former one into subjective parts. On account of this coincidence of the two divisions of the two wholes into the same parts, in which parts the twofold notion of part runs together, some people thought these two wholes are divided into parts of the same kind.

(107) As for the passage [(72)] taken from the Philosopher, it needs to be said that the Philosopher does not say a quantum is divided into parts of the same kind as the whole, but that "a quantum is divisible into what are in it, of which each or either one is naturally something and a 'this something' "

---

36. This is the fifth item on the program listed in **(75)**.
37. The argument in **(106)** will be much clearer if you compare it with the original argument in **(72)**.

[*Metaphysics* V. 13, 1020ᵃ7–8]. "Into what are in it," he says, as components of the whole they are in. Therefore, it is not so divided into subjective parts that are not so in it.

"Of which either one," if the division is into two, "or each," if into several, "is naturally something," that is, existing *per se* after the manner of the whole. For insofar as something is a quantitative dividing part, it is able, like the divided whole, to be *per se*. This is contrary to the division of a composite into matter and form. "And a 'this something' "—this is contrary to the division of a genus into species. If a number were composed of diverse numbers, it would not conflict with the notion of the number for it to be divided into numbers of a different kind than the whole. In the same way it does not conflict with an ell* that it would be divided into parts of a different kind than an ell if it were composed of two cubits and three cubits. (These differ in species from an ell.) So too the division of its subject into parts of a different kind does not conflict with a quantity.

(108) Therefore, I grant universally as a matter of fact that even though a whole does not require that it be divided into parts of the *same* kind as the whole, nevertheless it does not require them to be of a *distinct* kind either. For insofar as they are parts of the quantum, they are not of another kind. Even though the head, heart, and hand are quantitative parts and of a different kind than a man is, nevertheless they are not parts of another kind precisely *insofar* as they are parts of the quantum.

(109) Therefore, in the sense in which it is true (even though it could not be accepted by the Philosopher [(107)]) that a quantum is divided into parts of the same kind as the whole, it is completely beside the point. For it is not divided into parts in which the notion of the divided is included, but into parts that were in the divided.³⁸ They have one notion, not of the divided, but of something common to that and to these parts. But a species is divided into parts of the same kind as the species, because they include the notion of the divided species itself, and not something else that is of another kind but is common to the divided and to what divide it.

(110) Furthermore, I argue against the second line of reasoning [(73)–(74)]: The generator insofar as it generates, disregarding everything else, is distinguished from the generated insofar as it is generated, disregarding everything other than the generated. For it is unintelligible that the same thing generate itself. Even in the divine, a person of the Trinity does not generate itself. But the generator insofar as it generates does not include quantity as a proper generative principle. Neither does the generated insofar

38. As in the example of the head, heart, and hand in (108).

as it is generated include quantity as a *per se* or formal end-point of the generation. Therefore, disregarding either quantity—that is, the generator's and the generated's—this substance is distinguished numerically from that one.

[Scotus's own verdict]

(111) Therefore, I grant the conclusions of all the above arguments [(76)–(110)]: that it is impossible for substance to be individual through some accident—that is, that through something accidental to it it is divided into subjective parts and through this accident it is incompatible with it for it to be "not this."

[Reply to the preliminary arguments]

(112) To the first argument [(72)] in favor of the theory, it is clear from the fifth article [(105)–(109), especially (107)], how the argument takes the minor premise wrongly and in a sense that cannot be got from the Philosopher. And in the sense in which that minor premise can be taken as true, it is irrelevant to the point about the division of a whole into quantitative parts.

(113) Also, when it assumes further [(72)] that it is by means of the same factor that something is divisible and that it is distinguished through its dividing parts,[39] that is false. For a common nature is divisible of itself into individuals. But the dividing individuals are not distinguished by reason of the nature, but from their own distinguishing features. The same point appears in the case of a genus. For a genus is divisible of itself into several sub-genera and into several species, and yet the genus is not the reason for the distinction of the species. Rather the differences that constitute the species are the reasons for that distinction.

(114) To the second argument [(73)], it is clear [(110)] how it could be concluded from it that the same thing would generate itself. But to the form of the argument, I say that both premises are false. For even though another form is in another matter, nevertheless it is not on account of the otherness of the matter that it is another form. Rather, just as the entity of the form is prior, so too is its otherness.

---

39. This is not quite correctly put and does not reflect (72), which instead says that the principle of division in a nature is the same as the principle of distinction of the parts into which it is divided. The rest of (113) however gets the point right.

Likewise the other premise is false—namely, that it is another part of the matter on account of another part of the quantity. For whether the distinction of the parts of the matter in itself is quantitative or not, the distinction of the parts of the matter is prior to that of the quantity, because the subject of an accident like this is a "this something."

(115) To the proof, when it is said [(74)] that the generator does not generate except from matter quantified by another quantity, I say that whether this is so or not (more on that elsewhere [(208)]), at any rate for the parts of matter that are distinct according to the form of quantity, unity is a metaphysical attribute, so that the unity of matter naturally precedes any notion of quantity at all. For the notion of quantity precedes the kind of natural generator such that it externally requires its matter from which it generates and requires the quantity as accompanying the distinction of matter from matter. It ought to have been proven that quantity was the proper reason for such a unity—the unity of singularity in a substance. It was proven instead that it is a reason *sine qua non* with respect to the last item generated. Hence the form of the argument is faulty.[40]

(116) Suppose it is objected that from the confirming argument [(74)] at least it will be granted that quantity naturally precedes the individuation of a substance. (This is contrary to the conclusion of the second way [(82)–(83)] of disproving the theory.) For if the generator requires quantified matter before it generates, then the quantity of matter is naturally presupposed by the individuation of what is itself generated.

I reply and say that the quantity of what was corrupted, and all the accidents of what was corrupted, are presupposed in the order of temporal duration for the individuation of what is generated. For what was corrupted exists[41] beforehand together with all its parts. But nothing follows from this with respect to the minor premise [(74)], which affirms the natural priority of the quantity to the individuation of what is generated—that is, to the individuation of the substance the quantity is in. For the accidents of what

---

40. Hence . . . faulty: *Unde locus illius consequentiae nullus est. I. e.*, there is no "topical" *locus* governing the inference. This obscure paragraph in effect observes that quantity is not prior to the unity of the matter, as the argument in (74) appears to assume, but rather prior to the natural generating agent that requires both matter and an accompanying quantity. The mistake is hidden by a fallacy in the argument in (74). That argument only proves quantity is a *sine qua non*, whereas a stronger connection than that is needed to show that quantity is the principle of individuation.

41. Thus the edition. I conjecture the past tense 'existed', although the edition shows no variants here.

was corrupted, which temporally precede what is generated, follow on the substance they are in (even on that substance as singular). In the same way, the accidents of what is generated follow on the substance of what is generated.

(117) But the argument goes back still further. For, [it is claimed], it is not only as the quantity in what was corrupted that quantity precedes what is generated. It also naturally precedes *in* what is generated the form of what is generated. *Proof:* Otherwise, at the instant the generator induces the form, it would induce it not in a quantum. This seems to be contrary to the premise that a particular agent does not affect the substance of matter, but only affects matter precisely insofar as it is quantified [(74)]. Likewise, it seems to be contrary to Averroes in his treatise *On the Substance of the Sphere* [Ch. 1], where he seems to say quantity remains the same in the generated and the corrupted, because otherwise the generator would generate a body from a non-body.

(118) I argue against this: It seems first that this reasoning should not be brought up in favor of the theory. For [Godfrey of Fontaines], who seems to be the founder of this position,[42] appears to hold the contrary of what is claimed here. He holds that since quantity is not the first act of matter, neither does any form of corporeity remain the same in the generated and the corrupted. (Speaking about corporeity in the genus substance, he says [Godfrey, II.7],[43] no quantity remains numerically the same in the one and in the other.) Also, since he maintains that quantity immediately perfects the composite substance (and not merely the matter), as perfecting a subject, therefore he should maintain that the other quantity, the quantity of the generated, is naturally posterior to the generated, just as the quantity of the corrupted is naturally posterior to the corrupted. So this argument [(117)] about the priority of quantity to substance, or to the form of the generated, is not part of the theory of the one who holds this view—whatever is the case with Averroes.

This is *ad hominem.* But as for the conclusion in itself [(117)], I say (in agreement with him on these points) that [when fire by a substantial change becomes water], if no form of corporeity remains formally the same in the fire and in the water, then no accident whatever requiring a composite substance for its subject can remain the same in number throughout the

---

42. Godfrey did not originate the theory, but "founded" it in the sense of putting it on a solid "foundation."

43. The critical edition does not give a more precise reference, and I have been unable to locate a likely passage.

change. Instead each accident will either be in the corrupted as in its subject
or else in the generated as in its subject. Thus quantity and every other
accident will be naturally posterior to substance. So the quantity of the
corrupted, and every other accident of it, was naturally posterior to the
corrupted substance.

(119) I do not care very much about the premise [mentioned in (117)],
because it seems impossible. For to be the agent that affects the patient in
its aspect as patient seems to be nothing else than to induce in the patient
the act by which it is perfected. Now a particular agent induces the substantial
form by which matter insofar as it is matter is perfected—not matter insofar
as it is *quantified*, so that quantity is a mediating reason between the agent
and the patient. Therefore, the natural agent affects matter according to its
bare essence, as the patient immediately transmuted by it.

(120) To Averroes [(117)], I say that a body could be generated out of
what at some time was a nonbody, but perhaps a natural agent could not
generate a body out of a nonbody as out of what has been *corrupted*. A natural
agent is able, out of what was a body (with quantity inhering in it) up
until the instant of generation, to generate something else in that instant,
quantified by another quantity. For just as it is able to produce a substance
that was not there before, so it is able to produce all the accidents that follow
on that substance.

(121) If you say that even though it does not produce a body out of a
nonbody as out of what has been corrupted, nevertheless it will produce
another quantified body out of matter as nonquantified, I say in response
that it is necessary for a composite to be made or produced out of a non-
composite as a part, or else there will be an infinite regress. So out of matter
according to its substance absolutely, as out of a part, a body can be produced
that is a composite substance. Quantified substance accompanies this, because quantity is an attribute of the composite substance.

(This reply denies that an indeterminate dimension remains the same in
number in the generated and the corrupted. On that I will speak at greater
length elsewhere, if the occasion arises (W 8. 598, 620–621, 651). But it is
mentioned here because of the arguments [in (118)–(121)].)

[Reply to the main arguments]

(122) To the first main argument, from Boethius [(67)], I grant that the
variety of accidents is what makes a numerical difference in substance, in
the sense in which a form is said to make a difference. For all distinct forms
make some difference in this way in what they are in. But accidents cannot

make a specific difference in the substance they are in, from *Metaphysics* X, the penultimate chapter, [9, 1058ᵃ29–ᵇ25]. So they do make a difference in substances—a numerical difference. But they do not make the *first* numerical difference. Rather there is another, prior numerical difference. Neither do they *alone* make a numerical difference. The passage from Boethius makes neither of the two claims just denied. And unless one of them were granted, the point intended would not be established.

(123) But what about Boethius's meaning?

I say Boethius meant to prove there is no numerical difference among the divine persons. Although at the beginning of his little book *On the Trinity*, propositions like the ones quoted [(67)] can be found here and there, yet he seems to be arguing like this: The variety of accidents is what makes a difference in number. But in the divine persons there is no such variety of accidents, because a simple form cannot be a subject. Therefore, there is no numerical difference there.

(124) It seems at first that the argument is not valid unless Boethius meant that *only* accidents can distinguish numerically. For if numerical distinction could come about through some other means, then from the denial of accident there would not follow the denial of a numerical distinction.

I say in reply that a distinction of accidents accompanies every numerical distinction. Therefore, where there can be no variety of accidents there can be no numerical distinction either. On this basis Boethius's argument can claim that since in the divine there cannot be any accident (and so no *variety* of accidents), there cannot be any numerical distinction or difference there. The argument then is not as from a cause precisely denied to the denial of what it is the cause of, but rather as from the denial of a necessary accompaniment to the denial of what it necessarily accompanies.

(125) But how on this interpretation is it true that variety of accidents makes numerical difference?

I say it does make some difference, but not the first one, and it necessarily accompanies every numerical difference. The claim that they "make a numerical difference" has to be understood in this sense. This gloss does not seem a distortion of Boethius's text. Rather the text makes itself be understood in this way, since [those who appeal to Boethius here] necessarily have to explain what he himself adds there about place [(67)].⁴⁴ For place is not what primarily distinguishes individuals from one another—either in the

44. Godfrey of Fontaines, *Quodlibet* VII. 5, 319–320, cites only the first part of the passage, leaving out the remark about place.

sense of "place" that is an attribute of the locating[45] or in the sense of "place" that is an attribute of the located (that is, the "where" left behind in the located). Therefore, if on their view they have to explain "place" as quantity, what is wrong with explaining 'make a difference' as "making not the first difference but rather making *some* difference and accompanying the first difference?"

(126) To the second main argument, from Damascene [(68)], the reply is clear from Damascene himself at the end of that chapter, where he explains how he understands 'accident' there. He says the following [*Elementarium*, 103–104]: "Whatever are in some of the hypostases of one species and not in others are accidents and are adventitious." I grant therefore that whatever is outside the *per se* notion of a specific nature itself, and is not a *per se* consequent of that nature, is an accident of such a nature. In this sense, whatever is posited as individuating is an accident. But it is not properly an accident, as others understand it [(128)].

(127) That he does not mean "accident" properly is clear from Damascene himself, Book I of his *Sentences* [= *On the Orthodox Faith*], Ch. 8 [42–43]: "For we mean that Peter and Paul are of the same kind." Later on: "Hypostases have a great many separating factors in themselves. They are divided by mental acuity, and strength, and form (that is, shape), and habit, and complexion of humors, and privilege, and inventiveness, and by all their characteristic peculiarities." He adds a noteworthy remark: They are divided "by all these peculiarities," etc., "insofar as they are not mutually in one another but are separated. Hence they are called two and three men, and many. This can be seen also in every creature."

Note well: He says any created hypostases differ through "not being in one another but separated" more than they differ by their characteristic peculiarities. By way of opposite, in the same place he says: "The blessed hypostases of the Trinity *are* in one another." The reason for this latter is the unity of the nature, assuming the personal distinction (from distinction 2 of the Book I.[46] Therefore, the division of nature in created *supposita* is the first and greatest reason for their distinction.

(128) To the third argument, the one from Avicenna [(69)], I say he is mainly considering a quiddity insofar as it includes nothing that does not pertain to its *per se* notion. It is in this sense that "equinity is only equinity" and "neither one nor several" [Avicenna, *Metaphysics* V. 1, 86ᵛᵃ]. No matter

---

45. *I. e.*, of the containing body. See Aristotle's discussion of place as "the innermost motionless boundary of the container," *Physics* IV. 4, 210ᵇ32–212ᵃ30.

46. *I. e.*, of Scotus's *Ordinatio* (2. 344–349).

how much its unity is not another *thing* added on, but necessarily follows on that entity (as from every being, according to any entity whatever, there follows its unity), nevertheless that unity is not within the formal notion of the quiddity insofar as it is a quiddity. Instead it is so to speak an attribute following on the quiddity. Everything like that is called an "accident", according to him.

Even the Philosopher sometimes takes 'accident' in this sense (the "fallacy of accident" gets its name from this) for everything outside the formal notion of another. For everything like that is extraneous to that other and is based on a comparison to something else. The "fallacy of accident" comes about in this sense, and in this sense the genus is "accidental" to the difference, and whatever individuates it is an "accident" of the specific nature. But not as those [who appeal to Avicenna in (69)] understand accident. So there is an equivocation there about accident.

[Questions 5 and 6[47]

Question 5

Is a material substance a "this" and individual through matter?]

(129) Fifth, I ask whether a material substance is a "this" and individual through matter.

[Argument for the affirmative]

(130) Yes. For according to the Philosopher, *Metaphysics* V, the chapter on "one," [6, 1016^{b}32–33], "Those of which the matter is one are one in number." Therefore, etc.

[Argument for the negative]

(131) To the contrary, *Metaphysics* V. [4, 1014^{b}26–32], in the old translation:[48] "In the foundation of a nature, there is nothing distinct." Now what

47. Q. 6 is embedded in the structure of q. 5.

48. The text does not at all say what Scotus claims. Yet the reference to "the old translation" suggests Scotus means to be quoting, not just giving a loose paraphrase. No other nearby text seems likely.

is not in itself distinct or diverse cannot be the primary reason for the diversity or distinction of anything else. But matter is the foundation of a nature, a foundation altogether indistinct and indeterminate. Therefore, it cannot be the primary reason for the distinction or diversity of anything else.

[Other people's theory]

(132) Here it is said that yes. This is held especially on account of many passages from Aristotle that seem to sound like this.

One of these is in [*Metaphysics*] VII. [8, 1034^{a}4–8]: that the generator generates something else on account of the matter. "Callias," he says, "and Socrates are diverse on account of their matter (for that is diverse), but the same in species. For the species is individual."

(133) Again on the same basis, [*Metaphysics*] VII, the chapter on the parts of a definition [11, 1037^{a}33–^{b}5],: "The 'what-it-was-to-be' and the thing are the same in some substances. But what are in matter or are taken with matter are not the same." And again it appears in [*Metaphysics*] VIII. 3, [1043^{b}2–4]: "For soul and being a soul are the same, but man and being a man are not the same unless being a soul is also called a man." Therefore, it seems matter is outside the notion of the quiddity and of anything primarily having the quiddity. So since matter is something found in the realm of beings, it seems to be a part of the *individual*—that is, the individuation of the whole. Whatever in the individual is entirely incompatible with the notion of the quiddity can be posited as the primary reason for the individuating. Therefore, etc.

(134) Furthermore, in *Metaphysics* XII. [8, 1074^{a}31–38], Aristotle proves there cannot be several heavens. "For if there were several heavens as there are several men, the principle for each one will be one in species but many in number. But whatever," he says, "are many in number have matter. Now the primary 'what-it-was-to-be' does not have matter. For it is an actuality. Therefore, the first immobile mover is one both in notion and in number." This reasoning, by which the unity of the heaven is concluded from the unity of the mover and the unity of the mover (not only in species but in number) is concluded from the fact that it does not have matter, would not seem to be valid unless numerical distinction arose through matter. Therefore, etc.

(135) Moreover, *On the Heaven and the World* I. [9, 278^{a}3–15]: "When I say 'heaven' I indicate the form; when I say 'this heaven' I indicate the matter."[49]

---

49. Scotus is summarizing very loosely. Aristotle's authentic *On the Heavens* was often combined in the Middle Ages with the pseudo-Aristotelian work *On the World*.

[Against this theory]

(136) Against this I argue first from the texts of the same Aristotle.

According to the Philosopher, *Metaphysics* VII, the chapter on the parts of a definition [11, 1037ª5–10]: "It is plain that the soul is the primary substance, but the body is the matter. Now man or animal is what is made up of both soul and body as taken universally. But Socrates and Coriscus"—add 'are made up of these'—"as taken singularly, if 'soul' is said in two senses." And later on he adds: "But if this soul and this body [are what make up Socrates or Coriscus], then as the universal [is a composite], so is the singular."

(137) Earlier in the same chapter, [= 10, 1035ᵇ27–31]: "Man and horse and whatever are in singulars in this way are, taken universally, not the substance"—that is, the form—"but a certain whole"—that is, a composite—"made up of this matter together with this structure." Here by 'this' he does not mean uniform and singular matter, but determinate matter. Otherwise he would be contradicting himself. Thus he adds in the same passage: "as taken universally." And he adds later on: "Socrates is already made up of the ultimate matter," etc.

(138) The same point is also clear through the same Aristotle in [*Metaphysics*] XII. 2 [= 5, 1071ª27–29], where he says that the principles are the same, just as what are derived from those principles are also the same. "And the principles," he says, "of what are in the same species are diverse, not specifically but because they are the principles of singulars. Your matter and mover and species are not mine. But yet they are the same in universal notion." Therefore, he grants the distinction of form in the particular, just as of matter. And he grants the unity of matter in general, just as of form. Hence one must still ask what it is by which matter is a "this."

(139) Furthermore, as is proved from many passages in [*Metaphysics*] VII, the chapter on the parts of a definition [10, 1034ᵇ20–1035ᵇ3], matter belongs to the essence of the composite substance—say, of man—and so such a composite is not precisely the essence of the form. Therefore, just as the composite cannot of itself be a "this" (from the first question [(29)]), so neither will matter—which is its part—be of itself a "this." For the composite cannot be common and of the same kind in what are diverse unless everything belonging to its essence could be of the same kind as they are.[50]

(140) Furthermore, I argue from reason. Matter is the same in the generated and the corrupted. Therefore, it has the same singularity in the generated and the corrupted.

---

50. 'As they are' (= *cum eis*) is surprising. 'In them' (= *in eis*) would seem better. But the edition shows no variants.

(141) If you reply that it is not of the same species in the generated and the corrupted, I argue as I did before [(100)], against the theory of indeterminate dimension. So there will be a circular generation: first, of fire from water, and second, of water from fire. The water corrupted in the first instance and the water generated in the second have the same matter and are of the same species. Therefore, they are really "this water." Therefore, the first water naturally returns, the same in number. This counts against [those who hold that matter is the principle of individuation].[51]

[Question 6

Is a material substance individual through some entity that by itself determines the nature to singularity?]

(142) Because the solution to the passages from the Philosopher in favor of the opposite, affirmative side of the question, [(130), (132)–(135)], requires the solution of the sixth question, namely what it is through which a material substance is completed as an individual, therefore I ask sixth whether a material substance is individual through some positive entity that by itself determines the nature to singularity.

[Arguments for the negative]

(143) No. For in that case that determinant would be related to the nature as act to potency. Therefore, from the specific nature and that determinant there would result something truly and properly one. This is inconsistent. For the determinant is either matter or form or some composite made up of matter and form. Whichever is picked, there is an inconsistency. For then in the composite there would be another matter than the matter that is part of the nature, or another form than what is included as part of the nature, or another composite than what is the composite of the nature.

(144) Furthermore, in that case the singular composed of the nature and the *per se* determinant would be *per se* one, and therefore *per se* intelligible. This seems contrary to the Philosopher, *On the Soul* II. [5, 417^{b}22–23], and *Metaphysics* 7, [10, 1035^{b}33–1036^{a}8], where he seems to say plainly that intellection is of the universal, and sense and sensation are of the singular.

---

51. It was generally held that an individual cannot be destroyed and then come back again the same in number—at least not by any natural process.

(145) Furthermore, if the singular were *per se* intelligible, there could be demonstration and science concerning it. And so there would be a proper science of singulars insofar as they are singulars. The Philosopher denies this, *Metaphysics* VII, the chapter on the parts of a definition [*ibid.* & 15, 1039^{b}27–1040^{a}7].

(146) Again, if the singular included the specific nature and the *per se* determinant, it could be *per se* defined by these two factors included *per se* in its notion. So there would be one definition of the individual and another of the species—or at least a definition of the individual that adds onto the definition of the species, as the definition of the species adds onto the definition of the genus.

[Arguments for the affirmative]

(147) On the opposite side: Every inferior includes *per se* something not included in the understanding of the superior. Otherwise the concept of the inferior would be equally as common as the concept of the superior. And in that case the *per se* inferior would not be *per se* inferior, because it would not be beneath the common and superior. Therefore, something is *per se* included in the notion of an individual that is not included in the notion of the nature. Now what is included is a positive entity, from the solution of the second question [**(57)**]. And it makes something *per se* one with the nature, from the solution of the fourth question [**(111)**]. Therefore, it *per se* determines the nature to singularity—that is, to the notion of the inferior.

[Other people's theory]

(148) Here it is said, [Godfrey, VII. 5, 319 & 324–325], that **(a)** the specific nature is of itself a "this" and yet **(b)** it is through quantity that the nature can be common to several singulars. That is, quantity can be the reason why there are able to be several singulars under the nature.

(149) Point **(a)** is explained as follows: The most specific species is of itself atomic, and therefore indivisible.

(150) This is confirmed through Porphyry's statement [**P (31)**]: "Plato orders us, who are descending from the most general to the most specific, to stop there." But if it were possible for there to be a further division of the nature, we would not have to stop at that most specific nature. Therefore, etc.

(151) Likewise, Boethius in the his book *On Division* [877B–C], in counting up all the kinds of divisions, not only those *per se* but also accidental ones, does not count the division of the species into individuals. Therefore, the specific nature is not a "this" through something else.

(152) Again, if there were some reality in the individual beyond the reality of the specific nature alone, the species would not indicate the whole being of the individuals. This is contrary to Porphyry [P (37)].

(153) Point (b) [(148)] is explained as follows: For even though quantity is not the formal reason for the division of something into subjective parts, nevertheless when a quantitative whole is divided into quantitative parts, it is divided *per se* into parts that are of the same kind. Now the principle of division into divisors is the same as the principle of distinction among the divisors themselves. Therefore, just as quantity itself is the principle of division, so it is the principle of distinction in the divisors. But the latter are the subjective parts of the common nature. Therefore, quantity is the principle of distinction for such parts.

(154) How these two points [(148)] can hold at the same time is clear from an example. For according to the Philosopher, *Physics* I. [2, 185ᵃ32–ᵇ5], substance is of itself indivisible into parts, speaking about parts of the same kind. Yet when quantity is added, substance is partitionable into parts of the same kind. Indeed then it *has* such parts. In this way therefore, the nature of a species can be of itself a "this," and yet be both "this" and "that" through a nature attaching to it from outside.

[Refutation of this theory]

(155) It seems that this theory can be understood in two senses. In one sense, so that a material substance, insofar as it is essentially distinguished from quantity, remains the same and altogether non-distinct in individuals, according to the notion of its proper and essential entity. Yet it receives many quantities, and in receiving them it constitutes together with them many wholes at once. That is to say, in plain words, that the same material substance, not divided or distinct in itself, is informed by many quantities, and on this basis there are many individuals under the species.

(156) In the other sense, it can be understood that a material substance that is a "this" of itself, disregarding every quantity, will be a "this" and a "that" when the informing quantity is posited, so that it not only *receives* distinct quantities but also itself has a distinction *in itself* in its own substantial entity, in such a way that *this* substance, which is subjected to this quantity and distinguished from it essentially, is not *that* one, which is under another quantity and distinguished from it essentially. Nevertheless the fact that "this" is not "that" cannot hold without the quantity in the "this" and in the "that."

(157) The first interpretation seems impossible, because from it there follow inconsistencies in theology, metaphysics, and natural science.

(158) In theology there follows the inconsistency that it is not a property of the infinite divine essence for it to be a "this"—that is, it is not a property of it that it itself, existing as one and not distinguished in itself, can be in several distinct *supposita*. Yet this inability is generally understood to hold only in the case of the divine *persons*, who are distinct only relatively. Here however, under this first interpretation, it would be claimed that one substantial nature, in no way distinguished in itself, would have several *supposita* distinct by an absolute thing.

(159) Second, it follows that no substance of wine can be transubstantiated into the body and blood of Christ unless the whole substance of wine is transubstantiated. For the wine is not transubstantiated except according to its substance. (The quantity stays the same.) And according to you, the substance in this wine is the same as what is in that wine. Now the same substance cannot be both transubstantiated and not transubstantiated. Therefore, etc.

(160) There also follow inconsistencies in metaphysics. First the "Idea" that Plato posited would be established. For Plato claimed that an Idea is a substance existing by itself, a separated nature without accidents (as is attributed to him by the Philosopher), in which there is the whole nature of the species. This Idea, according to what Aristotle attributed to him, would be said of each individual by a formal predication that says "This is this." But this theory [(155)] held that this one substance is said of everything in its species by a predication that says "This is this," and yet is under this accident and that one. Therefore, the theory posits a community just as great as Plato posited in his Ideas.

(161) Second, according to those who hold this theory, two accidents of the same species cannot be in the same subject (if they are absolute accidents). For according to them a plain contradiction would follow, namely that the same thing would be in act and in potency in the same respect. But the opposite of this rule follows from the theory, because the same nature is in act according to many acts of the same species.

(162) On this point another impossibility could be inferred, a mathematical one insofar as a quantum pertains to the mathematician's consideration. Two dimensive quantities of the same kind would perfect the same subject at once. This goes against the proper notion of dimensive quantities of the same kind, speaking according to the mathematician's meaning.

(163) Third, there would follow two inconsistencies in natural science. First, no material substance can be generated or corrupted. Not generated, because if there is this stone, there will be in it all the substance that can be

in any stone. Yet this much quantity and that much numerically other quantity can be acquired by this substance of stone. But the acquisition of a new quantity is not generation. (This is clear from the terminal points of the [so-called] generation.) Therefore, etc.

Likewise, as long as this stone remains, the specific nature of stone remains in it. But every nature of stone is this nature. Therefore, as long as this nature remains, every nature of stone remains. Therefore, no material substance, [and in particular, no stone] can be corrupted while that stone remains, even though the quality or quantity is not the same.

(164) Second, it follows that although in accordance with the story from that damned Averroes about the unity of the intellect in all men, one can pretend the same thing about your body and mine as about this and that stone,[52] nevertheless holding not only in accordance with the faith but also in accordance with necessary philosophy that there is one and another intellective soul in distinct men, human nature cannot be of itself indivisible and yet one and another through quantity in distinct men. For in this man and in that man there is one substantial form and another substantial form, the latter being other by an otherness that naturally precedes quantity. So the proponents of this theory do not even try to reply to this counterexample, as though it were insoluble, but turn instead to other, "homogeneous" substances: stone or water. Yet if anything counted in their favor from the notion of an "indivisible" specific nature, they would have to draw the conclusion for man just as for stone. Therefore, they can see that the principles they proceed from are null and void, since plain impossibilities follow from them.

(165) The second interpretation [(156)] seems self-refuting. For what is of itself a "this"—in the sense in which something's being of itself a "this" was explained earlier [(48), (76)], that is, it is incompatible with it *per se* for it to be divided into several subjective parts, and it is also incompatible with it to be of itself "not this"—cannot be divided into several parts through anything added to it. For if it is incompatible with it of itself to be divided, it is incompatible with it of itself to receive something through which it becomes "not this." Therefore, to say that the nature is of itself a "this" (in the sense already explained of a nature that is of itself a "this"),[53] and yet

---

52. On Averroes' theory, see **K** Ch. 29. The present theory holds that there is one specific nature of stone, the same for all individual stones, and that individual stones are diversified by quantity. It would also presumably hold the same thing about the human body, that there is one for all men—much as "that damned Averroes" had held there is one soul for all men.

53. *I. e.*, "disregarding every quantity" (**156**) and "insofar as it is distinguished essentially from quantity" (**155**).

that it can be this and that by means of something else added to it, is to say contradictory things.

(166) This is clear in the example given in the statement of the theory [(154)]. For even though a material substance is not of itself divided into parts of the same kind as itself, nevertheless it is not of itself indivisible into such parts. For if it were of itself indivisible—that is, if division were incompatible with it—it could not receive a quantity by which it is formally divided into such parts. This is apparent. For a soul—or an angel, which *is* of itself indivisible in this sense—cannot receive quantity, just as it cannot be divided into parts either.

(167) There seems then to be a deception in the inference: "It is *not of itself* such and such; therefore, it is *of itself not* such and such" (a fallacy of the consequent). For according to a certain theory [Godfrey, VII. 5, 322], substance truly does not have of itself parts of the same kind as itself. Yet it does not of itself *not* have parts of the same kind as itself, in such a way that it is incompatible with it to have parts. For in that case it could not receive such parts formally through something added to it. So the nature of a most specific species is not of itself a "this," and anything else that is divisible from its nature is not of itself a "this" either. Yet it is not of itself *not* a this, in such a way that it is incompatible with it of itself to be divided into several parts. For in that case it could not receive anything by which such a division would formally belong to it.

[Scotus's own theory]

(168) To the question [(142)] therefore, I reply: Yes.

(169) To this I add the following reasoning: Just as unity in common follows *per se* on entity in common, so too does any unity follow *per se* on some entity or other. Therefore, absolute unity (like the unity of an individual frequently described above [(48), (76), (165)]—that is, a unity with which division into several subjective parts is incompatible and with which not being a designated "this" is incompatible), if it is found in beings (as every theory assumes), follows *per se* on some *per se* entity. But it does not follow *per se* on the entity of the nature, because that has a certain *per se* real unity of its own, as was proved in the solution of the first question [(30)]. Therefore, it follows on some other entity that determines this one. And that other entity makes up something *per se* one with the entity of the nature, because the whole to which this unity belongs is perfect of itself.

(170) Again, every difference among the differing is reduced ultimately to some items that are diverse primarily. Otherwise there would be no end to what differ. But individuals [in the same species] differ, properly speaking, because they are diverse beings that are yet something the same. Therefore, their difference is reduced to some items that are diverse primarily. Now these primarily diverse items are not the nature in this individual and the nature in that one, because what items formally agree by is not the same as what they really differ by, even though the same item can be really distinct from something and yet really agree with it. For there is a big difference between being distinct and being that by which something is primarily distinguished. Therefore, so it will be with unity.[54] Therefore, besides the nature [that is the same] in this individual and in that one, there are some primarily diverse items by which this and that individual differ, this one in this respect and that one in that. They are not negations, from the second question [(57)]. Neither are they accidents, from the fourth question [(111)]. Therefore, there are certain positive entities that *per se* determine the nature.

[Argument against the first line of reasoning]

(171) There is an objection against the first line of reasoning [(169)]. For if there is some real unity less than numerical unity, it belongs to something that is either in what is numerically the same or in something else. Not in what is numerically the same, because whatever is in what is numerically the same is numerically one. Neither is it in two, because there is nothing really one in those two. For that is a property of the divine *supposita*, as the passage from Damascene was explained above [(39)].

(172) I reply: Just as it was said in the solution of the first question on this topic [(32), (34)] that "nature" is naturally prior to "this" nature, so too the proper unity that follows on the nature as a nature is naturally prior to the nature's unity as "this" nature. The metaphysical consideration of the nature comes under this aspect, and under this aspect too its definition is assigned, and there are propositions *per se* in the first mode about it [(32)]. Therefore, in the same item that is one in number there is some kind of entity from which there follows a unity less than numerical unity is. Such unity is real, and what such unity belongs to is of itself formally one by numerical unity. I grant therefore that this real unity does not belong to anything existing in two individuals, but in one.

(173) If you still object, "Whatever is in what is numerically the same is numerically the same" [(171)], I reply first by giving another argument that is similar but plainer: "Whatever is in what is specifically one[55] is specifically

54. The role of this sentence in the argument is not clear.
55. Following the variant reading 'uno' for 'una'.

one. Therefore, color in whiteness is specifically one. Therefore, it does not have a unity less than the unity of the species."

That does not follow. For it was said elsewhere—namely, in Book I [of this *Ordinatio*, d. 8], the question on divine attributes, before the solution of the main argument about attributes, in solving the first doubt [4. 271]—that something can be called "animate" denominatively (for example a body), or *per se* in the first mode (for example a man), and so too a surface is called "white" denominatively, while a white-surface is called "white" *per se* in the first mode, because the subject includes the predicate. So too I say here that what is potential and contracted by the actual is informed by the actual, and for this reason is informed by the unity that follows on that actuality—that is, on that act. So it is one by the proper unity of the actual, but it is only denominatively one in this sense. It is not however *of itself* one in this sense, either in the first mode or through an essential part.

(174) Therefore, color in whiteness is specifically one, but it is not so of itself or *per se* or primarily but only denominatively. But a specific difference is primarily one, because it is primarily incompatible with it to be divided into what are several in species. Whiteness is specifically one *per se* but not primarily, because it is specifically one through something intrinsic to it (for example, through the difference).

(175) So I grant that whatever is in this stone is numerically one, either primarily or *per se* or denominatively. Primarily, say, as that through which such a unity belongs to this composite. *Per se*, the stone itself, of which what is primarily one with this unity is a *per se* part. Only denominatively, what is potential and is perfected by the actual and is so to speak denominatively related to its actuality.

[Further discussion of the theory]

(176) In explaining this solution [(168)–(170)] further, what this entity is by which that [individual] unity is completed can be explained through a comparison to the entity the specific difference is taken from. Now the specific difference—that is, the entity from which the specific difference is taken—can be compared to what is below it, to what is above it, or to what is alongside it.

(177) In the first case, it is *per se* incompatible with the specific difference and with that specific entity to be divided essentially into what are several in species or nature. Because of this, such division is also incompatible with a whole of which that entity is a *per se* part. So too here, it is primarily incompatible with this individual entity to be divided into any subjective

parts. And through this entity such a division is *per se* incompatible with a whole of which that entity is a part. The only difference is in the fact that the former unity, the unity of the specific nature, is less than the latter unity. Because of this, the former does not exclude every division according to quantitative parts, but only a division into essential parts. The latter however excludes every division according to quantitative parts.

(178) From this consideration alone, the present point is already confirmed well enough. For on the basis of the fact that every unity less than this [numerical] unity has its own entity on which it *per se* follows, it does not seem a likely story to deny to this most perfect kind of unity its own entity on which it follows.

(179) But comparing the specific nature to what is above it [(176)], I say the reality the specific difference is taken from is actual with respect to the reality the genus or the notion of the genus is taken from, in such a way that the latter reality is not formally the former one. Otherwise there would be unnecessary repetition* in a definition; the genus alone, or the difference, would sufficiently define the species. For it would indicate the whole being of the defined. Yet sometimes this contracting difference is other than the form from which the notion of the genus is taken, namely when the species adds some reality over and above the nature of the genus. But sometimes it is not another *thing*, but only another formality or another formal concept of the same thing. For this reason, one kind of specific difference has a concept that is not absolutely simple—that is, one taken from a form—and another specific difference has a concept that is absolutely simple, which is taken from the ultimate abstraction of the form. Concerning this distinction among specific differences, it was stated in Distinction 3 of the Book I [of this *Ordinatio*] how some specific differences include a being and some do not [3. 97–100].

(180) So too the reality of an individual is like a specific reality in this respect: It is so to speak an act determining the reality of the species, which is as it were possible and potential. But it is unlike it in this respect: It is never taken from an added form, but rather precisely from the last reality of the form.

(181) It is unlike it in another respect too, because the specific reality constitutes the composite it is a part of in its quidditative being. For the specific reality is itself a certain quidditative entity. On the other hand, this reality of an individual is primarily diverse from every quidditative entity. (This is proved from the fact that whatever quidditative entity is understood—speaking now about limited quidditative entity only—it is common

to many and it is not inconsistent for it to be said of many items each of which is it itself.) Therefore, this [individual] entity, which of itself is another entity than the quiddity or the quidditative entity, cannot constitute the whole of which is it a part in its quidditative being, but only in another kind of being.

(182) For Aristotle, a quiddity is often called a "form." For example, it is clear in *Metaphysics* V, the chapter on cause [2, 1013ᵃ26–28], and in many other passages, and in *Metaphysics* VII, the chapter on the parts of a definition [11, 1037ᵃ33–ᵇ4], that in whatever do not have matter the what-something-is is the same as what it belongs to. (As will be explained [(204)–(207)], he is talking about matter and form.) For him, whatever has a contracted quiddity is called "matter" [(206)–(207)]. Boethius too in his little book *On the Trinity*, [II. 28–48], says no form can be the subject of an accident, because form is said *in quid* of everything else. If humanity is a subject, therefore, nevertheless that fact does not pertain to it insofar as it is a form. Humanity is not the form of one part of the composite, of the form or of the matter, but of the whole composite that has a contracted quiddity—that is, in which there is a contracted quiddity. Therefore, every specific reality constitutes something in formal being, because it constitutes it in quidditative being. But the reality of an individual constitutes something precisely in material being—that is, in contracted being. From this there follows the logical claim that the former reality is essentially formal, the latter reality is material. For the latter constitutes something in the aspect of what can be a subject, whereas the former constitutes something in the aspect of precisely what is predicable. But a formal predicate has the aspect of a form, whereas what can be a subject has the aspect of matter.

(183) Third, comparing a specific difference to what is alongside it [(176)], namely to another specific difference, I say that even though sometimes one specific difference might be not primarily diverse from another one—for instance, as happens with the entity taken from the form [(179)]—nevertheless the ultimate specific difference, the one that has a concept that is absolutely simple, is primarily diverse from any other. And in this respect I say an individual difference is like a specific difference taken universally, because every individual entity is primarily diverse from every other one.

(184) From this the reply to the following objection is apparent. For it is objected: Either this and that individual entity are of the same kind or not. If so, therefore some entity can be abstracted from them. And this will be a specific entity. Therefore, one has to ask about it what it is through which it is contracted to this and that entity. If it is so contracted of itself, then by

the same reasoning we could have stopped at the nature of a stone.[56] If it is contracted through something else, therefore there will be an infinite regress. If on the other hand those individual entities are of different kinds, then what are constituted out of them will be of different kinds, and so they will not be individuals of the same species.

(185) I reply:[57] Ultimate specific differences are primarily diverse, and therefore nothing *per se* one can be abstracted from them. But it does not follow because of this that what are constituted out of them are primarily diverse and not of some one kind. For that some items are "equally distinguished" can be understood in two senses: Either because they are equally incompossible—that is, because they cannot be in the same thing—or because they equally do not agree in anything. In the first sense it is true that the distinguished are equally as diverse as their distinguishers. (For the distinguishers cannot be incompossible unless the distinguished are incompossible too.) In the second sense this is impossible in every case. For the distinguished not only include their distinguishers but also something else, so to speak potential with respect to the distinguishers. Yet the distinguishers do not agree in it.

(186) Just as was replied for primarily diverse specific differences, so I reply for individual entities: They are primarily diverse. That is, they agree in nothing the same. Yet the distinguished do not have to be absolutely diverse.[58] Nevertheless, just as those individual entities are incompossible, so too are the individuals having those entities.

(187) If you ask me what this individual entity is that the individual difference is taken from—is it matter or form or the composite?—I reply: Every quidditative entity (whether partial or total) in some genus is of itself

---

56. *I. e.*, if we are going to grant here that there is something of itself a "this," why not admit it at the outset, at the level of the specific nature *stone*? Then there would no need to have recourse to these "individual entities."

57. The main reply to the objection comes in (186). (185) is only a preliminary. It will help in understanding this section if you realize that the discussion concerns the various species under a common genus. The "distinguishers" are the specific differences that establish the species. The "distinguished" are the species themselves. The two senses of being "equally distinguished" may be loosely paraphrased as follows: In the first sense, *A* and *B* are equally distinguished if they cannot both be in any third *C*. In the second sense, *A* and *B* are equally distinguished if no third *C* is in both of them (they "do not agree" in any third *C*).

58. Here the "distinguished" are the individuals while the "distinguishers" are the individuating individual entities.

indifferent as a quidditative entity to this individual entity and that one, in such a way that as a quidditative entity it is naturally prior to this individual entity insofar as it is "this." As naturally prior, just as it does not belong to it to be a "this," so the opposite of being a "this" is not incompatible with it from its very notion. And just as a composite does not insofar as it is a nature include its individual entity by which it is formally a "this," so neither does matter insofar as it is a nature include its individual entity by which it is "this matter," nor does form insofar as it is a nature include its individual entity by which it is "this form."

(188) Therefore, this individual entity is not matter or form or the composite, inasmuch as each of these is a nature. Rather it is the ultimate reality of the being that is matter or that is form or that is the composite. Thus whatever is common and yet determinable can still be distinguished (no matter how much it is one thing) into several formally distinct realities of which this one is not formally that one. This one is formally the entity of singularity and that one is formally the entity of the nature. These two realities cannot be distinguished as "thing" and "thing," as can the reality the genus is taken from and the reality the difference is taken from. (The specific reality is taken from these.) Rather when in the same thing, whether in a part or in the whole, they are always formally distinct realities of the same thing.

[Replies to the main arguments]

(189) From this, the reply to the first main argument [**(143)**] is apparent. For when it is concluded that "every individual in which the nature is contractible is more composite than that nature,"[59] I say that "composition" can be understood either properly, as is a composition out of an actual thing and a potential thing, or else less properly, as is a composition out of an actual reality and a potential reality in the same thing. In the first sense, the individual is not a composite with respect to the specific nature. For it adds no reality,[60] because it adds neither matter nor form nor a composite, as the argument [**(143)**] goes on to show. In the second sense, the individual is necessarily a composite. For the reality the specific difference is taken from

59. This is not explicitly said in **(143)**. But it can be found in a parallel passage from Scotus's *Parisian Lectures* (18. 273).

60. One would have expected 'thing' here. The edition (484.17) reports one manuscript that corrects 'reality' into 'another thing' in another hand, and another manuscript that has 'thing'.

is potential with respect to the reality the individual difference is taken from, just as if they were two "things." For the specific reality does not of itself have the wherewithal to include through an identity the individual reality. Instead, only some third factor includes both of these through an identity.

(190) This composition is of a kind that is inconsistent with the perfect divine simplicity. For the divine simplicity does not allow a composition of actual "thing" and potential "thing" in itself, but neither does it allow a composition of an actual reality with a potential reality. For comparing any essential feature to anything else in the divine, the essential feature is formally infinite. Therefore, of itself it has the wherewithal to include through an identity whatever can be together with it. (This was often treated above in Book I.[61])

(191) The terms of the comparison in the divine are not precisely perfectly the same because some third thing perfectly includes them both, [but rather because of the formal infinity of one or both extremes].

But in the present case neither does the specific entity include the individual entity through an identity, nor conversely. Instead only some third item, of which both of these are as it were *per se* parts, includes both of them through an identity. Therefore, the most perfect kind of composition, which is between "thing" and "thing," is removed. But not every kind of composition is removed. For in general, whatever nature is not of itself a "this," but is determinable to being a "this" (whether in such a way that it is determined through another thing, which is impossible in every case, or in such a way that it is determined through another reality), is not absolutely simple.

(192) To the second main argument [(144)], I grant that the singular is *per se* intelligible as far as it itself goes. But if it is not *per se* intelligible to some intellect—say, to ours—more on that elsewhere [VII. 539–540]. At any rate, there is for its own part no impossibility that it can be understood, just as on the part of the sun there is no impossibility of seeing it, or on the part of vision in the owl, but only on the part of the owl's eye.

(193) To the point about definition [(146)], I say that even if some notion is able to express whatever accords with the entity of an individual, nevertheless that notion will not be a perfect definition. For it does not express the what-it-was-to-be. And according to the Philosopher, *Topics* I. [5, 101^{b}39], "the definition expresses [the what-it-was-to-be]." Therefore, I grant the singular is not definable by a definition other than the definition of the species. Yet it is *per se* a being and adds some entity to the entity of the species. But the *per se* entity it adds is not a quidditative entity.

---

61. Of Scotus's *Ordinatio* (2. 359–361; 4. 69–70, 269, 271, 272–274, 275–276).

(194) From this the reply is clear to the other point, about science and demonstration [(145)]. For the definition of the subject is the middle term in the most powerful kind of demonstration. Now the singular does not have its own definition, but only has the definition of the species. So there is no proper demonstration about the singular, but only a demonstration that is about the species. For it does not have its own attribute, but only the attribute of the species.

[Replies to the arguments for other people's theory]

(195) To the arguments in favor of the opinion [stated in (148)]:
When it is said first that a [most specific] species is atomic [(149)], I say it *is* atomic—that is, it is indivisible into several species. Yet it is not purely atomic—that is, absolutely indivisible. For indivisibility into several species is compatible with divisibility into several individuals of the same species.

(196) When indivisibility is proved through Plato's statement, which Porphyry gives [(150)], I say that the art of division ends at the most specific species. For to go further is to go on to an infinity, which must be "left behind" by the art of division, according to Porphyry [P (31)]. For the definite number of individuals does not come from the side of the individuals themselves. Rather they can be infinite in number. Their notion is not incompatible with this.

(197) If "division" is taken [(150)–(151)] strictly, insofar as it occurs in what requires parts determinate in multitude and magnitude, then in this sense the species is not divided into individuals. Now a genus requires a determinate multitude of species because, according to Boethius [*On Division*, 877C], the first divisible is into two. A quantum on the other hand requires a determinate magnitude, and when that is assumed there are halves in the whole that bounds the quantum. (There are two of them.) If "division" is taken strictly, insofar as it is into parts that have a proportion to the whole, which they either constitute or else are contained under it in a determinate multitude or magnitude, then a species is *per se* not divided into individuals. Both Plato and Porphyry can be explained on this basis.

But if "division" is taken broadly, insofar as it is into whatever are the participants of the divided nature (whether or not they have such a proportion to the whole in putting it together or in being subordinated to it), then the species is *per se* divided into individuals. For Boethius, this division of species into individuals is reduced to the genus, because the conditions and properties Boethius assigns [*On Division*, 878D–880A] to the division of a genus belong to this division too, which is the division of species into individuals.

(198) To the other point [(152)], that the species indicates the whole being of the individual, I say that there 'being' is taken for quidditative being, as Porphyry states in the chapter on difference [**P (45)**] where he says that *per se* the difference does not receive more or less. He proves this in the same passage: "For the being of each one is one and the same and is not receptive of intension or remission." He is taking 'being' for the quiddity, as the Philosopher does in *Metaphysics* VII. [3, 1043^{b}2]: "The soul and the being of the soul are the same." Because the entity the singular adds onto the species is not a quidditative entity, I say that the whole quidditative entity in the individual is the entity of the species. Therefore, the species indicates the whole being of the individuals. But the genus does not in this way indicate the whole being of the species, because the species adds a quidditative entity onto the genus.

(199) To the argument [(153)] for the other part of the claim [in (148)], about quantity, I say that the proposition 'The principle of divisibility is the same as the principle of distinction among the divisors' is false. The concept of what is in itself common to the species is the reason for its divisibility into the species. But it is not the reason for distinguishing the species from one another. Instead this species is distinguished from that one by a difference. In a quantitative division, on the other hand, the whole quantity insofar as it confusedly contains all the parts is the reason for divisibility in the whole quantum. But the reason for the distinction of the parts from one another is not like this. Rather that occurs insofar as this quantity distinctly in act is not that one in act that is in the whole.

(200) When it is also deduced further [(153)] that, when a homogeneous quantified whole is divided, there is a division by quantity, so be it. Nevertheless that division is not the primary division of the individuals. Rather this substance and that one have a division and distinction from one another, insofar as they are "this" and "that," naturally prior to the [quantitative] distinction, insofar as they were by accident parts of a distinct quantum. (For it was accidental to them to be parts.) Yet when a division is made according to quantitative parts, the division according to subjective parts occurs by accident.

[Reply to the fifth question]

(201) The solution to the preceding question, the fifth one, on matter [(129)], is clear from the arguments [(136)–(141)] against the theory [(132)]. For I grant that matter absolutely, insofar as it is matter, is not the reason for distinction or individuation. For whatever is a nature, whether total or

partial, in any genus at all is not of itself a "this." And therefore, one has to ask what it is through which it is a "this."

[Reply to the textual arguments from Aristotle]

(202) To the passage from the Philosopher, *Metaphysics* V. [6, 1016ᵇ32–33], ("One in number," etc., [(130)]), I reply: I say he is there taking "matter" for the individual entity that constitutes the individual in material being, not in formal being (insofar as the quiddity is called "form"). For that entity is not quidditative. This analysis is clear from what he adds [*ibid.*, 1016ᵇ33]: "One in species, of which the notion is one," etc. 'Notion' is here taken for quiddity, which is called a "form" with respect to the being of the individual.

(203) In the same way, the reply is clear to the passage from *On the Heaven and the World* [(135)] about "heaven" and "this heaven": It confirms the point.

(204) In the same way, the reply is clear to the passage from *Metaphysics* XII [(134)]. For I grant there cannot be several first movers, because in the first mover there is no matter. That is, there is nothing in it that contracts—like matter or something else. Rather the first mover is of itself a "this" without anything else contracting it. For such a contraction is inconsistent with perfect simplicity. Therefore, the quiddity of the first mover is of itself a "this."

(205) To the passage from *Metaphysics* VII [(133)], "In what are without matter the what-it-is[62] of the thing is the same as what it belongs to," I say that the what-it-is of a thing can be compared to what it belongs to *per se* and primarily, and also to what it belongs to *per se* and not primarily. In general, in the sense in which it belongs to something, it is the same as that something. For as the Philosopher argues in [*Metaphysics*] VII. 3 [= 6, 1031ᵃ17–18], "A singular," etc. "and the what-it-was-to-be is called the substance in the case of a singular." (For if the what-it-is is not a being, it is nothing.)[63] Now the what-it-is is what the thing primarily is. Therefore, it is *per se* the same as what the what-it-is belongs to *per se*. It is by accident the same as what it belongs to by accident, and therefore it is not absolutely the same as that. Thus Aristotle himself says in Ch. 3 [= 6, 1031ᵃ19–21] that

---

62. To a first approximation, throughout this intricate argument ((205)–(208)) the Aristotelian expressions 'what-it-is' and 'what-it-was-to-be' may be understood as "essence."

63. The role of this sentence in the argument is not clear.

for what are said by accident the what-it-is is not the same as what it belongs to. No surprise, because in Ch. 2 [= 4, 1029^{b}12–1030^{a}17] he explained that for none of them is there a what-it-is or a definition.

(206) Now what has the what-it-is can be understood as either the nature itself, to which the what-it-is belongs primarily, or else as a *suppositum* of the nature, to which it belongs *per se* but not primarily. In the first sense, the what-it-is, both in material and in immaterial cases, is the same as what it belongs to—and even primarily the same. For the nature primarily has the what-it-is. In the second sense, what has the what-it-is is not the same when it includes some entity outside the notion of its quiddity. For in that case it is not the same as the what-it-is primarily, because the what-it-is does not belong to it primarily, insofar as what has the what-it-is includes some entity outside the notion of what is primarily the what-it-is.

(207) To the Philosopher's point, therefore, I say that in what are not conceived with matter—that is, not with an individual entity that contracts the quiddity—the what-it-is is primarily the same as what it belongs to. For what it belongs to has no notion outside the notion of what is the what-it-is. But in what are conceived with matter—that is, with an individual entity that contracts the quiddity—the what-it-is is not primarily the same as what it belongs to. For what is primarily so conceived would not of itself have the what-it-is, but only through a part—namely through the nature, which is contracted through that individual entity.

(208) Therefore, one does not get from this the conclusion that the matter that is one part of a composite is outside the *per se* notion of the quiddity. Indeed matter truly pertains to the quiddity. And the species, and what has the form in the universal, primarily has the what-it-is and is primarily the same as it. Therefore, it does not follow that the matter that is one part of a composite is what individuates. Rather that only follows for the "matter" that is an entity contracting the quiddity, which I have granted [(206)]. But whether the lack of matter that is one part of the composite implies the lack of this kind of individual entity according to the Philosopher, I will talk about that in the following question [7. 505–507].

(209) To the Philosopher's point [(132)] that the generator generates something else on account of the matter, I say that the Philosopher's meaning there is that Platonic Ideas are not necessary for generation. For both the distinction between the generator and the generated and the likeness of the generated to the generator (both of which are required for univocal generation) can be had without Ideas. A particular agent gets from its form the fact that it likens the patient to itself, and so does the generator with respect to the generated. From the matter the generator gets the fact that

it is distinct from the generated. But it does not get this from the matter principally, even though it necessarily follows that it is distinguished from the generated by matter. For the generator does not perfect its own matter but another matter, through the form that terminates the generation. (Its own is already perfected by a form.) From the fact that the generator likens through the form, it perfects matter other than its own, and so its own matter is other than the matter that is deprived of such a form. But whatever has another matter than something else has is other than that something else, from the fact that matter is an essential part of a thing.

(210) I say then that the main reason for the likening or similarity is the form itself shared between the generator and the generated, not according to individual unity and identity insofar as it is "this" form, but according to a lesser unity and identity insofar as it is a form. The reason for generating is in accordance with this. Form also is a more principal reason for the distinction than matter is, because just as the form is more principally that by which something is a composite than the matter is, so it is more principally that by which a composite is one, and consequently not distinguished in itself and yet distinct from everything else.

(211) Nevertheless the form is properly assimilative (distinguishing 'assimilative' from 'distinctive'), so that the matter is not assimilative properly, because it is not a substantial or accidental quality. On the other hand, properly speaking, the matter is distinctive, because necessarily, from the fact that it lacks form, matter that does have form in advance is distinguished[64] from it, and so one composite is distinguished from another.

(212) There is another way too in which a composite can be understood to be "other" on account of matter, as on account of a pre-existing cause of otherness. For the form of the generated, even though it is a more principal cause of otherness in the composite than the matter is, nevertheless is not a cause that pre-exists this otherness. But the matter is, because it pre-exists in a state of privation. Therefore, it cannot be the same as the informed matter [that pre-exists in the cause].

64. Adopting a variant reading where the edition has 'distinguishes'.

William of Ockham

Five Questions on Universals
from His *Ordinatio*, d. 2, qq. 4–8

[Question 4

Is a universal a thing outside the soul, in individuals, really distinct from them, and not multiplied in individuals?]

(1) As for the identity and distinction of God from creature, it must be asked whether there is something univocal common to God and creature and essentially predicable of both. But because this question, along with much of what has already been said and is about to be said in the following questions, depends on a knowledge of univocal and universal nature, therefore in order to clarify what has been and will be said I will first ask some questions about universal and univocal nature.

(2) On this, I first ask whether what is immediately and proximately denominated by a universal and univocal intention [**K** Ch. 23] is truly some thing outside the soul, intrinsic and essential to what it is common and univocal to, and really distinct from them.

(3) Yes it is:

(4) First, it is truly a thing, essential and intrinsic to what it is common to. For according to the Commentator, *Metaphysics* V. comm. 7, [110I], "These two men, the universal and the particular—namely, the particular man of whom music is an accident—are essentially one." But what is essentially one with some real being outside the soul is itself truly a thing and essential to such a thing. Therefore, the universal man is truly a thing outside the soul, and essential to what it is common to.

(5) Second, it seems it is a really distinct thing. For it is impossible for the same thing to be both corruptible and incorruptible. But universals are incorruptible, and what they are common to are corruptible. Therefore, universals are not the same thing as singulars.

(6) On the contrary:

(7) The Commentator, *Metaphysics* XII. comm. 22 [= comm. 21, 307D]: "One and being are among universal things, which do not have being outside the soul." Therefore, according to him, universals do not have being outside the soul. But nothing that does not have being outside the soul is really the same as a being outside the soul. Therefore, etc.

[Walter Burley's Theory][1]

(8) On this question there is one theory that says every univocal universal is a certain thing existing outside the soul, really in each singular and belonging to the essence of each singular, really distinct from each singular and from any other universal, in such a way that the universal man is truly one thing outside the soul, existing really in each man, and is really distinguished from each man and from the universal animal and from the universal substance. So too for all genera and species, whether subalternate or not subalternate.

(9) So according to this theory, however many universals are predicable *in quid** and *per se* in the first mode* of any singular *per se* in a genus, there are that many really distinct things in that singular, each of which is really distinguished from the other and from the singular. All those things—not multiplied in themselves in any way, no matter how much their singulars are multiplied—are in each individual of the same species.

(10) There are many arguments in favor of this theory.

(11) First, from reason.

(12) First: Definition is primarily of substance and secondarily of accident, according to the Philosopher, *Metaphysics* VII. [4, 1030^{b}4–13]. But definition is not primarily of singular substance, according to him in the same place [15, 1039^{b}20–1040^{a}7]. Therefore, there is another kind of substance than singular substance, and it is what is primarily definable. But that other kind of substance is not separate from sensibles, because such a separate substance is not definable, according to the Philosopher himself in the same place. Therefore, that other kind of substance belongs to the essence of a singular.

(13) *Confirmation*: According to everyone, something in the genus substance is definable. But the individual is not definable. For if it were, then I ask what would be included in its definition. Nothing but substance, ac-

---

1. In q. 5 (6) Ockham says some people attributed this theory to Scotus. He is probably thinking of Henry of Harclay (see the text in Gál, "Henricus de Harclay." But in fact the view described here is not Scotus's, but rather Walter Burley's. See Walter Burley, 3rb–7rb. See also **K** Ch. 20.

cording to the Philosopher, *Metaphysics* VII. [4, 1030^{b}4–6]. Therefore, some substance would be included in its definition. But not singular substance, because then it would have to be either (a) the same singular substance itself. But that is impossible, because the same item does not define itself. Neither is it (b) another singular substance, because no singular substance is truly predicated of another singular substance. Therefore, some *universal* substance has to be included in its definition. Consequently the point is established.

(14) *Second confirmation*: A substance is defined by a definition properly so called, which is given by genus and difference. Then I ask: Is the genus a thing, or an intention of the mind? If it is a thing, it is not a singular thing, because no singular is a genus. Therefore, it is a universal thing. And it belongs to the essence of the defined species. For otherwise the species would be defined by means of something additional to it, since it would be defined by means of something outside its essence. Therefore, besides the singular thing there is some other, universal thing belonging to the essence of the singular thing.

(15) But if genus and difference are certain intentions of the mind, then to the contrary: A substance is only defined by means of substances, according to the Philosopher, *Metaphysics* VII. [4, 1030^{b}4–6]. Therefore, genus and difference are substances. Likewise, in that case a substance would be defined by means of something additional to it, since it would be defined by means of intentions of the mind that do not belong to the thing's essence.

(16) *Third confirmation*: A definition is truly predicated primarily of the defined. But it is not predicated primarily of any individual, since then it would be predicated of nothing other than that individual. Neither is it predicated primarily of something extrinsic to the individual, since nothing like that is truly a rational animal.[2] Therefore, it is predicated *per se* of something that is not any individual and yet is intrinsic to each individual. But nothing is like that except a universal thing really distinct from the individual and intrinsic to it.

(17) Second [(12)]: A real science is about true things outside the soul. For this is how real science is distinguished from rational science.[3] But no science is primarily about singular things. Therefore, there are some things outside the soul besides singular things. The minor premise is plain, ac-

---

2. Ockham is assuming we are talking about the definition of man.

3. On real and rational sciences, see William of Ockham, *Philosophical Writings*, 1–16.

cording to the Philosopher, *Posterior Analytics* I. [4–5, 73^{b}25–74^{a}13] and *Metaphysics* VII. [15, 1039^{b}20–1040^{a}7].

(18) Third: The word 'man' primarily signifies some thing outside the soul. For every univocal word has primarily one significate, since this is how it is distinguished from an equivocal word, which is one that signifies several things equally primarily. But the word 'man' does not primarily signify any intention of the mind, because then it would be a name of second intention. Likewise, in that case 'A second intention is a man' would be true without having to make any distinction, since a word is always able, in virtue of its being instituted to signify, to supposit for its significate. But it is plain that this proposition is either false or else has to be distinguished. Therefore, the word 'man' does not primarily signify an intention. Therefore, it signifies some thing outside the soul. It does not primarily signify a singular thing, because it does not signify one singular thing any more than another. There-fore, it signifies some thing other than a singular. Not one extrinsic to the singular. Therefore, etc.

(19) Fourth: The intellect can understand man without understanding any singular man. But by understanding man it understands a true thing. Therefore, some true thing is understood in that case and is distinct from any singular man.

(20) Fifth: The first adequate object of a real power is a true thing. But the first adequate object of any power at all, whether sensitive or intellective, is not some singular thing. For then nothing would be apprehended by that power except that singular thing, or except under the aspect of that singular. Both of these are plainly false. Therefore, some thing other than a singular thing is the first adequate object of a real power. The major premise is plain—especially in the case of a sensitive power—because nothing is appre-hensible by a sensitive power except a true thing; therefore, nothing is its object, either adequate or nonadequate, except a true thing.

(21) Sixth: The first subject of a real attribute is a true thing. But no singular thing is the first subject of any attribute at all, since then the attribute would belong to nothing but what that singular thing is said of, according to the Philosopher's procedure in *Posterior Analytics* I. [4, 85^{a}13–86^{b}30]. Consequently it would not belong to any other singular thing that has the same aspect. This is plainly false. Therefore, a real attribute primarily be-longs to another thing than a singular thing.

(22) The major premise is clear. For the subject is not more imperfect than its attribute. Therefore, if the attribute is real its subject will be real.

(23) *Confirmation*, from the Philosopher, *On the Soul* II. [7, 418^{b}7–9]: Transparency is in air and water not by reason of the water only, or by reason

of the air only, but by reason of a common nature. Therefore, the nature is in both. Therefore, there is some common nature in both, differing from both.

(24) *Second confirmation*, from *On Generation* I. [4, 319ᵇ22–23]: When air turns into water, there remains numerically the same transparency. This is not by reason of the matter, because in that case the transparency would always remain, just as the matter always remains. Neither is it by reason of a singular form, because no such form is the same [after the transformation]. Therefore, it is by reason of a common form. Therefore, there is some common form differing from each singular form.

(25) Seventh: In its acting, a natural agent aims at a true thing. And it does not aim at a singular thing. For by whatever reason it would aim at one, by the same reason it would aim at another too, since the agent is related equally to any other singular thing that has the same aspect as the first one as it is to that first one itself. Consequently it would aim at infinitely many singular things. So it would be frustrated in its intention, since it can never produce infinitely many things. Therefore, [since this is unacceptable], it aims at some thing distinct from singulars.

(26) Eighth: Either a most general genus is a true thing or else it is only a concept in the mind. If it is a true thing, then certainly no singular thing is a most general genus. For no such singular thing is predicated of all the things contained under a most general genus. Yet the most general genus is itself predicated of them. Therefore, the most general genus is another thing than a singular.

(27) If the most general genus is a concept in the mind, then since there can be several concepts, it would follow that there could be several most general genera *substance*.

(28) Again, ninth: According to Porphyry [P (32)]: "Species collects many into one nature." Therefore, species indicates one nature beyond the many collected things. Likewise, in the same place: "By participation in the species several men are one man." But they are not one singular man. Therefore, there is some universal besides particulars.

(29) Again, tenth: According to the Philosopher in the *Categories* [2, 1ᵃ20–21]: "Among things that are, some are said of a subject and are not in a subject." Such things are not accidents. (For according to him in the same passage [1ᵃ23–ᵇ3], accidents are in a subject.) Therefore, since they exist, they are substances. But they are not singular substances. For according to him in the same passage [1ᵇ3–4], singular substances "are neither in a subject nor are said of a subject." Therefore, etc.

(30) Again, eleventh: In the same work, the chapter "On Substance,"

[5, 2ª11–17]: One kind of substance is first substance and another second substance. First substances are singular substances. Therefore, besides singular substance there is another kind of substance, which is second substance—namely, genus or species.

(31) *Confirmation*: In the same passage [2ᵇ8–9], he says that among second substances the species is more substance than the genus is. Therefore, genera and species are substances. And they are not singular substances, because then they would be first substances. Therefore, there are other substances.

(32) Moreover, twelfth: In *On Interpretation* I. [7, 17ª38–39]: "Among things some are universals, others particulars." But one part of a dichotomy is not the other. Therefore, universal things are not particular things or conversely. Therefore, they are other things.

(33) Thirteenth: *Topics* I. [7, 103ª7–9]: " 'Same' is said in three ways: the same in genus, the same in species, and the same in number." On the basis of this, here is an argument: There is a threefold real identity here. But specific identity does not belong primarily to the individual, and neither does identity of genus. Therefore, they belong primarily to other things.

[Against this theory]

(34) This view is absolutely false and absurd. So I argue against it.

(35) First: No thing one in number, not varied or multiplied, is in several sensible *supposita* or singulars, or for that matter in any created individuals, at one and the same time. But a thing such as this theory postulates, if it were granted, would be one in number. Therefore, it would not be in several singulars and belong to their essence.

(36) The major premise is plain. For it is proper to the divine essence alone that without any division or multiplication it is really in several distinct *supposita*. The minor premise, that a thing such as this theory postulates is one in number, I prove like this: Whenever there are two equally simple really distinct things, neither of which includes in itself a greater intrinsic plurality of things than does the other, either each of those things is one in number or else neither of them is. For there is no greater reason why the one of them should be one in number than that the other one is. <Or, if one of them does include a greater plurality than the other one does, so that they are not equally simple, then if the one that includes the greater plurality and is the less simple is one in number, the one that includes in itself the lesser intrinsic plurality and is simpler will be one in number too.> But a universal thing and a singular one are, according to you, two really distinct and equally simple things, <or else the universal thing is the simpler>.

Neither does a universal thing include in itself a greater intrinsic plurality of things than does a singular thing. Therefore, if a singular thing is one in number, a universal things will be one in number.

(37) The first part of the minor of this syllogism, <namely, that a universal thing and a singular one are two really distinct things,> is granted by this view.

(38) The second part, <namely, that a universal thing does not include a greater plurality of things than does a singular thing>, I prove like this: If a universal thing includes a greater intrinsic plurality of things in itself, then this will be either a greater plurality (a) of universal things, or (b) of singular things. Not (a) of universal things. For I take one of those <included> universal things <and ask>: Does it include a greater plurality than a singular thing does or does it not?

(39) If it does, then I ask about one of those included things the same question as before. And so the stopping point of this line of questioning will be that some universal thing does not include a greater plurality of things than does a singular thing, or else there will be a regress to infinity.

(40) If it does not, therefore that universal thing, which does not include a greater plurality of things, will be one in number just like a singular thing. Consequently by the same reasoning, any other universal thing will be one in number too.

(41) Neither can a universal thing include a greater plurality (b) of singular things. For then it would not be distinguished from singular things except as a whole is distinguished from a part. This is impossible even according to them. For according to them, the singular essentially includes the universal and something more. Consequently the singular is a whole and the universal is a part, according to them.

(42) Likewise, the point [that the kind of universal this theory postulates would be something one in number] follows directly from alternative (b). For if each part is one in number, the whole will be one in number.

(43) *Confirmation*: According to them, whatever is included in a universal is included in everything contained *per se* under that universal. Therefore, whatever is included essentially in man is included essentially in Socrates, because whatever belongs to the essence of man belongs to the essence of Socrates. Therefore, a universal never includes a greater plurality of things, <singular or universal>, than does a singular. Consequently it is equally simple, and consequently one in number if a singular is one in number.

(44) If it is said that the universal includes many things, but not as intrinsic to it, and because of this it is not one in number, then to the contrary: Such

an inclusion or containing does not exclude numerical unity. For in this sense God, matter, and indeed any cause contains many really distinct things, and yet each such containing thing is one in number.

(45) If it is said that the universal thing is really communicable to many and really in many, but the singular thing is not, and therefore although the universal does not intrinsically include a greater plurality of things, nevertheless it is not one in number like a singular thing, then to the contrary I ask: How is it communicable to many? And how is it in many? Either it is communicated (a) through an identity with many and through its own real multiplication, in addition to the multiplication of the things it is in, or else (b) it is not multiplied or varied in itself and yet is communicated to many and is in them and always remains really distinct from them.

(46) If it is communicated (a) in the first way, then it is not distinct from the singulars, but rather indicates the singular things themselves, if it is communicated to them by identity.

(47) Likewise, there is an explicit opposition here if it is communicated to them by identity. For that is the same as to say that these very things are communicated to themselves.

(48) Likewise, if they are multiplied in addition to the multiplication of the individuals, then there would really be as many universals as singulars. And so none of them would be a universal.

(49) Even they assert the opposite of this, saying that the universal is absolutely another thing, not varied in itself and yet really existing in many.

(50) If it is said that a universal is communicated (b) in the second way, < namely, that it is not varied or multiplied in itself and yet is communicated to many and remains really distinct from them >, then such a communicability or existence in many does not exclude numerical unity. First, because matter, which is one in number, is really in diverse things in succession. And it is not any more one in number because it exists in diverse things in succession than it would be if it existed in the same things all at once without any variation in itself.

(51) Second, if the same form perfected several matters at once, it would not be any the less one in number.

(52) Third, according to the Commentator's tale [in his *Commentary on On the Soul* III. comm. 5, 387–413], although the possible intellect* is in many men, nonetheless it is one in number because it is really distinguished from each of them and is not multiplied in them, although the men it is united to are multiplied. Therefore, in the same way, although the communal man, which is claimed to be really distinguished, is in many singular men

from each of whom it is really distinguished, nevertheless if it is not multiplied in itself, but rather only the singular men it exists in are multiplied, then it will be absolutely one in number.

(53) Fourth, although the divine essence is communicated even by identity to distinct *supposita*, nevertheless because it is not multiplied in itself, but rather only the *supposita* it is communicated to are multiplied, it is one in number. Therefore all the more, if this communal man is communicated to many so that it is in many singular men, from each of whom it is really distinguished, nevertheless if it is not multiplied in itself, but only the singular men it exists in are multiplied, then it will be absolutely one in number.

(54) *Confirmation* of this argument [(45)]: Every thing that together with another thing makes up a number, so that it is true to say that they are many things, will either be numerically one thing or numerically many things. For it is impossible to have two or three things, unless there are many things each of which is one in number. But according to you, a singular thing and a universal thing are many (several) things. Therefore, a universal thing is either numerically one thing or numerically many things. Whichever alternative is given, the point is established.

(55) If it is said that the major [in (54)] is not universally true, because a one in number—like number itself—is not found in all things but only in continua, then to the contrary: This reply concedes the point. For it can just as truly and properly be said, according to this theory, that the universal thing is numerically one as that the divine essence is numerically one, and as the possible intellect the Commentator invents is numerically one, and as each angel is numerically one, and as the intellective soul [of any individual man] is numerically one according to the truth of the matter. So consequently, since every thing numerically one is truly a singular thing, every universal thing will be truly a singular thing.[4]

(56) *Confirmation* of the whole preceding argument [(54)–(55)]: Every thing that together with another really distinct thing makes up a number is numerically one thing or else numerically several things. But a universal thing such as this theory postulates, if it is granted, truly makes up a number together with a singular thing. Therefore, it is numerically one thing or numerically several things. But it is not numerically several things, because then it would be several singulars. For according to them and according to

---

4. The entire paragraph is puzzling. Why restrict number and numerical unity to continuous quantity? And how would this amount to conceding the point, as Ockham claims? Do not the examples he lists indicate that number and numerical unity apply to things other than continua as well?

the truth, every thing numerically one is singular, and therefore numerically several things are several singulars. But no universal thing is several singulars according to them, because according to them a universal is really distinguished from all singulars. Therefore, it is numerically one.

(57) The major of this argument is plain. For all the things that make up a number are numbered. Consequently each of them is one according to number.

(58) The minor is also plain. For according to them, a singular thing and a universal thing are several really distinct things. For example, Socrates and the universal the term 'man' signifies are several things. And they are not infinite in number. Therefore, they are finite. Therefore, they are two or three or four, or some definite number. And they certainly cannot be said to be anything but two. (That is clear by induction.*) Therefore, there are only two things here. Therefore, there will be a pair here just as truly as this man and this angel make up a pair. Therefore, each of these things—indicating this universal thing and this singular thing—is numerically one just as truly as both this man and this angel are numerically one.

< (59) *Confirmation* again: The two universals (namely, the universal man and the universal angel) are two really distinct things either by themselves or else through some features intrinsic to them. And they are not more than two. Therefore, each of them is truly one thing and not several. Consequently each of them is numerically one.

(60) *Confirmation* of all the above arguments [(35)–(59)]: I ask: What is the significate of the phrase 'numerically one'? One has to say either (a) it signifies whatever is one and not several. And then the point is granted. For each universal thing is one and not several.

(61) Or else (b) it signifies what is one and not several and in addition is not *in* several. In that case, no matter how much the [possible] intellect is one and not several, nevertheless if it were *in* several it would not be numerically one. Likewise the divine essence, since it is in several persons would not be numerically one. In the same way, if this form were in several composites through divine power, it would not be numerically one. All of which is false.

(62) Or else (c) one has to say it signifies what is one continuum and not several continua. And then an angel would not be numerically one. Neither would the divine essence or any intellective soul or any simple thing. These results are absurd.

(63) So from all the above [(35)–(62)] it is plainly clear that if there is a universal thing such as this theory claims it will truly be numerically one, just like an angel or a soul or any noncontinuous thing. >

(64) Second [(35)], I argue: Every thing prior to another thing really distinct from it can exist without that other thing. But according to you, this universal thing is prior to and is really distinct from its singular. Therefore, it can exist without the singular thing.

(65) I argue the same point in another way: When some thing really distinct from other things can in the course of nature exist without any one of them taken separately, and it does not depend essentially on any of them, then it can exist without all of them taken all together, at least by divine power. But according to them, without any given singular man, the universal thing signified by 'man' can really exist. Therefore, by divine power the universal thing could exist without every singular thing. This argument and the proposition on which it is based will be clarified elsewhere [**OT** 3. 309].

(66) *Confirmation* of the argument: An individual adds something to the nature, according to them. And this added feature is something that together with the universal thing makes something that is *per se* one. For if it did not, then it would be something that would be neither a substance nor an accident. Therefore, it does not seem to include a contradiction that the additional feature should be conserved by God without any advening universal nature. This seems absurd.

(67) Third: An individual of some species can be newly created no matter how many other individuals of the same species remain, created or produced earlier. But creation is absolutely from nothing, so that nothing essential and intrinsic to a thing absolutely precedes it in real being. Therefore, no nonvaried pre-existing thing in any individual belongs to the essence of that individual, if it is newly created. For if it did, something essential to the thing would precede it, and consequently it would not be created. Therefore, there is no universal thing belonging to the essence of those individuals. For if there were, it would pre-exist every individual produced after the first one. Consequently, all those produced after the one first produced would not be created, because they would not be from nothing.

(68) Moreover, every singular thing can be annihilated without the annihilation or destruction of any other singular thing on which it does not depend at all. Therefore, this man can be annihilated by God without any other man's being annihilated or destroyed. But in annihilation nothing intrinsic to the thing remains in real existence, either in itself or in anything else. Therefore, there is no such universal thing common to both this man and another one. For then it would be annihilated [when this man is annihilated], and consequently no other man would remain according to his whole essence. So each man would be corrupted at once, because when any part is annihilated the whole is destroyed.

(69) If someone quibbles against these arguments [**(67)**–**(68)**], that something is created or annihilated when everything in it that is numerically one in it is created or annihilated, but the nature common to it and to others does not have to be created or annihilated, then to the contrary: Creation is absolutely from nothing in such a way that nothing intrinsic and essential to the thing precedes it. Likewise, in annihilation nothing remains. Therefore, if something essential to the thing that can be created and annihilated precedes it and remains after its annihilation, the thing will not be annihilated or created.

(70) *Confirmation*: That universal thing is just as essential to the individual as any particular thing is. For according to them, Socrates is a man just as essentially as he has this matter and this form. Therefore, just as Socrates cannot be annihilated or created unless both this material and this form are created or annihilated, so too Socrates cannot be created or annihilated unless this universal thing that is essential to him is nothing beforehand or absolutely nothing afterwards.

(71) Likewise, this common nature is more essential and intrinsic to this individual than any matter or potency of matter is to a material form. But if a material form is produced in prime matter and from the potency of matter, the material form is not created. Or if matter or the potency of matter remains [after the material form is gone], that form is not annihilated, according to them. Therefore, all the more, if this universal thing intrinsic to this individual precedes or follows it, the individual is not created or not annihilated.

(72) Likewise, [if the above quibble is raised], I will just as easily say that this individual thing can be created even if what is added to the universal nature is not a pure nothing beforehand, provided that the nature itself is a pure nothing beforehand, since each is essential to the individual.

(73) Fifth:[5] Either this universal or communal man **(a)** belongs to the essence of Socrates, or **(b)** it does not. If **(b)** not, nevertheless it is certain according to them that Socrates does not belong to the essence of the communal man. For then this communal man would not remain without Socrates, which they deny. Therefore, there are two things neither of which belongs to the essence of the other. In that case I ask: Do they make up something *per se* one?

(74) If so, then Socrates is not an individual. Instead he will be a *part* of something *per se* one. Likewise, in that case he would not be essentially a

5. Where is the fourth argument? Compare **(67)**.

man any more than the matter is the form together with which it makes up something *per se* one.

(75) If they do not make up something *per se* one, and the one is not an accident of the other, then each will be subsistent by itself. So the universal man will be a Platonic Idea and will be a one subsisting by itself, even though it coexists with many individuals. Many other absurdities, which no one in his senses would accept, follow if that universal thing does not belong to the essence of Socrates or, together with something else, make up something *per se* one.

(76) Suppose it is said that (a) the universal thing does belong to the essence of Socrates, and yet is not the *whole* essence of Socrates, because then it would not be another thing than Socrates. Therefore, it is an essential part of Socrates.

(77) Many absurdities follow from this:

(78) First, then Socrates would be no more a singular thing than he is a universal. For a whole is not denominated more by one essential part of it than by another.[6] For example, a composite is not said to be more the form than it is the matter, or conversely (although the form is the more principal part).

(79) Second, then a singular thing would truly be the matter of a universal thing and the universal thing would be the form, or conversely. For either the added singular thing and the universal are of the same kind or of different kinds. They are not of the same kind, because then the one would not be more a universal than the other one is. If they are of different kinds, and all things that are of different kinds, if they make up something *per se* one, are related as form and matter, then the universal thing and the singular are related as matter and form.

(80) If it is said that this is not true except when each of those things is a singular, that is not valid. For I will say just as easily that when each of the things is a singular it does not have to be the case that the one is matter and the other form.

(81) Third, it follows that every accident would be truly and really composed of diverse really distinct things—namely, of such a universal nature and of something added to it. And in general it would follow that there would be as many really distinct things in any singular as there are universals predicable univocally of the same singular.

6. The idea seems to be that the other part of Socrates would have to be a contracting difference, which would be singular.

<(82) Again, then Socrates would be of another kind than Plato is. For what are added to the universals would be of different kinds.>

(83) Sixth [(73)]: Every thing outside the soul in the genus *substance* is susceptive of contraries. Therefore, if there is a universal substance, it will be truly susceptive of contraries. But no universal is susceptive of contraries. Therefore, no such universal is a real thing in the genus *substance*. The antecedent is clear from the Philosopher in the *Categories* [5, 4ᵇ17–18], when he says this is properly a property of substance.

(84) But that no such universal is susceptive of contraries, I prove like this:[7] For in that case, just as individual contraries can be in diverse individuals of the same most specific species, so too those common contraries would be in the same universal at once, which is impossible. The inference is clear, because those individual contraries cannot exist unless their common universals exist. Therefore, those common contraries have to be primarily in something susceptive of them. But they are not primarily in any singular or singulars. Therefore, they are primarily in some universal or universals. But they do not have to be in several universals, because it is possible that the singulars the singular accidents are in are of the same most specific species.

(85) For example, this intellective soul has knowledge with respect to one scientific conclusion, and another intellective soul is in error with respect to the same conclusion. In that case, the knowledge in general that precisely pertains to this conclusion, and the error in general that is contrary to that knowledge, are not subjectively in diverse universals belonging to these intellective souls. Therefore, they will be subjectively in the same universal. Consequently contraries will be together in the same primary subject.

(86) *Confirmation*: According to them, contrariety is primarily found among universals. Therefore, so too are inconsistency and opposition. Therefore, contrary universals will not be able to be in the same primary subject at all. <Yet this would follow if the above theory were true.>

(87) Likewise, it would follow that a universal thing would be primarily and *per se* transmutable. For what primarily and *per se* subjectively receives a thing is truly transmuted. But according to this theory, one would have to maintain that a universal nature primarily and *per se* receives a universal accident. For the universal is its primary subject. Therefore, it is primarily transmuted. The consequent is false, because, according to everyone, acts,

7. In fact the following argument proves something else: *if* there is a universal substance, it will be susceptive of contraries. This was already argued from authority in (83).

operations and transmutations primarily belong to singulars and not to universals.

(88) Likewise, a certain absurdity would follow in theology: Something intrinsic and essential to Christ would be damned and miserable both with the misery of guilt and with the misery of punishment. For the nature common to Christ and to other men is informed both by blessedness in general and by misery in general, both the misery of guilt and that of punishment.

<(89) Likewise, [if this view were true], then the same thing would be in diverse places at once.>

(90) Many other absurdities follow from this view, which would not have to be brought up against it—and neither would the ones mentioned above, on account of their unreasonableness and absurdity—except because this was the view of many people and is perhaps still maintained by many.

(91) *Confirmation* of the last argument [(88)]: When two really distinct things informed by contraries are in something, the whole is not denominated more by one of those contraries than by the other. Therefore, if the universal human nature existing in the essence of Christ is informed by misery, both of guilt and of punishment, then since it is certain that something belonging to the essence of Christ is informed by blessedness, therefore Christ is not denominated formally blessed any more than he is denominated miserable, which is absurd.

(92) *Second confirmation*: Everything essential in Christ is united to the divine Word. But nothing united to the divine Word is damned or miserable. Therefore, no such universal nature receptive of contraries (namely, of blessedness and misery) is in Christ.

(93) If you say it is not the Philosopher's meaning [*Categories* 5, 4^b17–18], that every substance is susceptible of contraries, but only primary substance, then to the contrary: As are the universals of substances, so too are the universals of accidents. Therefore, whiteness and blackness in general are in some subject or subjects primarily. But they are not primarily in singulars. Therefore, they are primarily in universals. Therefore, etc.

(94) The assumption is clear. For as a singular accident is to a singular subject, so a common accident is to a common subject. Therefore, just as a singular accident is in a singular subject, so a common accident is in a common subject. Consequently if the singular is susceptive of contraries, the most special species will be susceptive of contraries too.

[Ockham's own theory]

(95) Therefore, in reply to the question [(2)], I say otherwise: No thing really distinct from singular things and intrinsic to them is universal or

common to them. For such a thing is not to be posited except **(a)** to preserve the one's essential predication of the other, or **(b)** to preserve our knowledge of things and **(c)** the definitions of things. Aristotle, [*Metaphysics* XII. 4, 1078^{b}27–34], suggests these reasons for Plato's theory.

(96) But the first of these [**(a)**] is not valid. For by the very fact that the universal is claimed to be intrinsic to the thing and really distinct from the singular thing, it has to be a part of the thing. But a part cannot be essentially predicated of the thing, just as neither matter nor form is essentially predicated of the composite. Therefore, if it is essentially predicated of the thing, it must not supposit for itself but for a singular thing. But such supposition can be preserved by claiming that something is predicated that is not the whole thing or a part of the thing. Therefore, in order to preserve such predication, one does not have to claim that such a predicate is another thing and yet intrinsic to the thing.

(97) For example, the fact that the predication 'A man is an animal' or 'Socrates is an animal' is essential and *per se* in the first mode and *in quid* can be preserved just as much by claiming that the predicate is neither really the subject nor really a part of the subject as it can by claiming that the predicate is an essential part of the subject. For if it is claimed that the predicate is an essential part of the subject, then I ask: What is denoted by the proposition? Either **(i)** that the subject is essentially the predicate itself. And this is impossible, because a whole is never essentially or really its part. Or else **(ii)** it is denoted that what is truly a man is something that is truly an animal—that is to say, that what the term 'man' supposits for is the same as what the term 'animal' supposits for, no matter how much the predicate that supposits is not what it supposits for in the proposition.

(98) But all of this can be preserved equally well by claiming that the predicate is not the subject or a part of it as it can by claiming that it is a part of it. For it is equally possible that something extrinsic to something supposits for it as it is that its parts supposit for it. Therefore, in order to preserve this predication, one does not have to claim a common predicable of something is intrinsic to it.

(99) *Confirmation*: In the proposition 'A man is an animal' either the terms supposit for themselves or not. If so, then the proposition would be false, because the terms are distinct and the one is not the other. And according to the theory reported above [**(8)**] (and also according to the truth), if they do not supposit for themselves, then they supposit for things other than themselves. And so it can pertain to something extrinsic to supposit for something other than itself, just as it can for something intrinsic. Therefore, etc.

(100) Neither does one have to posit universals for the second reason **(b)**, by the same argument. For in order to preserve real knowledge, it suffices to have *per se* propositions in the first mode and the second mode, which can be had without any such other universal thing, as will be explained in replying to some arguments [(131)–(144)], and as was proved in the preceding argument [(96)–(99)]. Therefore, etc.

(101) Neither does one have to posit such a universal thing for the third reason (c), by the same argument, as will be clear later [(111)–(130)].

(102) The point [(95)–(101)] can be convincingly made on the basis of certain logical arguments. First, because what is universally denied of some genus is not a thing contained *per se* under that genus. For example, if 'No animal is *a*' is true, *a* will not be contained *per se* under animal. But every universal such as this view posits is universally denied of such a genus—say, of the most general genus substance. For 'No substance is *a*' is absolutely true. (Let *a* be the universal signified by 'animal', <or let it be a term that supposits for that universal>.) So too in every other case. Therefore, no universal is any thing really contained under the genus substance.

(103) The major is clear, because a genus is truly predicated of everything contained *per se* under that genus. The minor is clear, because I take the thing conveyed by 'animal', according to you. Let it be *a*. Then 'No substance is *a*' is true. For no incorporeal substance is *a*,[8] and likewise no corporeal substance is *a*. This latter is clear, because no inanimate body is *a*, and likewise no animate body is *a*. This latter is clear, because no insensate animate body is *a*, and likewise no sensate animate body is *a*. This latter is clear, because no man is *a*, no ass is *a*, and so on for all the species contained under sensate animate body. Therefore, no sensate body is *a*. This argument holds on the basis of the Philosopher's rule in *Topics* II. [4, 111ª33–34]: Whatever each species of some genus is denied of, that genus is denied of the same thing. Therefore, if 'No substance is *a*' is true, *a* is not *per se* a thing contained under that most general genus.

(104) Moreover second, from a *per se* inferior to its superior is a good inference <when, that is, superior and inferior supposit for the things contained under them, although it does not follow when they supposit for themselves>. Therefore, it follows: Man is a species; therefore, animal is a species. I ask therefore: How does 'animal' supposit in that proposition? Either it supposits (i) personally. And then the proposition is false, even

---

8. *a* is the universal *animal*. But *animal* is by definition a corporeal substance. So too, in the next sentence, it is claimed that *a* is not an inanimate body; animals are animate bodies. And so on down the Porphyrian tree.

according to them. For no animal is a species. Or it supposits (ii) simply. And then it is false again. For then 'animal' supposits for a common thing, according to them—namely, for itself—and that common thing is not a most special species but a genus.

(105) Moreover third, it follows: Every animal is corruptible *per se* and generable *per se*. Therefore, this thing (indicating the universal thing conveyed by 'man') is corruptible *per se*. And the same holds too for all the most specific universals contained under animal. The consequent is false; therefore, so is the antecedent. Consequently 'Every animal is corruptible *per se*' would be false. But no one denies that proposition, because by the same reasoning 'Every body is mobile' would have to be denied, and consequently too 'Every man is risible *per se*'. In general, every proposition in which an attribute is predicated of its subject with a mark of perseity would be false, which is absurd.

(106) The first inference [(104)] is clear, because from a distributed superior to each *per se* inferior, <which is to say, a thing contained under it,> is a good inference.

(107) If it is said that the superior is not distributed for all its *per se* inferiors, but only for singular ones, not for universals, then to the contrary: Every superior is distributed for the things that have it more immediately. Therefore, since those universals, according to you, are more immediate to the superior [universal than their singulars are], it will be distributed primarily for them.

(108) Moreover a genus is univocally predicated of a universal thing and of a singular thing. For if not, it is predicated of them equivocally, which they deny. Therefore, it is equally distributed for the one thing and for the other, because there is no reason to say it is distributed for one thing contained *per se* under it and not for another. I might just as easily say it is distributed for universal things as being the ones that are immediately contained under the genus, and not for singulars.

(109) Likewise, for the same reason that one universal is not distributed for such contents, neither is another. Therefore, 'being' is not distributed for other universals, but only for singulars. Consequently 'Some being is a universal' would be literally false. They deny this.

(110) Moreover fourth, if 'A most specific species is a substance' is true, either 'substance' supposits simply or personally. If simply, then the proposition will be false, because [if it were true] then a most specific species would be a most general genus. If it supposits personally, the proposition will still be false because then it supposits for its *supposita* and for singulars.

Consequently a most specific species would be some singular. Therefore, I say there is no such thing that is universal and intrinsic to the things it is common to.

[Replies to the arguments in favor of Burley's theory]

(111) To the other theory's first argument [(12)]: When it is assumed that definition is primarily of substance, I say that for a definition to be "primarily" of something can be understood in two senses: Either (a) it is of that of which the definition is primarily and adequately predicated, so that the defined and the definition are convertible. In this sense, definition is not primarily of substance. For of no substance is such a definition primarily and adequately predicated. Rather definition in this sense is primarily of some one term convertible with the definition, even though the term is not really that definition. (What that term is will be stated below, [q. 8, (22)–(85)].)

(112) For a definition to be "primarily" of something can be understood in another sense too, namely (b) because there is something the parts of which are primarily expressed by such a definition. This can be understood in two ways. For 'primarily', like any superlative, can be taken (i) positively or (ii) negatively.[9] If in the first way (i), I still say definition is of nothing primarily. For there is nothing primarily definable, because there is nothing the parts of which ought to be expressed except a singular. And the parts of one singular are not expressed by a definition more than the parts of any other singular are. In the second way (ii), I say definition is indeed primarily of substance, because the parts of a substance are primarily expressed by a definition.

(113) When it is said that definition is not primarily of a singular substance [(12)], I say this is true in sense (a). For of no singular substance is a definition primarily or adequately predicated. Yet in this last sense (b–ii), I say a definition is indeed primarily of a singular substance, because the parts of that singular substance are primarily expressed by the definition, and such a definition is not truly predicated *per se* of any other *suppositum*.

(114) For example, 'rational animal' is a definition. This definition is primarily of the term 'man', because it is predicated primarily and adequately

---

9. In the positive sense, x is most F if and only if x is more F than anything else is. In the negative sense, x is most F if and only if nothing else is more F than x is. The difference is that in the negative sense, but not the positive, there may be more than one thing that is most F.

of this term. For it is predicated of nothing except what the term 'man' is predicated of, and for everything the term 'man' is predicated of when it has personal supposition, the definition (if it supposits personally) is predicated of it. So the definition and the defined are converted. For this is what it is for some things to be convertible: whatever the one is predicated of, so too is the other, and conversely, if they supposit personally. (It is always necessary in the case of convertibles that something is predicated of the one, if it is taken as suppositing *otherwise* than personally, that is not predicated of the other, and conversely. For instance, man and risible are converted. Yet risible is an attribute of man, and man is not an attribute of man.)

(115) In sense (a), therefore, the definition 'rational animal' is primarily of the term 'man', and yet the parts of the term 'man' are not expressed by the definition. In the second sense (b–i), this definition is of nothing primarily. For nothing is expressed by the definition except the parts of Socrates and Plato. Just as nothing is a rational animal except Socrates and Plato (and so on for other singular men), so too the parts of nothing else are expressed by this definition. Yet the parts of Socrates are not expressed more than are the parts of Plato, or conversely. Therefore, the parts of none of them are expressed "primarily"—that is, in the sense that the parts of one are expressed more than are the parts of any other. In the third sense (b–ii), the parts of Socrates are indeed primarily expressed by this definition, and likewise the parts of Plato. For no one else's parts are expressed more.

(116) So understanding the phrase 'primarily defined' in this sense (b–ii), I say Socrates is primarily defined, and likewise Plato is too, and so on for every man. For of each such man the definition is truly predicated. And it is not predicated of anything else that supposits truly for itself, but only of those terms that supposit for singular men.

(117) Hence if, in the proposition 'Man is a rational animal', 'man' supposited for anything other than for a singular man, the proposition would be absolutely false. And so nothing imaginable is a rational animal except for this man or that one, and so on for other singular men. Consequently by the same reasoning, nothing's real parts are expressed by this definition except the parts of this man or that one, and so on for other singular men.

(118) Suppose it is said: A definition and the defined are the same thing. But the term 'man' is not the same thing as this definition. Therefore, the term is not what is primarily defined.

(119) Moreover the parts of no singular are primarily expressed by a definition. For a definition is the principle of perfectly knowing the thing the parts of which are primarily expressed by the definition. But of no singular are the parts perfectly known by a definition. For the parts of one

are no more perfectly known than are the parts of another, and so either the parts of none of them are perfectly known or else the parts of all of them are. But it is certain that the parts all of them are not perfectly known. Therefore, the parts of none of them are.

(120) Moreover the Philosopher says, [*Metaphysics* VII. 4, 1030^{b}4–13, & 15, 1039^{b}20–1040^{a}7], that definition is primarily of substance, and he says singular substance is not defined. And he is not equivocating. Therefore, it is another substance, one that is not a singular, that is defined.

(121) To the first of these [(118)], I say a definition and the defined are never the same thing. For just as they are not the same term, so too they are not the same thing. But this notwithstanding, they *supposit* for the same thing—and indeed for *precisely* the same thing. Neither is any thing signified primarily and principally by the one expression unless it is signified by the other. Nor is anything extrinsic connoted by either of them. This is what the authorities mean if they say a definition and the defined are one thing—that is, because they have the same significate. Even some modern authors, although some of them do not realize it, express this meaning quite well when they frequently say a definition and the defined convey the same thing and signify the same thing—and consequently are *not* the same thing, just as two signs or indications are not one significate or conveyed meaning.

(122) To the second argument [(119)], I say a definition is not always a principle of perfectly knowing whatever it is the definition of. Sometimes, as will be clarified later [OT 2. 478–480], what it is the definition of can be perfectly known even without any definition. But it is quite true that if you have the definition, the parts of something it is the definition of can be known to be in what it is the definition of.

(123) For example, when diverse men are known and their diverse circumstances are known, the definition 'rational animal' is finally taken on by the knower—that is, by knowing every man is a rational animal. When this definition is had by someone, if some man he had no knowledge of beforehand is presented to him, then by virtue of the knowledge of the definition mentioned, such a knower would know that this man, whom he did not previously know in himself except confusedly (because he did not distinctly apprehend each part of him), has really distinct parts—namely, a body and an intellective soul. He would not know this unless he had in mind and knew that the definition mentioned is a definition common to every man. So definition in this sense leads to a knowledge, a distinct knowledge in a way, of the singular thing it is primarily the definition of in the last sense (b–ii) explained above [(112)]. But it does not do this without a coexisting confused knowledge of

that singular thing. Yet that singular thing is not properly known distinctly by the definition, but improperly. For certain terms predicable of it are known that signify the distinct parts of the singular thing. How this occurs will be said later [(141) & OT 2. 478–480].

(124) To the third argument [(120)], I say there is nothing wrong with the Philosopher's equivocating in various places, especially when in one place he quite expressly states he is equivocating.

(125) Or it can be said with respect to the Philosopher's and the Commentator's meaning in *Metaphysics* V, in the various passages [cited in (12)–(15)], that he often takes 'substance' for a *name* or term signifying substance. In that case, I say definition is indeed primarily of substance—that is, it is primarily and adequately predicated of a name or common term precisely conveying singular substance. And in this sense, as was said [(111)–(116)], definition is not primarily of singular substance.

(126) To the first confirmation [(13)], I say no thing in the genus substance is definable in the first sense (a), but only in the third sense [(b–ii) of (111)–(116)]. And I say no *substance* should occur in its definition, but rather *terms* precisely signifying substances should occur there. In this sense, certain predicables are called "substantial"—that is, predicables conveying only substances. And in this sense the Commentator calls certain predicables "substantial" in *Metaphysics* VII. comm. 11 [161D–E], where he says there are only "three substantial predicables: genus, difference, and definition." That is, whatever is predicable of substance and does not convey anything but substance is either a genus or a difference or a definition. Yet these—genus and difference and definition—are not substances but are only signs conveying substances. *They* occur in the definition, not the substances conveyed by the genus and difference. For no substance is conveyed by the genus 'animal' except only a singular substance. Yet no such singular substance occurs in the definition.

(127) To the second confirmation (14), I reply in the same way. The genus and difference that occur in the definition of the species are not substances, but precisely *convey* substances without connoting any accident. Yet they do not belong to the essence of the species. But it does not follow because of this that such a definition is by way of addition. For a definition is said to be by way of addition, not because something occurs in the definition that does not belong to the essence of the defined, but because there occurs there something that conveys and signifies something outside the essence of the defined.

(128) For example, the definition 'White is the color that dazzles sight'

[*Topics* III. 5, 119ª30] is by way of addition. For the term 'sight' occurring here is outside the whole essence of whiteness and conveys something outside the whole essence of whiteness.

(129) When it is said [(15)] that, according to the Philosopher, substance is only defined by substances, I say this is to be understood as follows: Substance is only defined by predicables conveying precisely substances and not some accident.

(130) To the third confirmation [(16)], I say a definition is predicated of the defined in the first sense (a) described above, not suppositing for itself but rather for the defined in the third sense described there, [(b–ii) of (111)–(116)]. For in the proposition 'Every man is a rational animal', the subject is the defined in the first sense, and it does not supposit for itself but for a singular that is the defined in the third sense.

(131) To the second main argument [(17)], I say real science is not always about things as about what are immediately known, but about other things that nevertheless supposit only for things. To understand this, and on account of many statements that have been and will be made for the sake of some people inexperienced in logic, you need to know that any science, whether it is real or rational, is only about *propositions* in the sense of being about what are known. For only propositions are known. But a proposition, according to Boethius on *On Interpretation* I, [37.4–41.15], has three kinds of being: in the mind, in speech and in writing. That is to say, one kind of proposition is only conceived and understood, another kind is spoken, and another kind is written. So too, if there were any other signs instituted to signify in the same way words and letters are, there would be a proposition made up of those signs, just as there is of these.

(132) Therefore, just as a spoken proposition is truly put together out of words and a written proposition is truly put together out of inscriptions, so too a proposition that is only conceived is put together out of things conceived or understood, < or of concepts or understandings > of the soul.[10] So just

10. "*Conceptis sive intellectis < vel conceptibus sive intellectibus >* animae." '*Conceptis*' and '*intellectis*' are passive participles and mean "*the things* understood" and "*the things* conceived," whereas '*conceptibus*' and '*intellectibus*' are fourth-declension nouns meaning "concepts" and "understandings." Burley held that propositions can be made up of real things, "conceived" or "understood." (This is the theory of "real propositions.") By adding the extra words, Ockham distinguishes that theory from the view that mental propositions consist of purely mental concepts or "understandings," not of external objects. The fact that '*animae*' was in the original text and is not part of the addition suggests that the latter theory is what Ockham originally meant anyway, and that it was only later that he realized what he had written could be taken in a Burleian sense. See also the other addition, at the end of (132).

as every word can be part of a proposition in speech, so too everything understood can be part of a proposition in the mind, < according to one view, or a concept can be part of a mental proposition according to another view >.

(133) A word that is part of a spoken proposition can have many kinds of supposition—material, personal and simple—as is clear in the following propositions spoken and heard by the bodily ears: (a) 'Man is a monosyllabic word'. In this, the word is taken materially, because there the word, in the sense in which the proposition is true, stands and supposits for itself. Likewise (b) 'Man runs'. There it stands personally. For it supposits for the men themselves, not for the word, since the word cannot run. But (c) in 'Man is a species' the word supposits simply for something common. The same holds for a part of a similar proposition in the mind.

(134) Disregarding every spoken word (because a mental proposition belongs to no language—as Augustine says in *On the Trinity* XV. [10. 19], there is some word that belongs to no language), I say this part of such a mental proposition can have (a) simple supposition, and then it supposits for something common; or (b) it can have personal supposition, and then it stands and supposits for the signified things themselves, if it signifies things [so that it is not an "empty" term]; or (c) it can have material supposition, and then it stands and supposits for itself.

(135) On this basis, I reply to the argument [(17)]: The spoken proposition 'Every man is risible' is truly known. For as it is true, so it can be truly known, because everything true can be known. Now no one but a maniac can deny that some spoken propositions are true and some false. Who would say he had never heard a lie with his bodily ears? But nothing can be heard with bodily ears but a spoken word, just as nothing can be seen by bodily eyes but color or light. Therefore, some propositions put together precisely out of spoken words are true, like 'Every man is an animal', 'Every man is risible', 'Every species is predicated of several things differing numerically with respect to what they are', 'Genus is predicated of several things differing in species', and so on for other propositions that can be known. So too the proposition in the mind, which belongs to no language, is truly known.

(136) Now however, [no longer disregarding spoken words as in [(134)], the case is such that the knowledge of some such spoken propositions is real science, and of others it is rational science. Yet the known propositions and all their parts are truly spoken words. Nevertheless, because the parts of some of them supposit and stand not for themselves (that is, for the words) but for external things (that is, for their substances),[11] therefore the knowl-

---

11. Following a variant reading in the edition.

edge of such propositions is called "real science." But other parts of other propositions stand for the mental concepts themselves. Therefore, the knowledge of them can be called "rational" or "logical science." And the knowledge of the spoken propositions 'Man is a monosyllabic word' and 'Animal is a trisyllabic word' can be called "grammatical science."

(137) Yet all such propositions and all their parts are spoken words. They are only said to pertain to different sciences because the parts of different ones of them supposit for different kinds of things. Some supposit for things, some for concepts of the mind, and some for the words themselves.

(138) Therefore, analogously, it is the same way for propositions in the mind, which can be truly known by us in this life: All the terms of those propositions are only concepts and not the external substances themselves. Yet because the terms of some mental propositions stand and supposit personally for the external things themselves—as in 'Every mobile thing is partly in the beginning point [and partly in the end point]', 'Every man is risible', 'Every triangle has three [angles adding up to two right angles]', and so on—therefore there is said to be "real" knowledge of such propositions.

(139) But the terms of other mental propositions supposit simply—that is, for the concepts themselves. For example, 'Every demonstration is from primary and true etc.', 'Man is a species', and so on. Therefore, there is said to be "rational" knowledge of them.

(140) So it is irrelevant to "real" science whether the terms of the known proposition are things outside the soul or are only in the soul, provided they stand and supposit for the external things themselves. Hence one does not have to posit any such universal things really distinct from singular things to account for real science.

(141) On this basis, I reply to the actual form of the argument [(17)]: For science to be of things can be understood in three senses: Either (a) because the thing itself is known. And in that sense, no science is about substantial things, especially since nothing is known but a complex.[12] But a complex is not outside the soul, except perhaps in speech or in a similar kind of sign. In another sense (b), the things are parts of what is known. In this sense, real science does not have to be about external things. In a third sense (c), the things are what the parts of the known supposit for. In *this* sense real science is about things—but not about universal things, since there is no supposition for them. For in the mental proposition 'Every body is put together out of matter and a singular form', the supposition is not for any universal body, because no such body (even if there were any) is so put

12. That is, a proposition.

together out of singular matter and a singular form. Instead science in this sense is about singular things, because the terms supposit for those singulars.

(142) It is not in this sense that the Philosopher denies science is about singulars, but in the second sense (b). For the terms of the known propositions are not singular things, but are rather the universals about which there is science in the second sense (b), because universals are the *terms* of the known propositions. If sometimes one finds it said that science is about universal *things*, this should be understood in the sense that knowledge is about universal terms predicable of things.

(143) Therefore, in brief, as for what the Philosopher meant, it must be said that real science is not distinguished from rational science by the fact that real science is about things in such a way that these things are the known propositions or parts of the known propositions, while rational science is not about things. Instead, they are distinguished by the fact that the parts—the terms of the propositions known by a real science—stand and supposit for the things, while the terms of propositions known by a rational science do not. Rather in rational science the terms stand and supposit for other items, [namely, for concepts].

(144) There is a clear example in 'Every man is risible', 'Every man is susceptible of learning', and so on for other propositions known by a real science, and in 'Genus is predicated *in quid* of things differing in species', 'A most specific species is only predicated of individuals', and so on for other propositions known by a rational science.

(145) To the third main argument [(18)], I say the word 'man' does not primarily signify any thing, if 'primarily' is taken in the positive sense. But if it is taken in the negative sense, then I say it does signify a thing primarily. For it signifies primarily whatever singular thing it is predicated of. If it is said that in that case it would be an equivocal word, since an equivocal word is one that primarily signifies several things equally, I reply that for a word primarily to signify several things occurs in three ways. Either (a) because it is imposed on the one as if it were not imposed on the other, and it is imposed by two impositions, as holds for the name 'Socrates' if it is imposed on two men. For the one who imposed the name 'Socrates' on this man thought nothing about the other man, and in the same way the one who imposed the name on the other man thought nothing about this one. Such a word is equivocal, and is called equivocal "by chance."

(146) In a second sense (b), it happens that a word primarily signifies several things equally because it is imposed on many things equally, but by *one* imposition, in such a way that the impositor did not intend that it should signify this thing more than that other one. And if nothing else happens, this

can be called an equivocal word, although not by chance but rather in a way by "agreement."

(147) For example, if someone imposes the name 'Peter' on precisely these three men and does this by one imposition <which nevertheless is *equivalent* to several impositions>, then the name is not equivocal by chance. Neither is it properly univocal. For to any univocal word there corresponds only one concept convertible with it. But there is no concept convertible with the word in the example. For the lowest concept [on the Porphyrian tree] is either a specific one, and consequently common to *all* individuals of the same kind, [not just to the three named "Peter,"] or else it is a concept proper to some one individual. Consequently there is no middle ground, a concept that is common to precisely these individuals and not to others. So the word is not properly univocal but equivocal, by "agreement." This is because it is by a fixed deliberation that it is imposed on these men together.

(148) In a third sense (c), it happens that a word primarily signifies several things equally because by one imposition it is imposed on all the things the determinate concept had by the impositor is common to, in such a way that signs are so to speak ordered [by their corresponding concepts]. Not that the word primarily signifies the concept, but rather because it is imposed to signify primarily and precisely all the concept is predicated of, in such a way that if the concept is predicated of some things at one time and of others at another time, the word varies its significates in the same way. Such a word primarily signifying several things equally in this way is absolutely univocal. The word 'man' is like this, and so it is absolutely univocal. For the impositor of the word 'man' intended that it would signify every thing the determinate mental concept is predicated of, so that when the concept is predicated of a thing, the word would signify that thing, and when not, not.

(149) To the fourth argument [(19)], I say that <according to one theory> the intellect, in understanding man without understanding any singular man, does not understand any one thing in the genus substance but only understands a certain concept in the mind. (What this "concept" is will be said later [q. 8]. <But according to another view, each singular man is truly understood, not by a proper cognition or by any cognition equivalent to a proper one, but by a common one only.>

(150) To the fifth argument [(20)], I say that for something to be the adequate object of some power can be understood in two senses. Either because it is primarily apprehensible by the power, in such a way that nothing is apprehended by the power except under the aspect of that thing. In this sense, I say nothing is the adequate object of any power—especially of a sensitive power. For this color and that one are equally primarily appre-

hended by sight, and nothing is apprehended by sight prior to this color or that one. So too for the other sensitive powers.

(151) In a second sense, something can be said to be the adequate object of some power, not literally but insofar as that claim is equivalent to a claim about a signate act,[13] like this: 'Something is that of which being an object of such a power, or being apprehensible by such power, is primarily and adequately predicated'. In this sense for any sensitive power there is some adequate object. For there is some such thing of which being an object of such a power is adequately and primarily predicated. Yet that thing is not in reality the object of such a power and cannot be apprehended, either by itself or by accident, by such a power.

(152) For example, the common term 'color' is what 'apprehensible by the visual power' is primarily and adequately predicated of. For the common term 'color' is predicated of everything apprehensible by the visual power, and only of such. (This according to the view that claims light is not apprehended through itself [but only through color]. Whether that view is true or false is irrelevant to the present point.) Yet the common term 'color' cannot be apprehended, either by itself or by accident, by the visual power. For the visual power apprehends only a singular thing—or at any rate it does not apprehend a genus.

(153) When it is said [(20)] that nothing is the object of a sensitive power except a true thing, it must be said this is literally true. Yet insofar as it is equivalent to the signate act 'Being an object of a sensitive power is predicated of nothing except a true thing', <that is, one outside the soul,> it is absolutely false. For being an object of the visual power is predicated of the common mental term 'color' in saying 'Every color is visible'. Yet the common mental term 'color' is not a true thing <outside the soul>. The reason for this is that being an object of the visual power is not predicated of that common term for itself but rather for its inferiors. Therefore, in such a proposition it has personal supposition, not simple. For 'Color is visible' is not true except for a singular color.

(154) To the sixth argument [(21)], I say that 'real attribute' can be taken in two senses: In one sense (a), for something that is a true thing and an accident of another thing. In another sense (b), 'real attribute' is properly so called. It is properly called an "attribute" because it is predicable in the second mode of speaking *per se*. It is called "real" because it is an attribute

---

13. Signate = signified. Thus the following example turns a claim about powers and their objects into a claim about predication and so about signification. See also n. 14 below.

conveying a true thing outside the soul, even though it itself is not a thing outside the soul.

(155) In the first sense (a), I say the subject of a real attribute is a true thing, and a true singular thing. So the attribute is not predicated of several things any more than its subject is, which is a singular thing too. In the second sense (b), the subject of a real attribute is not a thing outside the soul, but is a certain mental concept suppositing for things outside the soul.

(156) This is clear for example in the proposition 'Every man is risible'. The subject is not some thing outside the soul, but is a certain mental concept suppositing precisely for the singular men themselves. For it suffices for the truth of this proposition precisely that 'risible' is truly predicable of each particular man. It is not required that it be predicated of any universal thing. For in that case, such a universal proposition could never be sufficiently induced,* which is contrary to true logic.

(157) From this fact an argument can be constructed in favor of the main conclusion [(95)]. For all universal propositions are equally induced from their singulars. But there is a universal proposition sufficiently induced from its singulars in such a way that the predicate is inconsistent with anything other than singulars. For example, 'Every man is singular and one in number'. Therefore, singulars are sufficient to verify such universal propositions in reality. Thus universal things such as [Burley's] theory postulates are posited to no purpose. The whole reason for this is that in such propositions the terms supposit personally and not simply. That is, they supposit for singulars and not for themselves.

(158) Suppose it is said: The proposition 'Man is primarily risible' is true. Therefore, it is true either insofar as 'man' has personal supposition. But in that case it is absolutely *false*, [not true], because no man is primarily risible. Or else it is true insofar as 'man' supposits for the concept. And in that case too it is false, because then it is denoted that the concept is primarily risible, which is plainly false. The concept cannot laugh, either primarily or secondarily. Therefore, the proposition has to be true insofar as 'man' supposits for something between the singular thing and the concept.

(159) I reply as was said to the fifth argument [(151)], that 'Man is primarily risible' is literally false, just as 'Something is the primary and adequate object of some power' is literally false. But it is true in the sense in which correct speakers understand it. For they understand by it a signate act: 'Of man *risible* is primarily predicated'. In this signate act 'man' has simple supposition and supposits for the concept. For of this concept being risible is primarily predicated, not for itself but for singular things. Therefore,

in the corresponding exercised act,[14] which is 'Some man is risible', 'man' will have personal supposition.

(160) For example, in the signate act 'A genus is predicated of a species', 'genus' supposits for the concept. For the concept of a genus is predicated of the concept of a species, not for itself but for things. Therefore, in the corresponding exercised act—which should not be exercised as 'A species is a genus', but for example as 'A man is an animal'—the terms have personal supposition.

(161) To the first confirmation [(23)], I say sometimes an attribute inheres in many things through a common nature outside the soul because there is something the same in them that stays in them *in succession*.[15] But sometimes it is said to inhere in them through a common nature, not by informing them but rather by predication. For it is predicated primarily of the common nature—that is, of something common to their natures. The Philosopher understands his statement in either of these two senses. More about this elsewhere [q. 6 (114)].

(162) I reply to the second confirmation [(24)] the same way: Numerically the same transparency does not remain unless numerically the same subject remains. For, even according to them, a numerically one accident is primarily in a numerically one subject.

(163) To the seventh argument [(25)], I say a natural agent does intend in its acting a true singular thing. For it intends what is *per se* and primarily produced. But a singular thing is *per se* and primarily produced. Therefore, etc.

(164) When it is said it does not intend one singular thing any more than another, since it is equally related to each, I reply that it does determinately intend one thing—the one that will be determinately produced. Hence because the same thing is intended by a prior and a posterior agent, therefore, since the first agent intended something determinately one, it is what is intended by the natural agent too. It is not the case that each singular is related to equally by the natural agent, just as neither is each one indifferently

---

14. See n. 13 above. The contrast is between *signified* (or signate) and *exercised* act. In 'Some man is risible', 'risible' is predicated of the subject 'man'. The proposition does not *say* (signify) this is what is going on in it, but it is what *is* going on. The predication is not being discussed (signified) there; it is actually being done (exercised). But in ' "Risible" is predicated of "man" ', the same predication is now being discussed (signified) but no longer actually being done (exercised).

15. Such a common nature is not a universal. See **B (18)**.

produced. But more will be said about this in the fourth book [**OT** 7. 3–19].

(**165**) Suppose a quibble is raised against this and against other things said above: 'Someone promises he will give someone else some horse' is true. In that case, I ask:[16] Does he promise the other person some singular thing, a universal thing, or a conceived thing? Not a singular thing, because he does not promise one any more than another. Thus either he promises no horse (and so he could fulfill the promise by giving no horse at all), or else he promises every horse (and so he could not fulfill the promise except by giving every horse). If he promises a universal thing, I have my point. If he promises a concept, that is not true. For he promises a true thing. Likewise, in that case he could fulfill the promise without giving any real horse but only a certain conceived one.

(**166**) This piece of sophistry would not have to be included here if certain people, who think they know logic, did not ponder such childishness and because of it maintain many absurdities about the supposition of terms. But it would be too long and boring to discuss this. So I dismiss it and say the promisor promises a true singular thing. For in the proposition 'He promises another person a horse', 'horse' supposits personally for singular horses. Hence such a person would never fulfill the promise if he were to give some universal, unless he were to give some particular horse too. Thus just as, in saying 'I promise you one particular horse', he promises a singular thing, so too in saying 'I promise you a horse'.

(**167**) When it is said he does not promise one singular thing any more than another, and therefore either he promises none or each of them, that does not follow. Instead it is a fallacy of figure of speech committed by changing one mode of suppositing into another, just as there is such a fallacy in arguing like this: "Every man is a singular man. But he is not one singular man any more than another. Therefore, every man is each singular man or none." For in the first premise, 'singular man' supposits merely confusedly, and in the second premise it supposits confusedly and distributively. So it is here too: In the proposition 'I promise you a horse', 'horse' supposits merely confusedly or in some such way, because it does not supposit confusedly and distributively. One can infer each singular under a disjunction in such a way that the consequent is a proposition with a disjoint predicate, not a disjunctive proposition. For it correctly follows: "I promise you a horse; therefore, I promise you this horse or that one or that one" and so on for all present and future horses. But the disjunctive proposition does not follow. For it does

16. The speaker throughout (**165**) is the "quibbler," not Ockham.

not follow: "I promise you a horse; therefore, I promise you this horse or I promise you that horse" and so on.

(168) So too it correctly follows: "Every man is an animal; therefore, every man is this animal or that animal" and so on for singular animals. But the disjunctive proposition does not follow: "Every man is an animal; therefore, every man is this animal or every man is that animal" and so on.

(169) So too in many other such cases. The predicate term often has merely confused supposition, or some similar kind of supposition with respect to predicates, without a preceding distributive sign. <Nevertheless I do not care for the present whether it literally has merely confused supposition or not. Therefore,> let us omit these details; they pertain to logicians. Yet ignorance about them makes for many difficulties in theology and in the other real sciences. If these and similar childish matters were fully known, such difficulties would be quite easy, or would even present no difficulty at all.

(170) To the eighth argument [(26)], I say a most general genus is a mental concept. But how it is one genus will be clear in the following [(175)–(177)].

(171) To the ninth argument [(28)], I say Porphyry means that the species is something one that collects many things into one nature—not a real nature, but into something one that conveys the natures of many things. Therefore, it is called one nature by signification, but it is one thing conveying many.

(172) It is the same way when he says "Several men by participation in the species are one man." Not numerically one man, or one communal man, because even according to them no man is a communal man. Instead he means that, of several men contained under one species (because no other participation is possible), there is predicated one man (that is, one term, of which 'man' is predicated when 'man' supposits simply). But if that one term is predicated of several men, it will supposit personally.

(173) To the tenth argument [(29)], it must be said that because the Philosopher in the *Categories* is speaking as a logician, he mainly discusses names and the terms of propositions. Therefore, he often attributes to a term of a proposition what is [literally] attributed to a thing, and conversely. The reason is that the pure logician does not have to say whether universals, which are the terms of propositions, are external things, or only in the mind, or in speech or in writing. And so he does not distinguish these alternatives.

(174) Therefore, I say his meaning there is this: Among things that are (that is, among names and terms conveying what are truly outside the soul and are true things), some are said of a subject (that is, of a primary substance, since the terms themselves are said of a primary substance, not for themselves but for the primary substance itself), and yet are not in a subject (that is, they

do not convey any thing existing in a subject). And contrariwise some are said of a subject (not for themselves but for the thing) and are in a subject (that is, they convey a thing existing in a subject). So in the signate act the term always has the same supposition, and yet in the two corresponding exercised acts it has various kinds of supposition, because in one it has simple or material supposition and in the other personal supposition.

(175) To the eleventh argument [(30)], I say there is no division of anything into distinct things when substance is divided into primary and secondary substance. Instead the division is into items included in a categorial line. Some of these can be true things, some are absolutely *not* things that are substances. The reason for this is that substance, which is a most general genus, is predicated *per se* and *in quid* of all such things in the categorial line, even though it is predicated *per se* of some of them (of things, <if a thing is predicated>), but predicated of others (of concepts) not for themselves but for things. For in such propositions the terms do not supposit simply and for themselves, but personally and for the singulars.

(176) For example, in the propositions 'Every man is an animal', 'Every animal is a body' and 'Every body is a substance', the terms do not supposit simply and for themselves, but personally and for the singulars. Yet each of these propositions is *per se* in the first mode. Likewise, the term 'substance' is predicated of each of the subjects of these propositions.

(177) In the same way and for this reason, these terms are included in the categorial line [for substance]. These terms alone, or similar ones, are related as superior and inferior. So the division of substance, which is a most general genus, is into what are predicated of many and into what are not predicated of many.

(178) To the confirmation [(31)], I say species are said to be more substances than a genus is because more imperfect things are conveyed by a genus than by a species, <or at least one of them is>. Also because species are closer in the categorial line to the individual, which is the only *thing* in the genus. And finally, on account of the Philosopher's own arguments he gives in the same passage.

(179) If it is said that the Philosopher assigns certain characteristics to be common to primary and to secondary substance, which characteristics can only belong to things (like being susceptive of contraries), it is to be said that he says they are common not by a real inherence but by a real predication. Such characteristics can be truly predicated of concepts, not for themselves but for things. For example, being an animal is truly predicated of the word 'man' when the proposition 'A man is an animal' is pronounced. But it is not predicated of the word 'man' for itself, but rather for a singular thing the

word 'man' supposits for. Thus it is not denoted that the word 'man' is an animal, but that the thing this word signifies is truly an animal.

(180) To the twelfth argument [**(32)**], I reply the same way: The division is of terms conveying true things. For some terms are universal, some are singular. They are called "things" because they convey true things.

(181) To the thirteenth argument [**(33)**], I reply that there are three kinds of real identity belonging to things:[17] **(a)** numerical identity, which belongs to one thing only. But **(b)** specific identity does not belong to one individual only. Instead it belongs to several individuals, in such a way that it is not predicated of each one of them but rather of several.[18]

(182) It is plainly clear that this is the Philosopher's meaning, since he says in the same place, [*Topics* I. 7, 103ª9–14]: Things are the same "numerically the names of which are several but the thing one, like a tunic and a cloak. But things are the same specifically which, although they are several, are indifferent according to species. For instance, a man is specifically the same as a man and a horse as a horse. For whatever are under the same species are called specifically the same. Likewise, whatever are under the same genus, like a man and a horse, are generically the same."

(183) It is clear from this that 'specifically the same' or 'generically the same' are not said of something that is not an individual. Instead they are said of the individuals themselves, in such a way that Socrates and Plato are specifically the same and this man is generically the same as this horse. That is to say, as Aristotle explains it [*ibid.*], Socrates and Plato are contained under the same species, and this man is contained under the same genus this horse is contained under. <So I grant there is some identity less than numerical unity or identity. But such identity is not the identity of some universal, but of the singulars themselves taken together. For example, Socrates and Plato are specifically one. >

[Reply to the preliminary arguments]

(184) To the first main argument [**(4)**], I reply: 'The universal man and a particular man are essentially one' is literally false. And the Commentator

17. I am deleting a colon in the edition and adopting the variants '*quae*' for '*quia*' and '*scilicet*' for '*sed*'. There is obviously some textual difficulty in the passage. The third kind of real identity is generic identity, although Ockham does not list it separately. (But it *is* mentioned in the passage from Aristotle in **(182)**.)

18. *I. e.*, we do not say *Socrates* is specifically identical, but that *Socrates and Plato* are specifically identical.

did not mean that. Instead he meant they are essentially one because the one is essentially predicated of the other and conveys the essence of the other, yet does not really belong to the essence of the other.

(185) To the second main argument [(5)], it must be said that universals, whether they are incorruptible or not, are not incorruptible *things*. Yet they can be *called* incorruptible, because according to what the Philosopher meant, being is always predicated of them in such a way that 'A man is' is always true < if that proposition is formed >.[19] But being is not always predicated like this of any sensible singular, according to what the Philosopher meant, because no matter what singular is indicated, 'This is' is contingent.

[Question 5

Is a universal a true thing outside the soul, really distinct from the individual, really in it and really multiplied?]

(1) Secondly, I ask whether the univocal universal is a true thing outside the soul, really distinct from the individual yet really existing in it, really multiplied and varied.

(2) Yes it is:

(3) First, that it is a thing outside the soul, really distinct from individuals. For according to the Commentator, *Metaphysics* VII. comm. 46, [198B]: "A universal does not signify just any substance, but a substance that a part signifies." Therefore, the thing signified by a universal is a part. But a part is really distinguished from the whole. Therefore, etc. Now it is clear from the same Commentator that a universal is multiplied and varied, because a part is varied according to the variation of the whole it is a part of. (This is so if it is a part of many wholes at once.)

(4) For the opposite:

(5) Every thing outside the soul, really distinct from an individual but really existing in it, really multiplied and varied, is either an essential part of it or else an accident of it. But between whole and part, and likewise between a subject and its accident, there is such a relation that if the one is singular the other will be singular too. Therefore, every such thing is truly singular and consequently is not universal.

---

19. The point of the insertion is that sentence-tokens (the bearers of truth value for Ockham) have to exist before they can have any features, including being true.

[One theory]

(6) On this question there is one theory attributed by some people to the Subtle Doctor [John Duns Scotus], just as the view reported and disproved in the preceding question is also attributed to him by other people.[20] This is the theory that the universal is a true thing outside the soul, really distinct from a contracting difference but really multiplied and varied by such a contracting difference.

[Against this theory]

(7) But to the contrary: This view seems to be absolutely false. For every thing really distinct from another thing is distinguished from the latter thing either by itself or by something intrinsic to it. But the humanity in Socrates according to this theory is really distinguished from the humanity in Plato. Therefore, it is distinguished from it either by itself or by something intrinsic. Therefore, even disregarding any contracting differences, these humanities are distinguished. But they are not distinguished in species. Therefore, they are distinguished numerically. Therefore, each of them by itself, without a contracting difference, is numerically one and singular.

(8) If you say these humanities are not *per se* in a species, because precisely individuals are *per se* in a species, and therefore the humanities are not distinguished numerically by themselves, I reply that this makes no difference. For even though forms are not *per se* in a species, but only composites are, nevertheless two forms, even when their matters are disregarded, are truly distinguished numerically. (Hence two souls separated [from their bodies] are numerically distinguished.) Therefore, despite the fact that these humanities of Socrates and of Plato are not *per se* in a species, they are nevertheless distinguished numerically, even disregarding whatever *make* them really different.

(9) If you say these humanities are not distinguished except by contracting differences, then to the contrary: Socrates' humanity according to you is really distinguished from the difference that contracts that humanity. Therefore, either it is really distinguished from that difference by itself or else by that contracting difference. Not by the contracting difference, because nothing is distinguished from *a* by *a* itself. (Rather by *a* it is *the same* as *a*.) Therefore, this humanity is distinguished by itself from the contracting difference. Therefore, there are two things here, really distinct from one

---

20. For example by William of Alnwick, an associate of Scotus.

another. But that is not possible unless each of them is numerically one. Therefore, that humanity, really distinct from the contracting difference, is numerically one. Therefore, it is numerically one and numerically distinct by itself. Therefore, it is not a this or numerically one through the contracting difference, but through itself.

(10) Likewise, when something is really distinguished by itself from something extrinsic to it, it is for the same reason distinguished by itself from anything else extrinsic to it. Therefore, if Socrates' humanity is really distinguished by itself from the contracting difference, it is for the same reason really distinguished by itself from Plato's humanity.

(11) *Confirmation*: It does not seem to be a contradiction that Socrates' humanity is separated from the contracting difference, and likewise Plato's humanity is separated from its contracting difference. In that case, I ask: Is the non-varied humanity that was Socrates' humanity really distinguished from the humanity that was Plato's humanity, or is it not? If so, the point is established: they are really distinguished by themselves. For they are not distinguished by contracting differences, since those do not exist.

(12) If they are not really distinguished from one another, then to the contrary: It is impossible for two things that do not make up something *per se* one to make or to be something *per se* one except by being really put together. Therefore, these humanities are really put together. Consequently the point is established: they are distinguished by themselves. For the parts of the same composite are always really distinguished by themselves, or through some factors intrinsic to them.

(13) Moreover it is not inconsistent that at least by divine power any absolute thing is intuitively seen [**K** Ch. 22] without any other absolute thing's being seen. Therefore, the humanity in Socrates can be intuitively seen without the contracting difference, and the humanity in Plato can be seen without its contracting difference in the same way. But such a seer will see that they are distinguished in place and orientation (whether by quantity or not I do not care, because that is irrelevant). Therefore, he will see they are distinguished. But no one knows distinctly and in particular that some things are essentially distinguished unless he knows in particular their intrinsic distinguishing principles. Therefore, these humanities are distinguished by themselves. Consequently they are by themselves "these."

(14) Second, I argue: If humanity is one thing and also another, therefore there will be as many most specific species as there are individuals. The consequent is false, because in that case there will necessarily be as many most general genera as there are individuals, which seems absurd. The inference is clear. For if humanity indicates a most specific species, it will

be either (a) Socrates' or Plato's humanity or (b) something neither the one nor the other. If the first (a), and it is not the one any more than the other, therefore there are two humanities here each of which is a most specific species. Consequently there are two most specific species. If the second (b) is granted, then I ask about the humanity that is neither the one nor the other: Is it a true thing outside the soul? In that case, the theory disproved in the preceding question is back again. Or is it only in the soul? In that case, no universal is outside the soul.

(15) One can argue the same way: If man is a species, I ask what 'man' supposits for [in the proposition 'Man is a species']. Either for a thing outside the soul or for a thing in the soul. If the latter, my point is granted. If the former, then either that thing is Socrates,[21] or else it is in Socrates and Plato and is not varied or multiplied there. In that case, the first theory, the one in the first question [q. 4], is back again. Or else it is in Socrates and Plato and *is* varied and multiplied in them. In that case, the point is established: there are as many most specific species as individuals. It also follows from this that no thing is a species. For no thing is common then, because neither the humanity in Socrates nor that in Plato is common. And, let us hypothesize, there is no humanity besides these. Therefore, etc.

(16) Moreover third, I argue: A thing that is determinate to one and is not indifferent to many is not a universal. But the humanity in Socrates is, according to you, determinate to one and cannot be found in anything else. And according to this theory, there is no humanity except what belongs to Socrates or Plato and so on. Therefore, no thing outside the soul is a universal.

(17) Suppose it is said that for the humanity in Socrates, it is not inconsistent from itself to be together with another contracting difference. But it is in fact determined to this individual by means of something extrinsic, and therefore as far as it itself is concerned it is indifferent and common.

(18) To the contrary: What cannot by any power be made to agree with several things is not really and positively common. Therefore, if the thing in Socrates cannot by any power be made to be in something else, it is not really and positively common. In fact it will be less common than this form or this matter, because each of them can by divine power be in several things—in succession at least.

(19) Moreover just as it is not inconsistent with a nature of itself that it

21. One manuscript adds 'or Plato'. The point is that there is nothing special about Socrates, who serves here only as an example of an individual. The unstated reason for rejecting this alternative is presumably that individuals would be species.

be together with another degree,[22] so too it is not inconsistent with that degree of itself to be together with another nature. Therefore, there will be a community in that individual contracting degree just as much as in the contracted nature.

(20) *Confirmation*: According to this theory, this individual contracting degree is really together with several contracted natures—that is, with the nature of all the genera and species predicable of that individual. Therefore, this degree will really be more common to diverse universal natures than any nature is to diverse individuals.

(21) If you say there is no community of predication here, but only a community of coexistence, that is not valid. For a precisely similar community can belong to a common nature with respect to its individuals, because according to this theory, the universal nature is really distinct from this individual. Therefore, it is not common by predication, but only by a certain coexistence, or as a part is common to wholes.

[Ockham's reply]

(22) Therefore, I say in response to the question [(1)]: In an individual, there is no universal nature really distinct from a contracting difference. Such a nature could not be posited there unless it were an essential part of the individual itself. But there is always a relation between whole and part such that, if the whole is singular and not common, then analogously each part in the same way is singular. For one part cannot be more singular than another. Therefore, either no part of the individual is singular or every part is. But not no part. Therefore, every part.

(23) Likewise, if two such really distinct factors were in the individual, it does not seem to involve a contradiction that the one could be without the other. In that case, the individual degree could be without the contracted nature or conversely, each of which is absurd.

(24) Likewise, almost all the arguments included in the earlier question [q. 4] against the view disproved there prove there is no such nature.

[Reply to the main argument]

(25) To the main argument [(3)], I say a universal in a way signifies a part when that universal is a genus of many composites distinct by specific forms. The reason for this is that then in each of its significates there is necessarily

---

22. The term seems to refer here to an individual difference.

found a part of the same kind, but also another part not like that. Therefore, the universal is said more to signify the former part than the other one. (It will be clear in what follows [**OT** 3. 195.10–199.9] how this is to be understood.) Therefore, a universal is not really a part, and so does not have to be really multiplied.

[Question 6

Is a universal really outside the soul, distinct from the individual, although not really distinct?]

(1) Third, I ask whether something universal and univocal is really outside the soul and from the nature of the thing distinct from the individual, although not really distinct.

(2) It seems so:

(3) For the nature of man is a this, and yet it is not *of itself* a this, because in that case it could not be in anything else. Therefore, it is a this through something added to it. Not through something really distinct, because then for the same reason the nature of whiteness would be a this through something added that is really distinct. In that case, this whiteness would be really composite, which seems false. Therefore, the nature is a this through something added that is formally distinct.

(4) For the opposite side:

(5) No nature that is really an individual is really a universal. Therefore, if this nature is really this individual, it will not be really a universal.

[Scotus's theory]

(6) On this question, it is said that in a thing outside the soul there is a nature really the same as a difference that contracts it to a determinate individual, and yet formally distinct from that difference. This nature is of itself neither universal nor particular. Rather it is incompletely universal in the thing, and completely universal according to the being it has in the intellect. Because this theory, I believe, is the theory of the Subtle Doctor [Duns Scotus], who surpasses all others in the subtlety of his judgment, therefore without changing the words he himself uses in various places, I want here to report distinctly the whole of the theory he sets out in bits and pieces in various places.

(7) It is part of this Doctor's theory [**S (30)**] that, in addition to numerical unity, there is a real unity less than numerical unity. It belongs to the

nature itself, which is in a sense universal. So the contractible nature can be compared first to the singular itself. Second, it can be compared to numerical unity. Third, it can be compared to being a universal. Fourth, it can be compared to that unity less than numerical unity.

(8) If it is compared to the singular itself, then this theory maintains that the nature is not *of itself* a this, but through something added [S q. 1]. Second, it maintains that what is added is not (question 2) a negation, or (question 3 [= S q. 4]]) some accident, or (question 4 [= S q. 3]]) actual existence, or (question 5) matter. Third, it maintains that what is added is in the genus substance and is intrinsic to the individual [S (147)]. Fourth, it maintains that the nature is naturally prior to the contracting difference. Thus he says: [**Ockham quotes S (187) (from after "I reply") and S (188) almost** *verbatim.*]

(9) It is clear from this passage that, with respect to the contracting difference, this theory claims: First, the individual difference is not quidditative. Second, the nature is naturally prior to this contracting difference. Third, the opposite of this individual difference—that is, another individual difference—is not inconsistent with the nature of itself, just as this individual difference does not belong to it of itself. Fourth, this is true both for a whole and for its parts. Likewise, the individual difference and the nature are not distinguished as one thing and another thing. Fifth, they are distinguished only formally. Sixth, he claims elsewhere [S (41)] that the nature is really one thing and another when it is combined with one contracting difference and another.

(10) Thus he says: [**Ockham quotes S (41) almost** *verbatim,* **from "every substance" to the end of the first paragraph.**]

(11) Hence, for this reason, he says the Idea attributed to Plato is not the substance of Socrates. Hence it follows in the same passage: [**Ockham quotes the second paragraph of S (41), from "the Idea."**][23] He maintains similar things elsewhere in various places [*e. g.,* W 11. 328–329, & W 4. 704].

(12) But if the nature is compared to numerical unity [(7)], then he likewise maintains that the nature does not from itself have a numerical unity, and is not what is immediately denominated by any real unity. Yet it is really numerically one. Neither is anything that is one, by any real unity, in two individuals, but only in one. Hence he says: [**Ockham quotes S (172) (from "I grant") and all of S (173)–(175) almost** *verbatim.*][24]

23. At the end of S (41), Scotus has 'according to him [= Plato]'. Ockham has changed this to 'according to him [= Scotus], namely, in Plato'.

24. The reference in S (173) to Scotus's *Ordinatio* 1, d. 8, is not described in as much detail as it is in Scotus's own text.

(13) But if, in the third way [(7)], a nature is compared to being a universal, then he maintains that of itself the nature is not completely universal. Rather it is completely universal only insofar as it has being in the intellect. Second, of itself community does belong to it, not singularity. Hence he says: [**Ockham quotes S (37) from "the universal in act" to the end.**]

(14) And he adds: [**Ockham quotes the second paragraph of S (38).**]

(15) Again, he adds in the same place [**Ockham quotes S (42) from "community and singularity" on.**]

(16) If, fourth [(7)], the nature is compared to the unity that is less than numerical unity, then he maintains this unity is not contained under the quidditative notion of the nature, but instead is predicated of it in the second mode of speaking *per se*. Hence he says: [**Ockham quotes the second paragraph of S (34) from "In this way" to "according to its primary entity."**]

[Arguments in favor of Scotus's theory]

(17) There are many arguments in favor of the main conclusion of this theory.

(18) First: [**Ockham quotes S (3) almost *verbatim* from 'Whatever' to 'this stone'.**][25]

(19) Second: [**Ockham quotes S (4) almost *verbatim*.**][26]

(20) Third: [**Ockham quotes S (7) almost *verbatim*, from 'An object' on.**][27]

(21) Fourth: [**Ockham quotes S (8)–(28) almost *verbatim*.**][28]

25. Ockham substitutes 'man' for 'stone' throughout.

26. He adds 'of itself' to the end of the passage.

27. After the words '*opposite* to the object's very notion', Ockham adds 'that is, insofar as it is a universal'.

28. The following differences are perhaps worth noting: Ockham omits 'Therefore, this unity is real' from the end of S (12). For 'numerical' in the first sentence of S (13), he has 'singularity'. In S (14), Ockham omits everything after 'For the Philosopher there means'. In S (18), he omits the phrase 'so that ... quality'. In S (19), between the words 'this opposition is real' and 'and one by some real unity', he breaks the sentence and adds 'Now insofar as it is an extreme'. These words are noted as a variant in the critical edition of Scotus. Ockham also omits the 'Therefore, etc.' at the end of S (19). In the first paragraph of S (22), after the words 'some real unity', he adds 'at least the object of one act of sensing'. He adds 'in its real unity' at the end of the paragraph and omits the rest of S (22). Everything from the words 'For according to the Philosopher' in S (13) to the end of S (28) Ockham added later while revising his *Ordinatio*. (That later addition is continued in (22)–(23) below.)

<(22) Moreover [compare **S** (31)] Avicenna, *Metaphysics* V. [1, 86va], says that equinity is only equinity, and that of itself it is neither one nor several, neither universal nor particular. Therefore, etc.

(23) Moreover [Scotus 2. 354–355], it is impossible for the same thing in virtue of entirely the same factor on the part of reality really to differ from something and really to agree with the same thing. But Socrates really differs from Plato and really agrees with him. Therefore, etc. >

[Against Scotus's theory]

(24) One can argue against this theory in two ways.

(25) First, because among creatures it is impossible for some things to differ formally unless they are distinguished really. Therefore, if the nature is distinguished in any way from the contracting difference, they have to be distinguished either as thing and thing, or as a being of reason and a being of reason, or as a real being and a being of reason.

(26) But the first alternative is denied by him [**S** (188)], and so is the second. Therefore, the third has to be granted. Therefore, a nature distinguished in any way from an individual is nothing but a being of reason.

(27) The antecedent is clear. For if a nature and the contracting difference are not the same in all respects, therefore something can be truly affirmed of the one and denied of the other. But among creatures the same thing cannot be truly affirmed and truly denied of the same thing. Therefore, they are not one thing. The minor is clear, because [if the same thing could be truly affirmed and truly denied of the same thing], every way of proving a distinction of things would be lost in the case of creatures. For contradiction is the strongest way to prove the distinction of things. Therefore, if among creatures entirely the same thing can be truly denied of the same thing, < or of the same term suppositing for the same thing, > and truly affirmed of it, no real distinction among them can be proven.

(28) *Confirmation*: All contradictories are equally inconsistent. But the inconsistency between being and non-being is so great that if *a* exists and *b* does not, it follows that *b* is not *a*. Therefore, so too for any contradictories whatever.

(29) Suppose someone says: It is true for primary contradictories that one can prove real nonidentity from them, but one cannot do this for other contradictories.

(30) To the contrary: Syllogistic form holds equally for every subject-matter. Now here is a good syllogism: 'Every *a* is *b*; *c* is not *b*; therefore, *c* is not *a*.' Consequently it is true of *a* and non-*a* that if this is *a* and this is not *a*,

then this is not this,[29] just as it is true that if this is and this is not, then this is not this. Therefore, so too in the present case, if every individual difference is of itself proper to some individual, and the nature is not of itself proper to some individual, it follows that the nature is not the individual difference, and this nonidentity is real.

(31) Suppose someone says: This argument is invalid. For the divine essence is the Son, and the Father is not the Son, and yet the Father is the essence.

(32) This reply is not enough. For just as it is unique to God that three things are numerically one thing, and therefore the numerically one thing is each of those three things, and yet the one of those three things is not the other, so too it is unique to God and surpasses every understanding that this inference does not follow: The numerically one essence is the Son; the Father is not the Son; therefore, the Father is not the essence. Hence that unique peculiarity should not be maintained except where the authority of Holy Scripture compels us to do so. Therefore, such an inference should never be denied in the case of creatures. For there no authority of Holy Scripture compels us, < since among creatures no one thing is[30] several things and also each one of them >.

(33) Suppose someone says: Such an inference is a good one if both premises are taken without any [syncategorematic] determination. Thus it correctly follows: "Every individual difference is proper to some individual; the nature is not proper to any individual; therefore, the nature is not really the individual difference." But in that case, the minor is false. On the other hand, the inference does not universally hold if the premises are precisely taken under some definite syncategorematic determination, like 'of itself' and '*per se*'.

(34) That is not valid. For as is syllogistic form in uniform syllogisms, both assertoric and modal ones (and likewise mixed syllogistic form made up of both assertoric and modal premises), so is syllogistic form, both uniform and mixed, for other propositions taken with other syncategorematic determinations, like '*per se*', 'insofar as' and the like. Consequently there is a syllogistic form in 'Every man *per se* is an animal; no stone *per se* is an animal; therefore, no stone *per se* is a man (and consequently in general no stone is a man)', just as there is in 'Every animal of necessity is a substance; no accident of necessity is a substance; therefore, no accident of necessity is an

---

29. Substitute 'this' for '*a*' and for '*c*', and '*a*' for '*b*'. The 'this' indicates the same thing throughout.

30. The edition has the plural but reports the singular as a variant.

animal'. Likewise, here is a good mixed syllogism: 'Every man *per se* is an animal; nothing white is an animal; therefore, nothing white is a man. Therefore, in the same way this will be another good syllogism: 'Every individual difference is of itself proper to some individual; the nature is not of itself proper to any individual; therefore, the nature is not the individual difference'. Likewise, this will be a good syllogism: 'No individual difference is really common; the nature is really common; therefore, the nature is not really the individual difference'. The premises are true; therefore, the conclusion is too.

(35) *Confirmation*: Just as from propositions about what is necessary there always follows an assertoric conclusion, so too from propositions with a note of perseity there follows an assertoric conclusion. This is because the *per se* is necessary. Therefore, just as it follows formally and syllogistically: "The nature necessarily is communicable; the contracting difference necessarily is not communicable; therefore, the contracting difference is not the nature," so too it follows: "The nature *per se* is communicable to many; the contracting difference of itself is not communicable to many; therefore, the contracting difference is not the nature."

(36) It is not valid to say that the conclusion is true—that is, that the contracting difference is not the nature—even though it is not really distinguished from the same nature. For it follows: "They are not really distinguished; and each is a thing; therefore, they are really the same; therefore, the one really is the other." And further: "Therefore, the one is the other." Consequently predicating the one of the other is true.

(37) The penultimate inference is clear. For 'really' is not a destructive or diminishing determination, and neither is 'formally'. Consequently, according to the Philosopher's rule in *On Interpretation* II. [11, 21ª21–24], there is a formal inference from something taken with such a determination to that same thing itself taken by itself.

<(38) *Confirmation* of the whole preceding reasoning: Just as the following syllogism is governed by the *dici de nullo* [*Prior Analytics* I. 1, 24ᵇ26–30]: "No difference is common; a nature is common; therefore, a nature is not a difference," so too this one is governed by the *dici de nullo*: "No difference is of itself common; a nature is of itself common; therefore, a nature is not a difference."›

(39) It can be argued in a second way [(25)] against the above theory: It is not true, even granting that there *were* such a [formal] distinction. First: Whenever one of a pair of opposites really pertains to something in such a way that it is truly and really denominated by that opposite (whether it

pertains[31] to it from itself or through something else), as long as the thing endures and is not changed, the remaining opposite does not really pertain to that thing. In fact, it is absolutely denied of it. But according to you [**S (34)** & **W** 4. 704–706], every thing outside the soul is really singular and one in number, even though one kind is singular of itself and another is singular only through something added. Therefore, no thing outside the soul is really common or one with a unity opposite to the unity of singularity. Therefore, really there is no unity except the unity of singularity.

(**40**) If it is said that these two unities are not really opposites, and in the same way singularity and community are not really opposed, then to the contrary: If they are not really opposed, then it cannot be concluded from any kind of opposition that the two cannot come together primarily in the same thing on the side of reality. Therefore, there is no way to argue sufficiently against the following conclusion: that the same thing is one both by this unity and by that one, and that this comes about through what is in all respects the same, and that the same thing is singular and common, and that this too comes about through what is in all respects the same.

(**41**) Moreover whenever consequents are inconsistent, their antecedents will be inconsistent too. But it follows: "*a* is common or one by only a lesser unity; therefore, a multitude opposite to a greater unity is consistent with *a*—namely, a numerical multitude." And it follows: "*a* is one with a greater unity; therefore, the opposite multitude is not consistent with *a*—namely, numerical unity." But 'A numerical multitude is consistent with *a*' and 'A numerical multitude is not consistent with *a*' are inconsistent. Therefore, '*a* is one with a lesser unity' and '*a* is one with a greater unity' are inconsistent. But according to you, '*a* is one with a greater unity' is true. For you say [**S (34)**] a nature is numerically one. Therefore, '*a* is one with a lesser unity' is false, always taking '*a*' for the very nature you say is always one with a lesser unity. And if the nature is not one with a lesser unity, much less is anything else. The assumption is clear from [Scotus], who says [**S (9)**], "The multitude opposed to the greater unity can go together with the lesser unity without contradiction. But this multitude cannot go together with the greater unity, because it is incompatible with it."

(**42**) Suppose it is said that this form of argument is not valid. For blackness goes together with a man, and blackness does not go together with the white. Yet a man is white, and *a* is a man and is white.

(**43**) This is not valid, because taking 'go together' in the same sense in

---

31. The edition has the plural but reports the singular as a variant.

both propositions, one or the other of them is false. For taking 'go together' actually, it is false that blackness goes together with Socrates, if Socrates is white. But taking it potentially, 'Blackness does not go together with the white' is false. For blackness can go together with the white,[32] just as the white is *able* to be black or to have blackness. Hence although blackness is inconsistent with whiteness, yet it is not inconsistent with what is white. Consequently it is not inconsistent with the white, because the two terms 'the white' and 'what is white' are converted.

(44) Furthermore, what he says—"The multitude opposed to the greater unity can go together with the lesser unity without contradiction"—seems to be inconsistent with the other claim [S (188)], where he says the nature and the individual difference are not really different. For when some two items are really the same, whatever can by divine power be really the one of them can also be the other. But this individual difference cannot be numerically several really distinct items. Therefore, neither can the nature that is really the same with this contracting difference be really several items. Consequently neither can it be any thing other than this contracting difference. So the nature cannot without contradiction allow in itself a numerical multitude.

(45) *Confirmation* of this reasoning: Everything really universal, whether it is completely universal or not, is really common to several things, < or at least is *able* to be really common to several things >. But no thing is really common to several things. Therefore, no thing is in any way universal. The major is plain, because a universal is distinguished from a singular by the fact that the singular is determined to one while the universal is indifferent to many, in the manner in which it is universal. The minor is also plain, because no really singular thing is common to several things. But every thing, according to them [S (34)], is really singular. Therefore, etc.

(46) Likewise, if some thing conveyed by the term 'man' is common to several, either it will be the nature in Socrates, or the nature in Plato, or some third nature other than these. It is not Socrates' nature, because that by which Socrates is really singular cannot be in Plato. Neither is it Plato's nature, for the same reason. Neither is it some third nature, because there is no such nature outside the mind. For according to them [S (34)], every thing outside the soul is really singular.

(47) *Second confirmation*: What cannot be communicated to several, even by divine power, is not really common. But (pointing to any thing whatever) *that* thing cannot be communicated to several, even by divine power, because

32. The edition repeats the phrase 'For . . . the white'.

it is really singular. Therefore, no thing is really and positively common.

(48) Suppose it is said that although it is inconsistent with this nature for it to be in several, yet this is not inconsistent with it *of itself* but because of something added with which it is one by a real identity [**W** 11. 329].

(49) To the contrary: This non-inconsistency of itself is not something positive, and consequently this community is not positive in such a way that it is something common. Rather it is only negative. Consequently there is no positive unity except numerical unity only.

(50) Moreover I can attribute a negative lesser unity like this to the individual degree. For it is certainly not numerically one from itself and *per se* (in the first mode of speaking *per se*). So, taking 'not inconsistent from itself or *per se*' insofar as it is the opposite of agreeing with something *per se* in the first mode of speaking *per se*, the proposition 'For this individual difference it is not inconsistent from itself to be in several' or 'It is not inconsistent with it from itself to be one by a unity less than numerical unity' will be true. For its opposite is false, according to them [**W** 4. 704]—namely, that this individual difference is numerically one *per se* in the first mode.

(51) My second main argument [see **(24)**] against the theory is this: If the nature were common in this way, it would follow that there would be as many species and genera as there are individuals. For Socrates' nature is a species, and for the same reason so is Plato's nature. Then I argue: Whenever some items are really several, and each of them can be called a species, there are several species. But this is so in the present case. Therefore, etc.

(52) *Confirmation*: From the multiplication of the proximate subject there follows a multiplication of its attribute. But, according to him [**S** (**34**)], this lesser unity is an attribute of the nature. Therefore, just as the nature is really multiplied so too the attribute, since it is real, will be really multiplied. Consequently just as there really are two natures in Socrates and Plato, so there will really be two lesser unities in them. But this lesser unity is either community, or at least inseparable from community, and consequently insep-arable from what is common. Therefore, there are two common natures in Socrates and Plato, and consequently two species. Consequently Socrates would be under the one common nature and Plato under the other. So there would be as many common natures—even most general ones—as there are individuals. These claims seem absurd.

(53) Suppose someone says: A thing is not completely universal, but only insofar as it is considered by the intellect.

(54) To the contrary: I ask about what is immediately denominated a universal. Is it precisely a true thing outside the soul, or is it precisely a being of reason, or is it an aggregate of a real being and a being of reason?

(55) If the first alternative is granted, the point is established: A singular thing is absolutely completely universal. (This is contrary to their own statement. For outside the soul, according to them [S (34)], there is no thing that is not really singular.) Consequently the same thing that is really singular is common, and not more one thing than another. Therefore, there are as many complete universals as there are singulars.

(56) If the second alternative [(54)] is granted, it follows that no thing is universal, either completely or inchoatively, either in act or in potency. For what cannot by divine power be reduced to completion and act so that it is such and such is not such and such either in potency or inchoatively. This is true where it is not the case that by the very fact that it is reduced to one act there remains a potency for another act (as for the infinite division of a continuum, and when something is in potency to contradictories). But that does not arise here. Therefore, if precisely a being of reason is a universal completely and in act, and in no way is a thing outside the soul a universal completely and in act, it follows that in no way is a thing outside the soul universal—one thing any more than another.

(57) If the third alternative [(54)] is granted, the point is established. For from the multiplication of any part there always follows a multiplication of the whole or aggregate. Therefore, if the completely universal is an aggregate made up of a thing and a being of reason, then as many as there are things outside the soul, each of which is a part of the whole aggregate, there will be that many such aggregates. So the point will stand: There will be as many most general genera as there are individuals.

(58) Moreover just as a universal is one in many and said of many, and is predicable of them, so too what is common is one in many and said of many and predicable of them. But that is enough to make something be completely universal, according to them [S (38)]. Therefore, everything common has whatever is required to make something completely universal, and consequently to make something completely a species or a genus. But according to them, as was quoted [(15)], community pertains to the nature of itself, outside the intellect. Therefore, being completely universal does too. Consequently from the fact that there are as many common natures as there are individuals, as was just proven, it follows that from the nature of reality there are as many most general genera as there are individuals.

(59) *Confirmation*: If the nature in Socrates is truly common, then since when Socrates is destroyed everything essential to him is destroyed, it follows that some common nature is truly destroyed and annihilated. But certainly some common nature remains in this case, insofar as another individual

remains. From a "contradiction" like this,[33] one can infer a real distinction, according to them [W 11. 261]. Therefore, the one of those common natures is not really the other, and consequently, when they both exist, they are several.

(60) Suppose it is said the nature is not common, insofar as it is appropriated to Socrates by a contracting difference.

(61) To the contrary: According to you [S (42)], this community pertains to the nature outside the intellect. I ask therefore: What does the term 'nature' supposit for in that proposition? Either for (a) a real being or for (b) a being of reason. But (b) cannot be granted, because ['being of reason outside the intellect'] would involve a contradiction. If (a) it supposits for a real being, then either (i) for a real being that is a singular or (ii) for some real being that is not really singular. If (i), then it is not common and consequently is not of itself common. If (ii) is granted, then there is something outside the soul that is not really singular. But they deny that. For they say [S (42)] the nature really is numerically one and singular.

(62) Third [(24)], I argue: The humanity in Socrates and the humanity in Plato are really distinguished. Therefore, each of them really is numerically one. Consequently neither is common.

(63) Suppose someone says: These natures are not distinct except through the added differences, just as none of them is numerically one except through an added difference. Therefore, neither of them is of itself singular. Rather of itself it is common.

(64) To the contrary: Every thing is essentially distinguished, either by itself or through something intrinsic to it, from every other thing it is essentially distinguished from. But the humanity in Socrates is essentially distinguished from the humanity in Plato. Therefore, it is distinguished from it either by itself or through something intrinsic to it, and therefore *not* through something extrinsic added to it. The major is clear, because to say Socrates is distinguished essentially from this ass through Plato is not to say anything at all.

(65) Likewise, to be the same and to be diverse follow immediately on being. Therefore, nothing is the same as or diverse from anything through something extrinsic.

(66) Likewise, according to the Philosopher, *Metaphysics* IV. [2, 1003[b]26–33], and the Commentator on that passage, [comm. 3, 67A–G], every being is one through its essence, and not through anything added.

---

33. Namely, that the one individual remains while the other one does not.

Therefore, nothing is numerically one through anything added. Therefore, the nature in Socrates, if it is numerically one, will be numerically one either by itself or by something essential to it.

(67) Likewise, if the nature is numerically one, then it is not common. Consequently it is not of itself common. For the determination 'of itself' is not a destructive or diminishing determination, and therefore there is a good inference from the negation of the determinable taken absolutely to the negation of the determinable taken with this determination. Therefore, just as it follows: "Socrates is not a man; therefore, he is not necessarily a man" so too it follows: "The humanity in Socrates is not common; therefore, it is not of itself common."

(68) *Confirmation*: [Sometimes something is said to pertain to something of itself, not positively but negatively.] For example, when it is said that a creature of itself is a nonbeing, or matter of itself is deprived of form. These and all similar propositions are literally false. But they are true insofar as they are equipollent to certain negative propositions—namely: 'Matter is not of itself formed', 'A creature is not of itself such and such a being'. Whenever something is said to pertain to something of itself in this way, not positively but negatively, then although it does not have to inhere actually in what it is said to pertain to, nevertheless absolutely it is *able* (at least through divine power) to inhere in it. For example, a creature is able to be a nonbeing, and matter is able to be deprived. Therefore, likewise the humanity in Socrates can be common to several men. The consequent is impossible. Therefore, the antecedent is too.

(69) Proof of the consequent's falsity: When some items are really the same, it is impossible that the one be really the same as the other unless the other be really the same as the one. This is true for creatures. It is even true in a way in God. For although it is not true to say that the Father is the Son, notwithstanding the identity of both the Father and the Son with the divine essence, nevertheless it is true to say that the Father is the thing that is the Son. Thus since the humanity in Socrates is really the same as the contracting difference, therefore if the humanity in Socrates can be really the same as the contracting difference in Plato, it follows that this contracting difference and that contracting difference could be one thing. Consequently some one thing could be Socrates and Plato, which involves a contradiction.

(70) Moreover whatever on the part of reality is distinguished from something else that does not belong to the formal understanding of it can be intuitively seen without that other item, according to this Doctor [Scotus, 2. 26–27, 352, 355]. He even claims the divine essence can be intuitively seen without the divine person. Therefore, the humanity in Socrates can be

intuitively seen without the contracting difference, and in the same way the humanity in Plato can be intuitively seen without any contracting difference. Consequently since these humanities are distinguished in place and subject, such an intellect can distinguish the one from the other without any contracting difference. This would not be possible if they were distinguished precisely by their contracting differences. Therefore, they are numerically distinguished by themselves.

(71) *Confirmation*: Such an intellect can form a negative proposition saying 'This is not that', and can know it to be true. Therefore, this thing by itself is not the other thing.

(72) *Confirmation*: According to this Doctor [Scotus, 2. 344], what are formally compossible or inconsistent are compossible or inconsistent by their formal notions. Therefore, for the same reason, whatever are distinguished or are the same are distinguished or are the same by their formal notions. Therefore, if these humanities—say, Socrates' and Plato's—are really distinguished, they are really distinguished by their own formal notions and by nothing added on. Consequently each of these of itself, without anything added, is really distinguished from the other. The assumption is clear, because he says [2. 344], "Note that, just as what are inconsistent are inconsistent from their own notions, so too noninconsistency or compossibility is from the compossibles' own notions."

(73) Suppose someone says: From the very fact that you[34] say 'these humanities' when you say 'These humanities are really distinguished', you include the contracting differences. For they are not "these" except through these contracting differences. Thus they are distinguished by their formal notions, because these differences belong to the formal notion of "these humanities" in such a way that if these differences are set aside, only an indistinct humanity remains.

(74) To the contrary: Whenever some items are distinguished in any way whatever on the part of reality, a term can be imposed that precisely stands for the one and not for the other. For otherwise there could be no true proposition denoting the distinction of the one from the other. Therefore, I impose the term '*a*' to stand precisely for what in Socrates is distinguished formally and not really from the contracting difference. For, according to you [S (188)], there is something in Socrates that is formally distinguished from the contracting difference, that is nevertheless really the same as that difference, and that therefore is really singular. I also impose the term '*b*' to stand precisely for what is formally distinguished from the contracting

---

34. *I. e.*, Ockham. The hypothetical objector is speaking here, on Scotus's behalf.

difference in Plato, and is yet really the same as that contracting difference. Then I ask: Are *a* and *b* really the same or not? If they are, then since they are not varied, they are not really distinguished at all. Consequently there is something indistinct really in Socrates and Plato. But they deny this [W 4. 704, 706]. For they maintain that nothing indistinct is really the same in Socrates and Plato. If they are not really the same, then they are really distinguished. Therefore, they are really distinguished by their own formal notions. But these do not include the contracting differences, by hypothesis. And so the point is established: They are distinguished by themselves.

(75) Furthermore '*a* is really inconsistent with Plato's contracting difference' is true according to you. Therefore, it is inconsistent with it by its own notion. Therefore, it is really distinguished from it by its own notion. Therefore, it is really distinguished by itself. And it is not distinguished except numerically, since it is not specifically or generically distinguished. Therefore, by itself it is numerically one.

(76) Suppose someone says: What are inconsistent or compossible are inconsistent or compossible by their own notions or else through some items really the same as what are inconsistent or incompossible.

(77) This is not valid. For as is clear from this Doctor [Scotus, 2. 344, 388–410], he is not talking there [see (72)] only about the inconsistency and compossibility of really distinct things, but also about the inconsistency and compossibility of what are only formally distinguished or compossible. (This is clear in the case of the divine essence and the divine relation in the Trinity.) Therefore, *a* and *b* will be really distinguished or the same even if their contracting differences are disregarded. They are not really the same, because if they were, they could never be really distinguished. Therefore, they are really distinguished by themselves.

(78) Fourth [see (24)], I argue: If the contracted nature were really distinct from every contracting degree, then the nature of itself would be numerically one, as was proved in the first question [q. 4 above]. Therefore, since this nature is no less one because of its real identity with the contracting difference, it follows that it will be numerically one of itself.

(79) *Confirmation*: The nature does not lose any unity through the fact that it is really the same as what is maximally one. Therefore, it will be no less one of itself through the fact that it is really the same as the individual difference than it would be if it were really distinguished from the individual difference.

(80) *Confirmation*: According to this Doctor [W 11. 12], whatever order any items would have if they were really distinct, they have the same order where they are distinguished in some other way but *not* really distinguished.

But if the contracting difference and the nature were really distinguished, they would have an order between them like that of two items, each of which would be of itself numerically one, and the one would be of itself a potency and the other an act. Therefore, they will have the same order where they are distinguished formally.

(81) This confirmation is plainer for the nature of genus with respect to specific differences. For if the nature of color were not really the same as the specific difference of whiteness, and the nature of color were not really the same as the specific difference of blackness, and yet these specific natures were distinguished by themselves, then they would have an order of the more perfect and the more imperfect. Therefore, where now they are not really distinguished from the specific differences, but they are really distinguished between themselves, they will have the same order by themselves. This is not possible unless they are distinguished by themselves. For it is a contradiction that some items are related by themselves as more perfect and more imperfect, unless they are distinguished by themselves, since the perfect and the imperfect are necessarily distinguished. Therefore, if now these specific natures by themselves have the order of more perfect and more imperfect, they will be distinguished by themselves.

(82) Fifth [see (24)], it would follow that the [individual] degree would be just as communicable as the nature—indeed, that it is *in fact* communicated to more universals. This is inconsistent with the relation between the nature and the individual differences. Therefore, it would follow that the individual degree is not less communicable than the nature, [as this theory says it is].

(83) Sixth [see (24)], the difference and the nature either have the same notion or different ones. If they have the same notion, then the one is no more one singular of itself than the other one is. If they have different notions, then to the contrary: Among creatures, items that are one thing do not have one notion and another. But the individual difference and the contracted nature are one thing. Therefore, etc.

(84) Likewise the similarity and agreement is greater, or at least equal, among what are one thing than it is among what are really distinguished. Therefore, they can agree more, or at least equally, in their characteristics and attributes, provided they are all equally simple or equally composite. Therefore, if the individual degree that contracts the nature of man and the individual degree that contracts the nature ass agree in this attribute—namely, that each is of itself a "this"—then the individual degree and the nature, which is really the same as that degree, will be equally able to agree in the same attribute.

(85) Likewise *a* and *b*, which are really the same, have no less the same notion than do *a* and some *d*, if the latter are really distinguished. But the nature in Socrates and the nature in Plato, which are really distinguished, have the same notion. Therefore, much more will the nature of Socrates and the contracting difference have the same notion.

< **(86)** Likewise, in that case Socrates would include something that has a different notion than everything in Plato. This is false. For in that case Socrates and Plato would not have absolutely the same notion. >

(87) Seventh [see **(24)**], if the nature were contracted in this way precisely by a contracting difference only formally distinct from the nature, then a real univocation[35]—that is, a univocation of something real and univocal to God and creatures—could be maintained on the part of reality, just as much as such a univocation can be maintained for creatures among any individuals whatever. The consequent goes against those who maintain, as my opponents on the other side do [Scotus, 4. 221–222], precisely that there is a *concept* univocal to God and creature, but not anything on the part of reality.

(88) The inference is clear. For such univocation should not be denied unless because there would follow a composition in God made up of something contracted and something contracting it. But by maintaining the formal distinction in God, such a composition does not follow. For what are only formally distinguished do not compose anything, as is clear with the divine essence and relation in the Trinity. Therefore, such univocation is not inconsistent with divine simplicity.

(89) *Confirmation*: There is no greater reason why these formally distinct factors compose something than there is that others do, even though these are distinguished more than the others are. For by whatever reason gradations are posited in the formal distinction, by the same reason gradations will be posited in composition out of formally distinct factors.

(90) *Confirmation*: Just as when some items are really distinguished (whether more or less does not matter), if they make up something *per se* one there is no greater reason why *they* compose it than there is that others do, even though they compose it *less* than those others do, so too if some items are formally distinguished and make up something *per se* one there is

---

35. *I. e.*, univocal predication. For Scotus nothing is really shared by God and creatures, even though it is possible to form a concept applying equally to both without equivocation or ambiguity (*e. g.*, the concept "being"). Ockham's objection is that on Scotus's theory there would in fact have to be something really shared by God and creatures, despite what Scotus says, just as there are really shared common natures among creatures.

no greater reason why *they* compose it than there is that others do. Therefore, either all formally distinct factors or constituents make up something *per se* one or none of them do.

[Against Scotus's statements]

(91) Again, in running through his remarks, many of them seem to be not correctly stated the way he puts them.

(92) First, his claim [S (187)] that the nature "is naturally prior to this individual entity insofar as it is a this." This is not true. For first, by the same reasoning, since there is a formal distinction between essence and relation in the Trinity, the essence would be naturally prior to the relation, which is false. Second, because according to his own statements elsewhere [W 11. 261], everything naturally prior to something else can by divine power come to be without that posterior something. But this is impossible in the case of the nature, since it is really the same as the contracting difference. The assumption is clear, because he claims that this is what it is to be prior to something else: to be able to be without that something else, and not conversely.

(93) Second, it does not seem a correct statement that the individual difference is not quidditative [(9)]. For everything that belongs to the essence of something *per se* in a genus belongs to its quiddity, and is consequently a quidditative entity. But this individual difference belongs to the essence of an individual that is *per se* in a genus. Therefore, etc.

(94) Suppose it is said that, [for this objection to hold], it is required that the entity be a communicable entity, since every quiddity is communicable.

(95) This seems to be a statement without any basis. For, just as you claim [Scotus, 7. 500] every quiddity is communicable, so I will claim just as easily that every real quiddity is communicable to specifically distinct items. Hence the specific entity will not be a quidditative entity.

(96) Therefore, it seems it has to be said that every entity belonging to the essence of some thing that is *per se* one and existing *per se* in a genus is a quidditative entity, so that whether it is communicable or incommunicable makes no difference. In fact, it ought more truly to be said, as will be clear [(166)], that no real quidditative entity is communicable except as a form is communicated to matter, or in the way in which a distinct thing is communicated to a distinct thing.

(97) Third, it does not seem a correct statement that the nature is indifferent of itself, and nevertheless that it is really the contracting difference [S (187)–(188)]. For as was argued [(34)–(35)], what is of itself indifferent is

indifferent. But the indifferent is not really the same as the nonindifferent. Therefore, the nature and the contracting difference are not really the same.

(98) *Confirmation*: If it is of itself indifferent, either it is really of itself indifferent or not. If not, then it is irrelevant to the present topic. If it is, then it can be really communicated, which was disproved earlier [(96)].

(99) From this it follows that it does not seem a correct statement [S (41)] that the nature is of itself indifferent and yet made proper through an identity. For if it is really indifferent, it is by this fact inconsistent for it to be in anything else. Therefore, it is not of itself common, except perhaps negatively.

(100) Fourth, it does not seem a correct statement that the nature is really numerically one even though it is of itself common, and that it is numerically one only denominatively [S (173)–(175)]. For when some items make up or constitute something *per se* one, then for whatever reason an attribute or characteristic of the one denominates the other, for the same reason this holds conversely as well. For example, for whatever reason a characteristic of matter is predicated denominatively of form, for the same reason a characteristic or attribute of form will be predicated denominatively of matter. Therefore, since the nature and the contracting difference make up something *per se* one, therefore for whatever reason numerical unity is predicated denominatively of the nature, so that the nature is really numerically one, for the same reason lesser unity, which is an attribute of the nature itself, will be predicated denominatively of the individual difference, so that the individual difference will really be common and one by a lesser unity. Consequently the whole singular for the same reason will be denominated by either unity. Hence the singular will be no more numerically one than the common will be, or else it will be one with a lesser unity.

(101) From this it is clear that the simile about color and whiteness [S (174)] works in favor of the opposite conclusion. For just as a specific difference cannot be called one by a unity that is less than specific unity is, so the unity of a genus cannot be called one by a unity greater than generic unity is.

(102) Fifth, what he says does not seem a correct statement, namely, that "the universal in act is what has some indifferent unity," etc. [S (37)]. For in that case, the universal in act would have to be one in many and said of many. Now I ask: Is that universal a being of reason? If so, then consequently it is not one in many singulars outside the soul except by predication (which is the same as being said of many). Therefore, if we distinguish being in many from being said of many, it is not true [that the universal in act is a being of reason]. But if the universal is outside the soul, then it is in reality according to some [numerical] unity.

(103) Sixth, it does not seem a correct statement that community and likewise singularity come together in the nature outside the soul [S (42)]. For nothing outside the intellect is common, since outside the intellect everything is really singular.

[Ockham's own answer to the question]

(104) Therefore, I say otherwise in response to the question.

(105) First, I show this conclusion: Every singular thing is singular *by itself*.

(106) I argue this as follows: Singularity immediately pertains to what it belongs to. Therefore, it cannot pertain to it through anything else. Therefore, if something is singular, it is singular by itself.

(107) Moreover, as what is singular is related to being singular, so what is universal is related to being universal. Therefore, just as what is singular cannot become universal or common through anything added to it, so what is common cannot become singular through anything added to it. Therefore, whatever is singular is not singular through anything added to it, but by itself.

(108) The second conclusion: Every thing outside the soul is really singular and numerically one. For every thing outside the soul is either simple or composite. If it is simple, it does not include many things. But every thing not including many things is numerically one, because every such thing and another precisely similar thing are two things. Therefore, each of them is numerically one. Therefore, every simple thing is numerically one. If it is composite, one will finally have to arrive at a certain number of parts. Consequently each of these parts will be numerically one. Consequently the whole composed of them will be either numerically one or else one by aggregation.

(109) This can also be argued in the following way: I take the thing you claim is not a singular thing, and I ask: Does it include several things or not? If not, then I take a really distinct but similar thing and argue: These things are really distinct, and there is not an infinite number of them. Therefore, there is a finite number of them. And it is plain that this can only be a pair. Therefore, there are precisely two things here. Consequently each of them is numerically one.

(110) But if the original thing does include several things, it does not

include infinitely many, and therefore it includes finitely many. Consequently there is a number of things there. Hence each of the included things will be numerically one and singular.

(111) From these arguments it follows that each thing outside the soul is singular by itself, so that it itself, without anything added, is what is immediately denominated by the notion of singularity. Neither are any items whatever possible on the part of reality, distinct in any way at all, one of which is more indifferent than another, or one of which is more numerically one than another—unless perhaps the one is more perfect than another (as, for example, this angel is more perfect than this ass).

(112) Hence each thing outside the soul will be by itself a this. One does not have to look for a cause of individuation (except perhaps the extrinsic and intrinsic causes, when the individual is composite). Rather one has to look more for a cause why it is possible for something to be common and universal.

(113) Therefore, I reply to the form of the question: What is universal and univocal is not really anything on the part of reality formally distinct from the individual. For it is clear it is not merely formally distinct, because in that case whenever a superior would be predicated of its inferior, the same item would be predicated of itself. For the superior and the inferior would be the same thing, [if they are only formally distinct]. The consequent is false. For then the same genus would never be predicated of diverse species. Rather there would be one predicate for one species and another for another species, which seems nonsense.

[Replies to Scotus's arguments]

(114) To the first argument in favor of the other theory [S (3)], I say "being in something" can be of two kinds: either really or according to predication, as when it is said that the predicate is in the subject it is said of. In the first sense it is true that whatever something is in, it is in it in every instance. In the second sense this does not have to be so, if the subject is a common term. Therefore, it does not follow, if the nature of man[36] of itself is a this, that whatever the nature of man is in, it is "this man."

(115) Yet the proposition 'The nature of man is of itself a this' has to be

---

36. Much of the argument in this and the following paragraphs will be clearer if you remember that Latin has no definite or indefinite article, so that the phrase '*natura hominis*' can to be translated 'the nature of man' or 'a nature of a man', etc., depending on the context.

distinguished (even though perhaps not literally), insofar as 'nature of man' can supposit simply or personally—that is, insofar as the term can stand for a thing outside the soul, or for itself. If the latter, then in that sense 'The nature of a stone is of itself this' is false.[37] For in that case it is denoted that a concept of the mind, which is universal, is of itself this stone. And that is false, because this concept cannot, either of itself or through any power whatever, be this stone, even though it can be truly predicated of it, not for itself but for the external thing. But if 'nature of man' is taken in the former sense, then in that sense 'A nature of a man of itself is this man' is true. Yet it is compatible with this that a nature of a man of itself is that other man—indeed, that a nature of a man of itself is *not* this man. For since 'nature of man' is a common term, both those propositions could be true as two subcontraries each of which is verified of one singular or another. For in that case they are equipollent to these particularly quantified propositions: 'Some nature of itself is this man', which is verified of this nature, and 'Some nature of itself is not this man', which is verified of another nature that is not this nature.

(116) In the same way, just as 'A man is Socrates' and 'A man is Plato' are compatible, so too 'A nature of a man is of itself this man' and 'A nature of a man is of itself that man' are compatible.

(117) When he says [S (3)] "If the nature of man is of itself this man, then whatever the nature of man is in, it is this man,"[38] I reply that this does not literally follow formally. Instead it is a fallacy of figure of speech [Aristotle, *Sophistic Refutations* 4, 166^{b}10–21, & 22, 178^{a}4–179^{a}10], insofar as one mode of suppositing is transformed into another. For in 'A nature of a man of itself is this man' the term 'nature of a man' supposits determinately, whereas in the consequent it instead supposits merely confusedly. But whatever happens about that, 'A nature of a man is such that, whatever it is in, that thing is this man' is true because it has a true singular: 'This nature of a man is such that, whatever it is in, that thing is this man.' And in that case, in arguing "A nature of a man is such that, whatever it is in, that thing is this man; a nature of a man is in that man; therefore, that man is this man," there is a fallacy of the consequent, because it argues from all indefinite propositions.[39]

---

37. The change from 'man' to 'stone' is a mere slip, without significance.

38. Ockham substitutes 'man' for Scotus's 'stone'. See the remark at (18).

39. Propositions in which the subject has no explicit quantifier. For syllogistic purposes indefinite propositions were treated as particularly (existentially) quantified. A valid syllogism must have at least one universally quantified premise (affirmative or negative). Hence a syllogism in which all the premises are indefinite is invalid.

(118) But as for the diversity between the indefinite propositions in the above argument, one of which is denied and the other granted, the same has to be said as for 'Each man's ass runs' and 'An ass belonging to each man runs'.[40] <Now you need to know that when one says 'A nature *of* a man is of itself this man', it should be understood as being an intransitive construction—that is, as 'A nature *that is* a man is of itself this man'.>[41]

(119) To the second argument [(4)], I grant that whatever one of a pair of opposites belongs to, the other opposite is inconsistent with it of itself. Therefore, because a nature of itself is a "this" (insofar as 'nature' supposits personally), I grant accordingly that numerical multitude is inconsistent for a nature—that is, (a) it is inconsistent for a nature to be in anything else, and (b) it is inconsistent for a nature to be in many.

(120) The first of these (a) is verified of one singular, because it is inconsistent for *this* nature to be in something else. Yet this is compatible with its not being inconsistent for a nature to be in something else—in fact it belongs to a nature of itself to be in something else, <that is, it belongs to a nature to *be* something else>. This is verified of another singular. For as was said [(117)], these two propositions are indefinite. Consequently since the subject in them supposits personally, they are equipollent to two particular propositions each of which has some true singular, and consequently each is absolutely true.

(121) But (b) 'It is inconsistent for a nature to be in many' is true for any singular, because it is inconsistent for any nature to be in many.

(122) Suppose it is said: It is not inconsistent for a nature to be *predicated of* many. Therefore, neither is *being in* many inconsistent with it.

(123) I reply: The antecedent has to be distinguished, insofar as (a) the subject can supposit personally. In that case, the proposition is absolutely false because each singular is false—that is, 'It is not inconsistent for this nature, etc.', 'It is not inconsistent for that nature, etc.', and so on for other singulars. Or (b) the subject can supposit simply. In that case, the antecedent is true, because then it is denoted that the common term 'nature', which is not in reality but only in the mind, can be predicated of many, not for itself but for things. In sense (a) the inference is a good one, because the subject

40. In Latin, the difference is only in word order: '*Cuiuslibet hominis asinus currit*'/ '*Asinus cuiuslibet hominis currit*'. These standard examples were interpreted as in effect: 'Every man owns some ass that runs' and 'Some ass such that every man owns it runs', respectively. The point of the examples was to illustrate the importance of the order of quantifiers.

41. In short, the genitive in 'nature of a man' is a "genitive of apposition."

supposits personally both in the antecedent and in the consequent. But in sense **(b)** it is invalid, because in that case the subject in the antecedent supposits simply and in the consequent personally, and so there is a fallacy of equivocation according to the third mode of that fallacy.[42] Nevertheless, even if the subject of the consequent could have simple supposition, the consequent and the inference would have to be denied anyway, if we take 'being in' for 'being in something really and subjectively'. For in that sense the nature is in no singular. That is to say, this common [concept] is subjectively in no singular.

(124) Suppose someone says: Something is a "this something" and is distinguished from every other "this something" by the same item. But a nature of itself is not distinguished from any other this something. For then it would not be that stone. Therefore, stone of itself is not this stone.

(125) I reply as before, that 'A nature of a stone is of itself distinguished from every other this something' is true of one singular insofar as the subject supposits personally. Likewise, 'A nature of a stone is of itself another stone than this one' is true of another singular. Therefore, it does not follow that the other stone is not a stone, just as it does not follow: "A man is distinguished from Socrates, or a man is not Socrates; and a man is Socrates; therefore, Socrates is not Socrates, or is distinguished from Socrates."

(126) Also the second main argument [**S (4)**] proves the opposite [of what was intended]. For just as, when one opposite belongs to something of itself, the other opposite is inconsistent with it of itself, so too when one opposite belongs to something, then as long as that opposite belongs to it the other opposite is inconsistent with the same item. For example, if being white belongs to Socrates, then as long as Socrates is white the other opposite cannot belong to him (namely, that he be black). Therefore, if a nature of a stone is this, then a nature of a stone, as long as it is this, cannot be in anything else. So as long as it is this stone, it cannot be any stone that is not this one.

(127) So it is clear that the argument goes against him. Therefore, one has to reply as has been said, on his side and on mine.

(128) To the third main argument [**S (7)**], it must be said that one kind of object is naturally prior to the act, and another one not. So the universal is never naturally prior to the act, and the universal in act is not the proper aspect of the object of the intellect. For as will be clear elsewhere [**OT** 3. 492–496], the first object of the intellect (first by a primacy of generation)

---

42. On the modes of the fallacy of equivocation, see Spade, "Synonymy and Equivocation in Ockham's Mental Language."

is the singular itself under its own aspect, and not under the aspect of a universal.

(129) To the fourth main argument [S (8)–(10)], I say there is no unity of the nature existing in this stone unless it is equally primarily the unity of the stone. Yet I make a distinction about unity: In one sense 'unity' is said insofar as it denominates precisely something one and not several, and not one in comparison to something else really distinct from it. In this sense, I say every real unity is numerical unity. In another sense 'unity' is said insofar as it denominates several items, or one item in comparison to another one really distinct from it. In this sense, specific unity denominates Socrates and Plato, and the unity of a genus denominates this man and this ass. It does not denominate anything in any way distinct from these individuals. Instead it immediately denominates the individuals themselves.

(130) Hence just as it is truly said that Socrates and Plato are specifically one and the same and Socrates is specifically the same as Plato, so it is truly said that this man and this ass are generically the same and that this man is generically the same as or one with this ass. That is to say, they are contained under the same species or under the same genus. The Philosopher explicitly gives this analysis in *Topics* I, the chapter "On the Same," [7, 103^{a}6–14], as was said in the first question on this issue [**q. 4**].

(131) In this sense, I grant that not every real unity or identity is numerical. But this unity does not belong to a nature distinct in any way from individuals. Instead it belongs immediately to the individuals themselves, or (what is the same) to one in comparison with the other.

(132) But because the supporting arguments [S (11)–(28)] go against what was first understood [(113)?], I reply to them:

(133) To the first one [S (11)–(15)], when it is said following the Philosopher that "in every genus there is something one and primary that is the metric and measure of all the others in that genus," I say that, as will be clear in Book II, [q. 9, **OT** 5. 164.9–166.11], a measure is sometimes a true thing outside the soul. For example, cloth is measured by the ["ell"* or] elbow. Sometimes the measure is only a certain concept in the mind. The first kind of measure must be one by numerical unity.

(134) But the proposition 'In every genus there is *only* one entity that is the measure of all the others' is false. If Aristotle's statement is to have any truth, it must be understood in the sense that in every genus there is something that is the measure of all things *specifically distinct* from it. It does not have to be the measure of all other things whatever, whether they are specifically distinguished or not. In this sense, there are several things each of which is a measure of all other things specifically distinct from it. And each of them is one by numerical unity.[43]

(135) When it is said [S (12)] that "the unity of what first measures is real," I say: If 'first' is taken positively, then this is false, because it has a false presupposition. For nothing is what "first measures" in this sense. But if it is taken negatively, I grant it. For the "first measures" in that sense are many—namely, each individual of the species, especially if each one is equally simple.

(136) When it is said [S (13)] that in a genus "No singular is the measure of all that are in that genus," I grant there is none for individuals of the same species. But there is one that is a measure of all items specifically distinct from it. That is enough to make the point.

<(137) Nevertheless you need to know that the Philosopher is speaking [*Metaphysics* III. 3, 999ª12–13] mainly, or perhaps only, about what are in the same species, as is clear from his examples there, and about species that have individuals some of which are greater and others less. He means that something that is less than the others is a measure of the others—not of all the individuals of that species, but only of those that are not as small.>

(138) To the second supporting argument [S (16)–(17)], I say comparison occurs in an indivisible species not because of the unity of the concept, or precisely because of numerical unity, or precisely because of specific unity—whether specific unity is held to be like what was claimed at the beginning of the solution to this argument [(129)], or whether it is maintained according to some other people's way of imagining falsehood [S (16)–(17)]. For in that case, there would be comparison in *every* indivisible species. Instead a comparison occurs because several individuals of the same species can make up one individual. Therefore, where many items <not distinct in place and subject> can make up something one, such a comparison is to be maintained there and not anywhere else. Because this is possible for individuals of the same species and not for individuals of diverse species, therefore comparison is held to occur in an indivisible species and not in a genus.

(139) For example, this white thing is called whiter than another white thing because it has more parts of whiteness <in the same primary subject>. And if in this way more parts of whiteness and of blackness came together at the same time in making a *per se* one color, that color could be called "more colored" than the other.

---

43. The point is that, within a given genus, things in one species may be a measure of things in other species, but not of one another.

(140) When it is said [S (17)] that this comparison is not made according to numerical unity, that is true in the first sense of speaking about numerical unity [(129)]. Therefore, it is made according to specific unity. For it is made according to two things, each of which is numerically one. No third something, distinct in any way from these two, is required.

(141) To the third argument [S (18)], I say: If one claims similarity is a relation really distinct from its extremes, then it must be said that there are two similarities here, having two real foundations, each of which foundations is numerically one. So the one foundation is not the basis for founding the similarity between the same thing and itself, but is instead the basis for founding its similarity to the other extreme.

(142) Now it is clear what the Philosopher thought about the numerically one. For after he explained how 'similar', 'same' and 'equal' are said in relation to 'one', he afterwards adds [*Metaphysics* V. 15, 1021ª12–13]: "Now one is the principle and measure of number." Therefore, he is not thinking about any unity of anything not numerically one.

(143) But does it have to be granted that this unity is the basis for founding this relation?

(144) It must be said that, according to those who hold that these relations [of similarity, sameness and equality] are really distinguished [from their foundations—see Scotus, W 6. 635], one should not any more claim unity is the proximate basis for founding similarity than that it is for founding relations of any other kind. But the difference lies in the fact that for these relations, there is required some "real unity" in the second sense discussed at the beginning of the solution of this argument [(129)], a real unity of a sort not required for other relations of any other kind. For at least specific unity is required for these relations, and it is not necessarily required for others, even though sometimes such a specific unity is there.

(145) To the fourth argument [(19)], I say: For items to be the primary extremes of a real opposition can be understood in two senses: Either **(a)** because they are items of which being really opposed is primarily predicated in a positive sense. But it is not predicated of them for themselves insofar as they have simple supposition, but for singulars insofar as those items have personal supposition. Or **(b)** because in reality they are really contraries. In sense **(a)**, the extremes of a real opposition are not real, because the term 'being really opposed' is not predicated primarily and adequately of any things at all, but only of concepts *for* things (if the predication is in the mind), or of words *for* things (if the predication is in speech), and so on. It should not be granted that they are literally contraries. Instead one must speak in the same way as what was said earlier [q. 4, (150)–(153)], about the primary adequate object of a sensitive power and about the primary subject of a real attribute.

(146) In sense **(b)**, there are not just two extremes of a real opposition. Rather there are many, just as there are many real oppositions. Hence this whiteness and this blackness are really opposed. Likewise, that whiteness and that blackness are really opposed. In precisely these cases is it true that one of a pair of contraries destroys the other. And each of them is numerically one. For nothing destroys anything but what is numerically one.

(147) And when it is said [**S** (**19**)] "In that case this white thing would be the primary contrary of the black," I say: The white is not properly contrary to the black. Rather whiteness is contrary to blackness. I grant that this whiteness is primarily contrary to blackness, insofar as 'primarily' is taken negatively. For it is contrary to blackness, and nothing is more contrary to blackness than it is. But insofar as 'primarily' is taken positively, in that sense nothing is primarily contrary to blackness.

(148) Suppose it is said: **(i)** "To one thing there is one contrary" [*On the Heavens* I. 2, 269ª14–15; *Metaphysics* X. 4, 1055ª19–20]. Therefore, it is not the case that there are many things contrary to blackness. Likewise **(ii)**, contraries can be in the same item [*Categories* 11, 14ª15–16], but two individuals cannot. Likewise **(iii)**, contraries are furthest apart from one another [*Metaphysics* X. 4, 1055ª27–28]], but two individuals are not furthest apart from one another.

(149) To **(i)**, I say: The Philosopher is talking about what is one according to species, not according to number. It has already been stated [(**129**)] how specific unity is real and on the part of reality. For it is nothing else than for there to be on the part of reality several items contained under the same species, according to the Philosopher, *Topics* I. [7, 103ª10–12].

(150) To **(ii)**, I grant that contraries can be in the same item—at least successively. So I say it is not a contradiction that water should be hot in the highest degree, just as it is not a contradiction that it should be cold in the highest degree (if there is a gradation of degrees in such forms).

(151) To **(iii)**, I say: Contraries are furthest apart by the kind of "distance" that can be between individuals of diverse species. But what kind of "greatest specific distance" is required for contrariety, and what kind is not, that will be stated elsewhere [**OP** 2. 233–234].

(152) To the fifth argument [**S** (**20**)–(**22**)], I say: The object of one act of sensation is one by numerical unity. When it is said that "the power that cognizes the object in this way—that is, insofar as the object is one by this unity—cognizes it insofar as it is distinct from everything else," I say it does cognize what is distinct from everything else. And it cognizes it under the aspect by which it is distinguished from everything else. For that aspect, which is the very thing itself, immediately terminates the act of cognizing. Yet the power does not on this account have to be able to discern or distinguish the thing from everything else, because more is required for a discriminating cognition than for a merely apprehensive cognition. A discriminating cognition never actually occurs except with respect to distinct items. And this still does not suffice for the distinct items to be apprehended, unless in themselves they are dissimilar or distinguished in place and orientation. (This is true when all such apprehended items are naturally prone to make up something *per se* one, as holds for sensible qualities, but not for any acts of intellection, or for the will's acts of love, or for intelligences[44] or souls.) Thus, however much such items are apprehended, they do not have to be able to be discerned, because of the high degree of similarity among them.

(153) Yet if the power is an intellective one, it can recognize that this item *x* is distinct from everything else, even though, indicating some definite item *y*, it does not have to be able to recognize that this *x* is distinct from this *y*. For a universal proposition can be known and yet many of its singulars not be known. But a sense power is not properly able to recognize *x* to be distinct from anything, because this ability pertains to the complex knowledge by which it is known that this is not that. Nevertheless a sense power is able to *discern*[45] this *x* from one item and not from another, and sometimes it can discern this from that and at other times not, on account of some variation on the side of reality.

(154) *Confirmation* of this reasoning: Sense discerns the more white from the less white. I ask then: Does it apprehend either of these precisely under the aspect of the common, or under the aspect of singularity?

(155) If the former, then they agree in that aspect. Therefore, they are not discerned through it. If the latter, the point is established: It is apprehended under the aspect of singularity. Not that the mental intention "singularity" is the aspect terminating the sense power, but what is immediately denominated by this intention immediately terminates the sense power.

(156) To the confirmation [S (22)]: The primary object of the intellect by primacy of generation is one by numerical unity, and that object does precede. But the primary object by primacy of adequation, if there is any such object, is not one by numerical unity and does not precede, as will be stated later [**OT** 3. 388–389].

44. That is, angels.

45. The point is that "recognizing" is an intellectual act while "discerning" may be merely sensitive.

(157) To the sixth argument [S (23)–(27)], I grant that every real diversity is numerical in the sense in which every real unity is numerical, because even specific diversity is numerical. For according to the Philosopher, [*Metaphysics* V. 9, 1018ª4–11], whatever are generically diverse are specifically diverse, and whatever are specifically diverse are numerically diverse. Hence numerical diversity occurs in more cases than specific and generic diversity do. For it follows: "They are generically or specifically diverse; therefore, they are numerically diverse." But not conversely.

(158) When it is said [S (23)] that "every numerical diversity, insofar as it is numerical, is equal," I say this is absolutely false. For then it would follow that every diversity would be equal, since 'insofar as' is not a destructive determination. Nevertheless if the consequent is understood in the sense that all things that differ *only* numerically are equally diverse, it can be granted for things that do not admit of more and less or greater and less.

(159) If it is said that every numerical unity is equal, and therefore every numerical diversity is equal, I say the consequent does not follow in the sense in which the antecedent is true, just as it does not follow: "Whatever are equal are equally equal (for equality does not admit of greater and less); therefore, whatever are unequal are equally unequal." This reply holds where one opposite admits of greater and less and the other does not. And that is so in the present case.

(160) As for what he intimates in the argument—that if every diversity were numerical, then the intellect could no more abstract anything common from Socrates and Plato than it can from Socrates and a line, and that every universal would be a pure figment of the intellect [S (23)]—I say to the former that from the very fact that Socrates and Plato differ by themselves only numerically, and Socrates is most similar in substance to Plato, even disregarding everything else, it follows that the intellect can abstract something common to Socrates and Plato that will not be common to Socrates and to a whiteness. One does not have to look for any other cause of this than because Socrates is Socrates and Plato is Plato and each is a man.

(161) Suppose someone says: Socrates and Plato really agree more than Socrates and an ass do. Therefore, Socrates and Plato agree in something real in which Socrates and an ass do not really agree. But they do not agree in Socrates, or in Plato. Therefore, they agree in something distinct in some other way. And that is common to each.

(162) I reply: Literally it should not be granted that Socrates and Plato agree *in* something or somethings, but that they agree *by* somethings, because they agree by themselves. And it should be granted that Socrates agrees with Plato not "*in* something," but "*by* something," because he agrees by himself.

(163) If it is said that Socrates and Plato agree in man, I say: 'Man' can supposit simply or personally. In the former sense, the statement can be granted, because this is nothing else than saying 'man' is one common term predicable of Socrates and Plato. But if 'man' supposits personally for some thing, in that sense the statement is absolutely false. For in no man do they agree. Neither in any thing do they agree. Rather they agree *by* things, because they agree by men, because they agree by themselves.

<(164) To the form of the argument [S (23)], therefore, I say Socrates and Plato by themselves really agree more than Socrates and an ass do, but not *in* anything real.>

(165) To the other point, about the figment [(160)], it is clear how a universal is a figment and how it is not [see q. 8, (22)–(54)].

(166) To the first confirmation of this argument [S (26)], I say: For some items to be "primarily diverse" can be understood in two ways: Either because nothing is one and the same in both of them, but whatever is in the one simply and absolutely of itself is not anything in the other. In this sense, I grant that all individuals are primarily diverse by themselves—unless perhaps the case is otherwise for individuals one of which is generated from the other, because of a numerical identity of the matter in each.

(167) But some things are said to be primarily diverse in another sense, when the one is immediately and primarily denied of the other. Hence when the one is not immediately denied of the other, so that the negative proposition composed of those terms is not immediate [see *Posterior Analytics* I. 15, 79^{a}33–^{b}22], then they are different and not just diverse. In this sense all individuals of the same species are primarily diverse. For an immediate negative proposition is composed of them. Likewise, all the species contained immediately under some genus are primarily diverse, because an immediate [negative] proposition is composed of them. Hence Socrates and Plato are primarily diverse in this sense. But Socrates and this ass are not primarily diverse. For this is an immediate proposition 'Socrates is not Plato'. But this one is not immediate 'Socrates is not this ass', because this is more immediate 'No man is this ass'.

(168) Therefore, the common saying [*e. g.*, Aquinas, *Summa theologiae* I. 90. 1. ad 3], that the primarily diverse are what agree in nothing, while the different are what agree in something, is not a correct statement. Rather primarily diverse things are those neither of which differs from the other through anything more common of which either is denied beforehand, whereas different ones are those one of which is denied of the other because something more common than it is denied beforehand of the same thing.

<(169) That is, primarily diverse things are those had when nothing

more common than either of them is the means[46] of concluding a negative proposition denying the one of the other. Different things are those had when something more common than one of them is the means of concluding a negative proposition in which the one is denied of the other. For example, this man and this ass differ because 'man' is such a means, and 'ass' is likewise. For "No man is an ass; this man is a man; therefore, this man is not this ass" is a good syllogism. >

(170) That this is the Philosopher's meaning is clear from the Philosopher himself, *Metaphysics* X. [3, 1054[b]23–30],[47] where he says: "Difference is other than diversity. For the diverse and what it is diverse from are not necessarily diverse *by something*." That is, it is not necessary that there be something more common than what is diverse, of which what it is diverse from is immediately denied before it is denied of what is diverse. For example, for Socrates to be diverse from Plato there does not have to be something more common than Socrates, of which Plato is immediately denied, whereas he is denied of Socrates only mediately. Instead 'Socrates is not Plato' is an immediate proposition.

(171) The Philosopher gives the reason for this: "Now everything either diverse or the same is a being."[48] That is, every being, whether it has anything more common of which another being is denied earlier or does not, that being is the same as or diverse from any other given being whatever. "But what differs from something is different by something." That is, everything *x* that differs from something *y* differs through something prior and more common of which the other item *y* is immediately denied, whereas *y* is denied of *x* only mediately. For example, this man differs from an ass through 'man', of which 'ass' is immediately denied, and 'ass' is denied of this man only mediately. < You need to know that when I say this man differs from an ass through 'man', I am taking 'differ through something' as I analyze it in the eighth distinction [OT 3. 231.15–21], when I analyze how something differs from another through an essential difference. Hence 'to differ through something' is taken equivocally in different places. >

(172) This is what he means when he adds, "Hence there is necessarily something the same by which they differ." This should not be understood

---

46. This might also be translated "middle term" (of a syllogism). So too throughout the paragraph.

47. This reference applies to the entire phrase-by-phrase commentary Ockham gives in (170)–(175).

48. I follow Ockham's Latin here, although the passage as he quotes it does not seem to agree in sense with his own explanation in the next sentence.

in the sense that there is something the same by which each differs from the other, because that is impossible. For in that case they would agree more than differ by it. Instead it should be understood in the sense that there is something the same by which, as through a middle term, this differing thing is shown to differ from that one. For example, through 'substance' as through a middle term it is shown that man is not a quantity, as follows: "No substance is a quantity; man is a substance; therefore, no man is a quantity." Thus the middle term is more common than the differing extreme is, because the middle is always its genus or species.

(173) This is what the Philosopher says: "Now this very same thing"—fill in: by which the differing thing differs from the other—"is a genus or a species"—fill in: is a genus or a species with respect to that differing thing, and is not its difference. "For everything that differs differs generically or specifically."

(174) Hence to say differing things differ by their differences and agree in genus (if they are in a genus) is to say nothing at all. Instead it should be said that they differ by their genera or by their one or several species, not on the part of reality but rather in the one's mediately or immediately being denied of the other.

(175) The Philosopher gives an example, saying: "By genus indeed"—fill in: some things differ—"for which there is no common matter or generation from the one to the other, as for whatever belong to one and another kind of category." Observe that what are in distinct categories differ by genus, and consequently differ by species. Those differ "by species, however, of which the genus is the same," and yet the species are diverse.

(176) Thus I say man and whiteness differ by their genera, because each has a genus above it through which a negation can be made of the one from the other, according to the procedure the Philosopher gives in *Posterior Analytics* I. [15, 79^{a}33–79^{b}22]. But whiteness and substance differ by a genus, because even though whiteness has a genus through which a negative proposition can be shown to be true in which whiteness is denied of substance or conversely, nevertheless substance does not have such a genus.[49] But the common notions *substance* and *quality* do not differ by genus or by species. The same thing is to be said, analogously, for what differ by species.

(177) Since the Philosopher says all differing things (insofar as differing things are distinguished from diverse ones) differ by genus or by species [(173)], and since Socrates and Plato differ neither by genus nor by species,

---

49. The text seems to have reversed the 'even though'- and 'nevertheless'-clauses.

it is plain that they do not differ at all. But Socrates and this ass differ, because they differ by species.

(178) Suppose it is said this goes against the Philosopher's meaning because he immediately adds in the same place [*Metaphysics* X. 3, 1054ᵇ30–31]: "What is called a genus is what two things differing according to substance are both called." Therefore, it seems according to him that what are immediately contained under a genus are different.

(179) Likewise, the Commentator on the same passage, comm. 12 [260I]: "What differ through formal differences are the things for which the genus is one."

(180) Again, *Metaphysics* V. [9, 1018ᵃ12–15]: "What differ are said to be whatever are diverse, being something the same. They differ not only by number but also either by species or by genus or by analogy. Further, things are also called different for which the genus is diverse, and also contraries and whatever have diversity in their substance."

(181) To the first of these [(178)], I say: A genus is what, while staying the same, is predicated of some things differing according to substance. For every genus is predicated of several things differing by species. Yet not *all* the things of which it is predicated differ. For from some of the things of which it is predicated there is put together an immediate [negative] proposition, and from others there is not.

(182) To the second [(179)], I say: Some things differing through formal differences have the same genus. In general, all things outside the soul that are really different through formal differences have the same genus. For such things are nothing but the individuals of diverse species. Yet things having the same genus do not all have to differ through formal differences, as will be clear elsewhere [**OT** 3. 207.10–209.19].

(183) To the third argument [(180)], I say the Philosopher takes 'differ' there insofar as it precisely belongs to things. In that sense, all things whatsoever are diverse and are "being something the same," not by identity but by essential predication. That is, something the same is predicated of them truly and *in quid*. He goes on to say, "They differ not only by number." That is: and those things are not only diverse according to number as individuals of the same species are, but "also"—fill in: they are diverse—"either by species or by genus or by analogy." Diverse things like this, I say, are different. Yet not all diverse things are different. For a real being and a being of reason are diverse. Nevertheless they are not different, because nothing the same is predicated of them *in quid* <according to the view that claims a being of reason has only objective being. But according to another view, something

is indeed predicated of them *in quid*.[50] > Later on [*Metaphysics* V. 10, 1018[a]20–[b]8, and X. 4–10, 1055[a]3–1059[a]14], he sets out other ways of being different.

(184) Suppose it is said: If things that are different agree more than do things that are only diverse, then this man and this ass would agree more than this man and that man do.

(185) I say: Taking 'different' as the Philosopher takes it in *Metaphysics* X. [3, 1054[b]25–28], different things do not always agree more than what are precisely diverse do. Rather it is enough that they differ in more ways—that is, one of them is truly denied of more terms truly said of the other. For example, this stone is denied of more terms said of this man than this other man is. Thus that man and this stone are different, but this man and that man are not.

(186) To the other confirmation [S (27)], I reply the same way.

(187) To the other argument [S (28)], I say: Even if no intellect existed, there would be some real unity between the generating fire and the generated fire, on account of which unity it would be called univocal generation. But that unity would not be said of any one thing. Rather it would be said of several really distinct things, as has been stated [(129)]. Therefore, etc.

(188) To the citation from Avicenna [(22)], I say it should not be understood that equinity is only equinity in the sense that equinity is neither one nor several, neither in the intellect nor in act, because equinity really is in act and really is singular. For just as equinity is really created by God, and likewise equinity is really distinct from God, so too equinity is really and truly singular. Instead Avicenna means these features do not pertain to equinity *per se* in the first mode. None of these features is included in its definition, as he himself expressly says, [*Metaphysics* V. 1, 86[va]].

(189) Suppose it is said, in accordance with Avicenna, and in accordance with other philosophers too [*e.g.*, Henry of Ghent, *Summae* a. 28, q. 5, 1. 168[v], & *Quodlibet* III. 9, 58[v]–62[r]], that equinity is of itself indifferent to being singular and to being universal. I ask: How is this true? Either insofar as 'equinity' supposits simply, or insofar as it supposits personally. If it supposits simply, then this concept is *not* indifferent, because it can in no way be singular. Therefore, it is not simple supposition when a term supposits for a concept, which is contrary to what was said above, [q. 4 (139)]. If the term supposits personally, then the proposition is false. For then the term supposits for singulars. But nothing singular is indifferent in this way. There-

50. On these two views, see q. 8 below.

fore, it seems that besides supposition for a concept and supposition for a singular thing, one has to posit a third kind of supposition, namely when a term supposits for the quiddity itself, absolutely indifferent to both universality and singularity.

(190) I reply, in conformity with some of what was said above [**(188)**], that 'Equinity is not of itself universal or particular, but rather indifferent to being universal and to being singular' [compare **(22)**] is not true except insofar as a signate act is understood by it—namely, "Of equinity there can be indifferently predicated being universal and being singular." In this signate act, 'equinity' has simple supposition. But in the two corresponding exercised acts, 'equinity' will have different kinds of supposition. In the one (in 'Equinity is a universal'), it will have simple supposition, and in the other (in 'Equinity is a singular'), it will have personal supposition.

(191) For example, 'Of man there is predicated a word and running' is true. In it 'man' has material supposition. For both are predicated of the word 'man'. To this signate act there correspond two true exercised acts: 'Man is a word', in which 'man' supposits materially, and 'Man runs', in which 'man' supposits personally.

(192) To the last argument [**(23)**], I say: When what agree and what differ are compatible with one another, it is not inconsistent for them to come together in the same thing in the same respect. So when some things agree specifically and yet differ numerically, there is no inconsistency.

(193) This is clear from his own example. For it is certain that the contracted nature really agrees with the individual difference, because it is really the same thing. Yet the nature is distinguished in some way from the contracting difference. I ask then: Does it agree and differ in the same respect, or does it agree in one respect and differ in another? If it is in the same respect, I have my point: The same thing in the same nondistinct respect both really agrees with and is formally distinct from the same thing. In that case, I will just as easily say that Socrates in the same respect both specifically agrees with Plato and is numerically distinguished from him. So too generally in all such cases.

(194) But if it agrees in one respect and is distinguished in another, then I ask about those "respects." They are distinguished somehow, and yet agree because they are one thing. Therefore, do they agree and are they distinguished in the same respect, or is it that they agree in one and are distinguished in another? So either there will be an infinite regress or else it will stop at some point where the same thing in the same respect both agrees in such and such a way with something and is distinguished in such and such a way from it. And in that case, I will just as easily say that the same thing in the same respect both agrees specifically with something and is numerically distinguished from it.

(195) Suppose is it said [W 4. 698]: Disregarding every intellect, there is still a greater agreement from the nature of things between Socrates and Plato than between Socrates and this ass. Therefore, from the nature of things, Socrates and Plato agree in some nature in which Socrates and this ass do not agree.

(196) Likewise [W 4. 698], unless there were a greater agreement between Socrates and Plato than between Socrates and this ass, a specific concept could no more be abstracted from Socrates and Plato than from Socrates and this ass.

(197) To the first of these [(195)], I say: The inference drawn is not valid, just as it does not follow: "An intellectual nature agrees more with God from the fact that it is an image of God than an insensible nature does that is not an image of God. Yet[51] they do not agree in anything real in any way distinct from them, even according to these people [Scotus, 4. 190]. Rather it is surely *by themselves* that they agree more."

(198) So it is in the present case. Socrates and Plato by themselves agree more than Socrates and this ass do, disregarding everything else. Likewise a real being agrees more with God than a being of reason does. Yet God does not agree *in* anything with a creature—except perhaps in a concept.

(199) From this, the answer to the second point [(196)] is clear. There is a greater agreement between Socrates and Plato than there is between Socrates and this ass, but not on account of anything in any way distinct from them. Instead they agree more by themselves.

(200) This reply is confirmed by their own statements [(195)–(196)]. For I take two individual differences contracting the nature of man. These differences agree more than do an individual difference contracting the nature of man and an individual difference contracting the nature of whiteness. *Proof of this*: The individual difference contracting the nature of man agrees with the contracted nature. For it is really the same thing with it. But that contracted nature—say, Socrates' nature—agrees more with Plato's nature than with the nature of whiteness. Therefore, it agrees more with Plato's individual contracting difference. Consequently, from first to last, Socrates' individual difference agrees more with Plato's individual difference than it does with the individual difference of this whiteness. Now Socrates' individual difference is certainly really distinguished from the individual difference of this whiteness. Therefore, it is either

51. Ockham seems to have forgotten the structure of his argument here. At first he says "it does not follow," so that we expect an inference *If P then Q*. But what he gives us is not an inference but an observation: *P, yet not-Q*.

in the same respect that it agrees more with the one than with the other, or in another respect. If it is in the same respect that it agrees with the one and is really distinguished from the other, then the point is established: Something can in the same respect both agree with something and be distinguished from the same thing. If it agrees in one respect and is distinguished in another, therefore the individual difference would include many factors and there would be an infinite regress, both of which are nonsense.

(201) Suppose it is said: This individual difference—say, Socrates'—does not through itself or from itself agree more with Plato's nature and with Plato's individual difference than it does with the nature of this whiteness, but rather it does so through the contracted nature.

(202) To the contrary: As Socrates' individual difference agrees more with Plato's nature, so conversely Plato's nature agrees more with Socrates' individual difference than with the individual difference of this whiteness. Therefore, it agrees more (a) by itself, or (b) through Socrates' contracting individual difference, or (c) through Socrates' nature. If (a), then since Plato's nature is certainly distinguished by itself from Socrates' individual difference, therefore the same thing in the same respect is distinguished from and agrees with the same thing. But (b) cannot be granted, because in that case the individual difference would agree more with one individual difference than with another. Neither can (c) be granted, because nothing is ever really the same with something through something extrinsic to it and really distinct from it.

(203) Suppose it is said: Although it agrees by itself with this individual difference, nevertheless it is not distinguished from it except through another individual difference.

(204) To the contrary: The nature by itself is distinguished from every individual difference. For according to them [(8), **point 4**], by itself it is not inconsistent with it to be without any individual difference. Moreover two individual differences, from the very fact that each is a creature, agree more with each other than this creature and God do. Now it is certain that they are distinguished from one another. Therefore, either one has to grant that the same item in the same respect is distinguished from and agrees with the same item, or else one has to grant an infinite regress.

[To the main argument]

(205) To the main argument (3), it is clear that a nature of a stone is of itself "this," and so a nature of a stone cannot be in anything else. Yet it is compatible with this that a nature of a stone of itself is *not* "this" but rather "that," and in something else. For these are two indefinite propositions, verified of diverse singulars.

<(206) Nevertheless you should know that literally 'A nature of a stone is in a stone' is false. Instead it should be granted that a nature of a stone *is* a stone. (Yet in the case of Christ it can be granted that a human nature is *in* Christ.) Yet 'A nature of a stone is in a stone' is commonly granted. But if it is understood that a nature of a stone is truly in a stone, as in something distinct in any way, then that is absolutely false. If however it is understood that the nature *is* the stone then it is true.>

[Question 7

Is there anything univocally universal and common in any way at all really on the side of reality outside the soul?]

(1) Fourth, I ask whether what is univocally universal and common is in any way at all really on the side of reality outside the soul.

(2) Yes it is:

(3) According to the Commentator, *Metaphysics* VII. comm. 11, [161E], "A definition is the same as the substance of the thing." Therefore, it is in some way outside the soul. Consequently all its parts are in some way outside the soul. But a definition is composed of universals. Therefore, etc.

(4) On the opposite side:

(5) Opposites cannot belong to the same thing. But every thing outside the soul is absolutely singular. Therefore, none is in any way universal.

[Three forms of the common view]

(6) In coming to a conclusion on this question, all those I have seen agree in saying that the nature that is somehow universal (at least in potency and incompletely) is really in the individual, although some say it is distinguished really from the individual, [qq. 4–5], some only formally [q. 6], some that it is in no way distinguished on the side of the nature of the thing, but only according to reason or through the consideration of an intellect.

[The common view: first version of the third form]

(7) Hence some[52] say that in creatures there is a certain kind of form that according to its own reality and nature has no unity in itself at all. Rather

---

52. The critical edition cites a pseudonymous work attributed to Thomas Aquinas and also Hervaeus Natalis's *Commentary on the Sentences*, but remarks that Ockham's actual wording is to be found in neither source.

in itself it is naturally divided. It has a unity only according to the reason's understanding, in such a way that it subsists in no individual with only that most basic kind of unity, without the addition of any positive formal feature. For example, the form of a genus, which is in reality only as divided by the forms of species.

(8) There is another kind of form, which according to its own reality and nature is in itself one and individual and divided from every other form, in such a way that it subsists in *supposita* with nothing formal added to it. For example, the form of any most specific species, the unity of which is only according to reason. Such a specific form is undivided, I say, with respect to its subjective parts as far as it itself is concerned.

(9) Therefore, this theory holds that the form of a genus is not one simple form of itself, but of itself is divided. But the form of a species is one simple form of itself, and as such it is universal. That very same form, as designated in this *suppositum*, is particular. Thus this theory holds that both the form of the genus and the form of the species subsist in these singulars, although in different ways.

[The common view: second version of the third form]

(10) Others[53] hold that a thing according to its actual being is singular. The same thing according to its being in the intellect is universal. Thus the same thing according to one being or according to one consideration is universal, and according to another being or according to another consideration is singular.

[The common view: third version of the third form—Henry of Harclay's theory]

(11) But some moderns[54] maintain that the same thing under one concept is universal and under another concept is singular. Thus they say: "Superiority and inferiority belong to a thing only in comparison with the intellect. For according to Avicenna, *Metaphysics* I [= V. 1–2, 87rb–87va], one and the same thing under one understanding or concept is singular and under another is universal. In this sense, I say every thing posited outside the soul is by that

---

53. The critical edition cites an anonymous Paris manuscript, and also Durand of St. Pourçain's *Commentary on the Sentences.*

54. Henry of Harclay. Ockham is quoting Henry's *Quaestiones disputatae* q. 3, virtually *verbatim*. See Gál, "Henricus de Harclay," 216–217.

very fact singular. This singular thing is naturally apt to move the intellect both to conceiving it confusedly and to conceiving it distinctly. I call a 'confused' concept that concept by which the intellect does not distinguish this thing from that one. Thus Socrates moves the intellect to conceiving him to be a man. Through that concept the intellect does not distinguish or distinctly recognize Socrates as distinct from Plato. Now I say what is superior to Socrates—say, man or animal—does not signify any other thing but the thing that is Socrates—but as it is conceived confusedly, and as it moves the intellect to conceiving him in a confused way. So I say 'Socrates is a man' is the predication of a superior of an inferior, which is nothing other than the fact that Socrates is Socrates. Socrates is absolutely a man, as conceived confusedly. Hence in reality Socrates is a man, an animal, a body. All these are really one. There is no superior and inferior, except according to the intellect that considers things in the way described."

(12) So then all these views maintain that the universal and the singular are the same thing really, and do not differ except according to reason. In this respect, they disagree with the three opinions reported in the three preceding questions [qq. 4–6]. Yet they *all* agree on the fact that universals are somehow on the side of reality, so that universals are really in singulars themselves.

[Arguments in favor of the common view]

(13) One can argue in many ways in favor of this general conclusion.[55]

(14) First: What is really divided into true things is a true thing. But the form of a genus and likewise the form of a species are really divided into true things, as into their subjective parts. In the same way, every universal is divided into its real subjective parts. Therefore, every such thing is a true thing outside the soul.

(15) Second: Everything that is truly an essence of any thing, and is included essentially in the quidditative understanding of any thing outside the soul, is a true thing outside the soul. But every genus, every species, and in general every universal predicable *in quid* of a true thing outside the soul belongs to the essence of its inferior, and is included essentially in the quidditative understanding of anything *per se* inferior to it. Therefore, etc.

(16) *Confirmation*: Every thing outside the soul can be truly, perfectly and

---

55. Ockham's editors observe that these arguments are not found *verbatim* and in this order in any other known author, although some of them are found individually in one author or another.

distinctly understood without what is not in any way a true thing or intrinsic to it. But no individual can be understood truly or distinctly if what is *per se* superior to it is not understood. For example, Socrates cannot be understood if animal or man or any other superior notion is not understood. Therefore, whatever is superior to Socrates belongs to the essence of Socrates and consequently is a true thing outside the soul. For no being of reason belongs to the essence of an existing thing outside the soul.

(17) Third: In reality there is something that is communicable to several by identity. But such a thing can only be a universal. Therefore, the universal is something really existing in reality.

(18) Fourth: All items in a categorial line are true things and not just beings of reason. But both genera and species are included in a categorial line. Therefore, both genera and species are true things outside the soul. The major is plain: First, because a genus is predicated *in quid* and univocally of all that are contained *per se* under that genus. But nothing is predicated univocally of a real being and a being of reason. Therefore, all that are *per se* in a categorial genus either are real beings or are beings of reason. They are certainly not all beings of reason. Therefore, they are all real beings.

(19) Second, because nothing *per se* contained under one of a pair of notions *per se* dividing something common is *per se* contained under anything contained under the other one of those dividing notions. For example, if substance is divided by corporeal and incorporeal substance, nothing *per se* contained under corporeal substance will be *per se* contained under anything contained under incorporeal substance. But being, by its first division, is divided into being outside the soul and being of reason [*Metaphysics* V. 7, 1017ª22–35]. Therefore, no being of reason can be contained under any category. For real being outside the soul is divided into the ten categories. Therefore, since genera and species are contained under substance, which is a category, they will not be able to be contained under being of reason. Consequently they are not beings of reason, but rather real.

(20) Third, because if genera and species were beings of reason, then since beings of reason are varied according to the variation of the understandings of them, it follows that genera and species are varied according to the variation of the understandings of them. Hence there will be as many genera *substance* as there are understandings.

(21) Moreover, fifth [see (18)], there is some distinction between *suppositum* and nature. Otherwise 'Man is humanity' would be true, just like 'Man is man'. But a *suppositum* is on the side of reality, and likewise a nature is too. For otherwise there would be no distinction in reality. Therefore, the universal is in some way on the part of reality.

(22) Moreover the view can be supported by authorities:

(23) Boethius, [*Second Commentary on Porphyry*, 215.19–216.2], says a species is the whole being of its individuals. Therefore, a species is the same thing as its individuals. Therefore, it is on the side of reality.

(24) Moreover the author of the *Six Principles* [I. 7–9, 36–37][56] asks the question: Do universals arise from nature or from art? He replies that they arise from nature. But nature works mysteriously in the case of universals. For in producing singulars it produces universals. Therefore, every community, as he says, proceeds from singularity. From this it is argued: What arises from nature has being outside the soul. But a universal arises from nature. Therefore, etc.

(25) Again, *Topics* IV. [4, 124^{b}11–12]: If the genus is destroyed, the species and individual are destroyed too. But the destruction of a being outside the soul never follows on the destruction of a being in the soul. Therefore, genus is outside the soul.

(26) Again, the Philosopher, *Posterior Analytics* I. [8, 75^{b}24–25]: Demonstrations are about the perpetual and incorruptible. And [Robert Grosseteste] the Lincolnite,[57] says on the same passage, [*Commentary on the Posterior Analytics* I. 7, 98–99], "It is plain that demonstration occurs about universals found in singulars." Therefore, universals are truly outside the soul.

(27) Again, the Philosopher, [*Posterior Analytics* I], Ch. 18 [= 31, 87^{b}32–33]: The universal is always and everywhere. And the Lincolnite says on the same passage, [*Commentary on the Posterior Analytics* I. 18, 143–148], "If we understand universals, as Aristotle does, as forms found in the quiddities of singulars or particulars, by which particular things are what they are, then for the universal to be everywhere is nothing but for it to be in every particular. For being everywhere is being in each of its places. But the places of those universals are the very singulars the universals are in."

(28) Again, the Philosopher, *Physics* I. [1, 184^{a}21–23], says confused things are more known to us. But beings in the soul are not more known to us. Therefore, universals are not precisely beings in the soul.

(29) Again, the Commentator on *Physics* I. comm. 4, [7G]: "He means by universals the most universal that can be found in these things belonging to the realm of nature." Therefore, universals are in singulars.

---

56. The anonymous *Book of Six Principles (Liber sex principiorum)* is a discussion of the last six of Aristotle's ten categories, mentioned but discussed only cursorily in the *Categories*.

57. Grosseteste was so called because he was bishop of Lincoln diocese.

(30) Again, in the same place, comm. 13, [12K]: "The intentions of which the name 'being' is said, namely the universal and the individual, are very different." Therefore, the universal is truly a being.

(31) Again, in the same place, comm. 15 [12M]: "The name 'being' is said of the universal and the particular intention—that is, the individual."

(32) Again, *Metaphysics* III. [4, 999^{b}34–1000^{a}1]: "We call singular the numerically one, but universal what is in these."

(33) Again, *Metaphysics* V, the chapter "On the same," [9, 1018^{a}3–4],: "Socrates is not in many, for which reason one does not say 'every Socrates'."

(34) Again, *Metaphysics* VII. [1, 1028^{a}10–12]: Being signifies what a thing is and the individual. Therefore, each of those is a real being.

(35) Likewise in the same place, the Commentator, comm. 1 [= 2, 153G]: "It is plain that the first thing of which the name 'being' is said absolutely and principally is what is said in reply to the question 'What is this given individual that exists *per se*'? And this question is about substance." From this it can be argued: What is more principally being than any accident is a being outside the soul. But a universal is like that, according to the Commentator.

(36) Likewise, what is given in reply to the question "What is it?" asked about a substance is not just a being in the soul. For that does not belong to the quiddity of an external thing. Instead one replies to the question 'What is the individual?' by giving the universal in the category of substance, not by giving the individual. Therefore, etc.

(37) Likewise, he says "this question is about substance." But this question is about the universal, as its reply is also given by way of the universal. Therefore, etc.

(38) Again, comm. 3, [154D]: "These"—that is, quiddities—"are substances, because they are parts of the substances that are substances in reality—that is, of particulars."

(39) Again, comm. 4, [155A]: "A sign of the fact that for us substance is more manifest than accidents—that is, universal substances than universal accidents—is that to know an individual substance by its substantial universals is more perfect than to know it by its universal accidents."

(40) Again, comm. 10, [160H]: "Let us consider this substance the definition signifies." Therefore, the metaphysician considers the substance the definition signifies. But he does not consider any individual. Therefore, etc.

(41) Again, comm. 11, at the beginning [161D]: "The substance of a thing is what is said in response to the question 'What is this individual substance?' And therefore, we described that substance by a dialectical description, saying it is what the expression signifies that gives the essence of the thing. This[58] expression is the definition and is what is said *per se*—that is, what is predicated essentially. Aristotle suggests the first kind of essential predicables: definition." From this text it is clear that definition signifies the substance that is predicated essentially and in the first mode. But such a predicate is only predicated of several things. Therefore, etc.

(42) Again, comm. 40, [192I–K]: "It is explained there what the substance is that is a quiddity, and how this substance is predicable of what is a substance, and that this pertains to it insofar as it is universal." Therefore, some substance is predicable insofar as it is universal.

[Against the common view]

(43) Against this view:

(44) First, against its conclusion. It does not seem that any thing outside the soul that is a substance is universal except perhaps by voluntary institution. First, because opposites require distinct things to belong to primarily. But universality and singularity are opposites like this, according to all [who say universals are somehow in singulars]. Therefore, what are primarily and immediately denominated by universality and singularity are distinguished. Therefore, either they are distinguished formally, which was disproved earlier [q. 6]. Or they are distinguished as one thing and another thing, and consequently the first [q. 4] or the second [q. 5] theory disproved in the first questions is back again. Or else they are distinguished as one being of reason and another being of reason, or as a real being and a being of reason. But it is certain that what is primarily and immediately singular is not a being of reason. Therefore, what is primarily and immediately denominated a universal is only a being in the soul. Consequently it is not in reality.

(45) Second: Either really and formally the same thing is singular and universal or it is not. It cannot be said that it is not, as was proved in the three preceding questions. But if it is, then to the contrary: The thing that is singular is not predicable of several. But what is universal is predicable of several. Therefore, it is not the same. This amounts to arguing as follows: It is impossible for contradictories to be primarily verified of the same item. But being predicable of several and not being predicable of several are verified of the singular and the universal respectively. Therefore, they are not the same.

---

58. Adopting the variant 'qui' for 'quae'.

(46) Suppose it is said: The universal is not predicated of several except through an act of a composing intellect, and therefore the thing that *of itself* is not predicated of several can be predicated of several through an act of a composing intellect.

(47) That is not valid. For not only are being *predicated* of several and not being *predicated* of several contradictory, but being *predicable* of several and not being *predicable* of several are contradictory too. Likewise, to be able to be predicated of several and not to be able to be predicated of several are contradictory. But before any act of the intellect, the universal is able to be predicated of several, and the singular is not predicable and is not able to be predicated of several. Therefore, even without any act of the intellect, the universal is not the singular.

(48) Moreover I argue by means of the Philosopher's own reasons [*Metaphysics* VII. 13, 1038^{b}9–11], the ones he relies on to demonstrate the conclusion that no universal is a substance. I argue as follows: The substance of a thing is proper to what it is the substance of. But the universal is proper to nothing, but instead common. Therefore, the universal is not a substance.

(49) Suppose it is said: The Philosopher intends to prove that a universal is not first or proper substance. (Thus the Commentator argues as follows in [*Metaphysics* VII.] comm. 45, [197K]: "The substance of any given thing is proper to it. But a universal is common to several. Therefore, a universal is not a proper substance.") So it is not proven absolutely that a universal is not a substance, but that it is not a *proper* substance.

(50) This reply is not valid. For it is part of the Philosopher's purpose to argue against those who claim universals are substances—as the Platonists did. But they, as he attributes to them [*Metaphysics* VII. 14, 1039^{a}24–261], do not claim universals are proper substances, but instead common substances. Thus they say certain substances are particular and certain ones common. Therefore, it is not enough for him to prove against them that universals are not proper substances, unless he also proves that they are not substances at all. Hence it is argued [*ibid.*, 13, 1038^{b}12–15]: If the universal that is common to several is a substance, either it is the substance of all of them or of one. Now it is impossible for it to be the substance of all of them. Therefore, it will be the substance of one. Consequently all the things it is common to will be that one thing, which is impossible.

(51) Again, he argues [*ibid.*, 1038^{b}15–16]: A universal is what is predicated of some subject. But substance is in fact not predicated of any subject. Therefore, a universal is not a substance.

(52) Third, he argues [*ibid.*, 1038^{b}23–27]: Just as it is impossible for an individual to be composed of qualities, because then quality would be prior to the individual substance, so it is impossible for an individual to be composed of a non-"this-something." Therefore, no universal is a part of a substance and consequently, since it does not exist by itself, it will not be a substance at all.

(53) Fourth [*ibid.*, 1039ᵃ3–6]: Nothing comes to be from two ingredients in act. Therefore, when ingredients are distinguished <and make up something *per se* one, > one has to be a potency and the other an act. Consequently if a universal were a substance and something were added to it, they would have to be related as act and potency, which is nonsense.

(54) Fifth [*ibid.*, 1039ᵃ2–3]: There would be the Third Man.

(55) Again, *Metaphysics* X. [2, 1053ᵇ16–17]: The Philosopher says it is impossible for any universal to be a substance. Here the Commentator says, comm. 7 [= 6, 255I–M]: "Since it was explained in the treatment of substance and the genera of being that it is impossible for any universal to be a substance, it is plain that the universal *one* is not a substance." He continues: "And since universals are not substances, it is plain that the common *being* is not a substance existing outside the soul, just as the common *one* is not a substance." He goes on: "One and being, as predicates, are universals that do not have being except in the soul." He continues: "Since universals are not substances, therefore neither are genera substances." He goes on: "Neither are substances genera, because genera are universals." From this entire passage, it is clear that universals do not have being except only in the soul. Therefore, they are not in external reality.

(56) Likewise, from the fact that being and one are universals Aristotle [*Metaphysics* XII. 4, 1070ᵇ7–9] proves they are not substances. Therefore, no universal is a substance.

(57) Again, the Commentator, *Metaphysics* XII. comm. 22 [= 21, 307D–E]: "One and being are among the universal things that do not have being outside the soul." Therefore, the universal is not outside the soul.

(58) Again, comm. 28 [= 27, 311H]: "A universal principle does not exist outside the soul. Rather individuals do." He continues: "No universal generates or is generated." Therefore, the universal is not in reality.

(59) Again, comm. 29 [= 28, 312F]: "There is no demonstration about the particular even though in reality only this is a being." Therefore, in reality a universal is not a substance or a being outside the soul. He says the same thing at *Metaphysics* VII. comm. 2, 20, 21, and 30, [= 2–3, 20–21, & 28, 153F–154F, 169D–171K, & 177M–182L], and in almost infinitely many other places.

[Against the first version of the third form of the common view]

(60) Against the first way [(7)–(9)] of holding the third form of the common view I ask: How are the nature and the designation[59] of the nature distinguished? If they are not distinguished at all, then the nature is no more universal than the designated nature is. If they are distinguished somehow, then it will be either according to reality[60] or according to reason. If the former, that was disproved earlier [**qq. 4–6**]. If the latter, it follows that one of them is only a ["reason" or] aspect, as was said in the question on divine attributes [**OT** 2. 265.1–6]. It will[61] also be clear in the same place [**OT** 2. 19.3–20.9] that there is no middle, third kind of difference among creatures.

[Against the second version of the third form of the common view]

(61) Against the second way [(10)] of holding the third form of the common view, I argue: When something precisely denominates something else because of something extrinsic, then whatever the extrinsic feature can belong to, the denominating feature will accordingly be able to belong to it too. Therefore, if the thing that really is singular is universal according to its being in the intellect, which is not possible except because of an act of intellection, then any thing that can be understood can likewise be universal in the same way. So Socrates can be universal and common to Plato according to his being in the intellect. Likewise, the divine essence according to its being in the intellect will be universal, even though according to its real being in act it is most singular. All these results are absurd.

(62) *Confirmation*: When something from the nature of the thing is inconsistent with another, it is not able to belong to the latter according to anything extrinsic. But it is inconsistent with any thing of itself that it be common to another thing. Therefore, community can belong to no thing according to anything extrinsic. Hence whether the thing that is singular is understood or not understood, it will not be able to be common or universal according to any kind of being it has.

---

59. The individuation, making it a designated "this."

60. *I. e.*, the distinction is "on the side of reality," either a real distinction or a Scotist formal distinction.

61. Even though the reference is to an earlier passage, the future tense makes some sense here, since the discussion there is a later addition.

[Against Henry of Harclay's view]

(63) In the same way, it is clear that the third way of holding the third version of the common view is absolutely false and unintelligible, the way maintaining that the same [singular] thing confusedly conceived is universal [(11)]. For if a confusedly conceived thing is universal, I ask: What is that thing? Let it be *a*. Therefore, *a* confusedly conceived is universal. Consequently *a* confusedly conceived is common to *b*. Therefore, '*b* is *a* confusedly conceived' is a case of predicating the superior of the inferior. So Socrates is Plato confusedly conceived, and God is a creature confusedly conceived.

(64) To this it is said [Harclay, Gál ed., 218–219] that it does not follow. For 'Animal is Socrates confusedly conceived; Plato is an animal; therefore, Plato is Socrates confusedly conceived' is invalid because of a variation in the middle term. The claim in the minor is about another animal than in the major, because in reality there is nothing common to them. For just as 'animal' signifies Socrates confusedly conceived, so it signifies Plato confusedly conceived.

(65) But this is not a true or logical statement. For when 'Animal is Socrates confusedly conceived' is said, either 'animal' supposits simply or personally. If personally, then animal is not only Socrates confusedly conceived, but animal is Socrates distinctly conceived too. For then the proposition is an indefinite having one true singular: 'This animal is Socrates distinctly conceived', indicating Socrates.

(66) But if 'animal' supposits simply, then either it supposits **(a)** for some true thing, or **(b)** for a being only in the soul, or **(c)** for an aggregate of the two. If **(a)** for a thing,[62] then some true thing is common. Consequently a true thing is predicated truly of another thing. And so just as 'Socrates is an animal' or 'An ass is an animal' is absolutely true, so too 'An ass is Socrates as conceived' will be true. For according to you, the common thing for which 'animal' supposits in 'Animal is Socrates confusedly conceived' is Socrates as conceived, and is in no way distinguished from Socrates as conceived. Therefore, whatever the one is predicated of, so is the other. If each supposits personally, then just as 'An ass is an animal' is true insofar as 'animal' supposits personally, so 'An ass is Socrates as conceived' will be true insofar as the predicate supposits personally.

(67) Furthermore his claim above [(11)], that superiority and inferiority belong to a thing through a comparison with the intellect, is absolutely false.

---

62. Alternatives **(b)** and **(c)** are never addressed.

For no thing is superior, however it might be considered, just as no thing is indifferent, however it might be considered.

(68) *Confirmation*: If something extrinsic makes Socrates be white, then something in reality is truly white, even though it is not white of itself but only through an extrinsic cause. Therefore in the same way, if the intellect makes a thing superior, then the thing will be truly superior and indifferent, even though not of itself but only through an intellect conceiving the thing confusedly. So in saying that the same thing is superior and inferior, and that nothing in reality is common or indifferent, two contradictories are said.

(69) Furthermore his claim that a thing under one concept is singular and under another is universal [(11)] is false. For a thing that is of itself singular is in no way universal, under any concept. The reason is that there is always a formal inference from a determinable taken with some nondestructive and nondiminishing determination to the same determinable taken absolutely [*On Interpretation* 13, 22ª14–23ª26]. Thus it formally follows: "A thing under such and such concept is universal; therefore, a thing is universal." The consequent is false, just as 'A thing is indifferent' is false according to them [(11)]. Therefore, the antecedent is absolutely false.

(70) Suppose someone says: This *is* a destructive or diminishing determination. For 'to be understood', 'to be conceived' and the like are destructive or diminishing determinations. Therefore, just as "Caesar is thought of; therefore, Caesar is" does not follow so "A thing under such and such a concept is universal or indifferent; therefore, a thing is universal or indifferent" does not follow.

(71) Likewise, according to you[63] it does not follow: "Man in general or communal man is a concept of the mind; therefore, man is a concept of the mind."

(72) The first of these is not valid. For they are not destructive or diminishing determinations. The reason for this is that a determination is a diminishing one when a part denominated by the determination, a part of some whole, is expressed. For example: "An Ethiopian is white with respect to his teeth." There the denominated part is expressed, and if the denomination of such a part is not enough for the denomination of the whole, then the determination is a diminishing one. In that case there is a fallacy *secundum quid et simpliciter* [Aristotle, *Sophistic Refutations* 5, 166ᵇ37–167ª20 & 25, 180ª23–ᵇ39], not by arguing to the determinable taken absolutely but by arguing to the determination taken absolutely. For example, in arguing: "An

63. *I. e.*, Ockham. The objector is speaking.

Ethiopian is white with respect to his teeth (that is, he has white teeth); therefore, the Ethiopian is white," there is a fallacy *secundum quid et simpliciter*. Yet the fallacy is not in inferring the determinable taken absolutely, as if the conclusion were: 'Therefore, the Ethiopian has teeth'.

(73) But in the present case such a part is not expressed when 'A universal is Socrates confusedly conceived' is said. Therefore, there is no diminishing determination here.

(74) Likewise, if there were a diminishing determination, one could infer the determinable taken absolutely, by inferring "Therefore, the universal is Socrates." There would be a fallacy *secundum quid et simpliciter* in inferring the absolute determination, by inferring: "Therefore, the universal is confusedly conceived." And so the point would be established.

(75) Likewise, these determinations are not destructive ones. For a determination is destructive when it is absolutely inconsistent with the thing it is added to, or at least with the existence of that thing, but denominates it because it properly and truly denominates something that was its part. This is clear with 'dead', when one says 'dead man'. For it is impossible that a man be and yet that he be dead. Nevertheless according to common usage in speech it is said that "A man is dead," because the body that was a part of him is truly dead. But it is clear that this cannot be said in the present case. Therefore, these determinations are not destructive.

(76) From this the reply to the counterexample [(70)] is clear. For there is no destructive or diminishing determination in 'Caesar understood'. Therefore, it follows absolutely: Caesar understood is; therefore, Caesar is." And likewise it follows: "Caesar in someone's thought is; therefore, Caesar is."

(77) Suppose someone says: According to the Philosopher, *Sophistic Refutations* I. [5, 166^{b}37–167^{a}20],[64] this is a fallacy *secundum quid et simpliciter*. But such a fallacy occurs always when one argues from something taken in a certain respect to that same thing taken absolutely, or conversely.

(78) I say: 'Caesar in thought is; therefore, Caesar is' is not a fallacy *secundum quid et simpliciter*. Rather it is a formal inference. But here is a fallacy *secundum quid et simpliciter* according to Aristotle [*ibid.*]: 'Caesar is in thought; therefore, Caesar is.'[65] Neither is the fallacy *secundum quid et simpliciter* always when one argues from a determinable taken with a diminishing

64. In the Middle Ages, Aristotle's *Sophistic Refutations* was divided into two books; Book II began at what is now Ch. 16.

65. The example is of course not Aristotle's, since Caesar came later. The difference between this example and the preceding one is in word order, and so in the scope of the intentional operator 'in thought'.

determination to that same determinable taken absolutely. That way of arguing is only one mode of the fallacy. Another mode occurs when one argues from some proposition having a predicate to a proposition making an existence-claim. For example arguing like this: "Socrates is in thought; therefore, Socrates is." Likewise: "When a rose does not exist, a rose is nevertheless understood; therefore, a rose is." And likewise according to the Philosopher in the same place [*ibid.*, 167ª2–4]: "The white is not a man; therefore, the white is not." It is plain that this is a fallacy. For certainly the inference is not valid, and therefore commits *some* fallacy or other. But it is clear by induction* that it commits no other fallacy. It would most seem to commit a fallacy of the consequent; but that is not true, because it does not follow one way or the other. For just as it does not follow: "Caesar is in thought; therefore, Caesar is" so too it does not follow the other way.

(79) The same thing is clear for the second example [(70)]. Therefore, always when there is some predicate that can equally belong to a being and to a non-being, whether one argues affirmatively or negatively, there is always a fallacy *secundum quid et simpliciter*. This is what the Philosopher says [*ibid.*]: to be *something* is not the same as being absolutely. For example, being in thought is not the same as being. Likewise, not being something is not the same as not being absolutely. For example, not being a man is not the same as not being absolutely. Yet being in thought, like not being a man or like being a man, is not a diminishing or destructive determination.

(80) Therefore, the rule [(69)] holds when one argues from a determinable taken with a determination that is neither diminishing nor destructive (in the sense described [(72), (75)]) to the same determinable taken absolutely, if the determination is affirmative, not negative. For example, it follows: "Socrates is a white man; therefore, Socrates is a man." Yet it does not follow negatively: "Socrates is not a white man; therefore, Socrates is not a man." In general it does not follow negatively, but it does affirmatively.

(81) To the second counterexample [(71)], I say it is not valid. For in the consequent 'Man is a concept of the mind', the subject can have simple or personal supposition. If it has simple supposition, there is a good inference. If it has personal supposition, the inference is not valid because of a variation in the supposition. For in the first proposition it supposits simply, and in the second personally. So there is a fallacy of equivocation according to the third mode. Therefore, just as 'Some man is a species or a universal' is to be absolutely denied, because in it 'man' can only have personal supposition because of the added particular sign,[66] so in the same way 'Some thing confusedly conceived is universal' is to be absolutely denied. Hence it is

66. The existential quantifier 'some', the sign of "particularity."

impossible that the same thing under one concept is universal and under another concept is singular.

(82) From these considerations it is clear that the following common claims are not correct statements: that the same thing under one mental intention is singular and under another universal, or that according to such and such a being it is a man and according to another kind of being it is not a man but something else, and many other claims like these. For example, if a thing is considered in such and such a way then it is this, and if it is considered in another way or under another consideration then it is something else. For such propositions with such determinations imply propositions taken absolutely without those determinations. Otherwise I could just as easily say that a man according to one kind of being or under one consideration or mental intention is an ass, and under another is an ox, < and under another is a lion, > which is absurd. Therefore, these are overly improper ways of speaking and abandoning every scientific manner of speech.

[Ockham's view]

(83) Therefore, I say otherwise to the question [(1)]: No thing outside the soul is universal, either through itself or through anything real or rational added on, no matter how it is considered or understood. Thus it is just as great an impossibility that some thing outside the soul be in any way universal (except perhaps through a voluntary institution, as the word 'man', which is a singular word, is universal) as it is an impossibility that a man be an ass through any consideration or according to any kind of being whatever. For when something belongs to something only denominatively, whether through something informing it or through something absolutely extrinsic to it, then everything the informing or extrinsic factor is related to, the denominating feature accordingly belongs to it equally. For example, if something dazzles sight precisely because of the whiteness informing it, then whatever is equally white will equally dazzle. Therefore, if a thing is universal through the consideration of the intellect, which consideration is something completely extrinsic to the thing, then whatever is equally understood will be a universal. So everything understood will be a universal.

(84) Suppose someone says: A thing is not universal when it is understood in just any way, but only when understood confusedly. So not every thing is universal. (This is the third view reported above [(11)].)

(85) This reply is not valid. First, because when the thing is precisely understood distinctly, a proposition can be formed in which a superior is predicated of its inferior. For example, if Socrates is intuitively seen and whatever is in Socrates is intuitively seen (at least by divine power), still such an intellect can know that Socrates is a man and that he is an animal. Therefore, without any confused intellection proper to something, its superior is had by the intellect, and consequently so is the universal or common.

(86) Moreover in that case God would truly be a universal. For according to you, God can be confusedly understood. Therefore, if a universal is just a thing confusedly understood, then God will truly be a universal. (Or God as confusedly understood will truly be universal.)

(87) Moreover sight can see something confusedly. Therefore, for whatever reason the universal is had when a thing is confusedly understood, for the same reason the universal is had when a thing is confusedly seen, which is absurd.

(88) Moreover, as will be explained elsewhere [OT 2. 459, 476], no simple thing can be confusedly understood if it is understood at all, and yet there truly is a universal with respect to simples.

(89) So I say: Nothing can come to belong to a thing through any consideration or mental intention, except only by extrinsic denomination. And what belong by extrinsic denomination are precisely those features that belong primarily to an act of intellection or consideration. Thus the thing can be said to be "understood." It can also be said that the thing is "conceived" and that the thing is a "subject" and that the thing is a "predicate," <according to one view [q. 8]>. For this is nothing other than for the thing to be understood by such an intellection. So whatever can be understood by an intellection can be truly called a subject, and a predicate, and a part of a proposition <according to that view> and so on. All of these can be predicated just as much of the divine essence as they can of a creature.

(90) Therefore, if some thing is universal and another is not, the intellect is not what makes this so. For it can regard all things the same way. Instead it will be from the nature of the thing, and because of some diversity in reality, in such a way that one thing in reality is related of itself to being universal otherwise than the other one is. Consequently there is in reality some distinction or nonidentity between what is denominated by the mental intention of universality and what is denominated by the intention of singularity. The opposite of this was proved in the preceding questions, [especially q. 6].

(91) Furthermore, I argue: Socrates is not a universal according to any kind of being or consideration. Neither is Plato or this ass or that one, and so on for the singulars (indicating all singular things). Therefore, no thing is universal according to any kind of being or intention or consideration. The inference is clear as a case of arguing from all the singular propositions to

the universal proposition. The antecedent is clear because there is no greater reason for one singular proposition to be true than for another. But this is true: 'Socrates is not a universal according to any kind of being or consideration or intention or mode'. For if he were, then for the same reason I could say that Socrates under some mode is Plato, and a man under some mode is an ass, and a stone, and a whiteness. All of these are absurd.

(92) Likewise, if the same thing were really universal and singular, then in every case of predicating a superior of its inferior the same thing would be predicated of itself. For the universal would be predicated of the particular, and they are the same thing according to you. This is absurd.

(93) Therefore, I say a universal is not in the thing itself of which it is a universal, either really or subjectively, any more than the word 'man', which is a true quality, is in Socrates or in what it signifies. Neither is a universal a part of the singular with respect to which it is a universal, any more than a word is part of its significate. Yet just as the word is predicated of its significate truly and without any distinction, not for itself but for its significate, so too the universal is predicated truly of its singular, not for itself but for its singular.

(94) This is the Philosopher's meaning, and the Commentator's, and indeed all philosophers' who judge correctly about the universal. Thus the Commentator says, *Metaphysics* VII. comm. 44, [197C–D]: "Since he"—that is, Aristotle—"has explained that what definitions signify are the substances of things, and definitions are composed of universals predicated of particulars, he begins to investigate whether universals are the substances of things or whether they are not, but instead there are only the substances of the particulars the universals are predicated of. This is necessary for explaining that the forms of individual substances are substances, and that in the individual there is no substance but the matter and the particular form it is composed of."

(95) From this text come some of the statements made in this question and in the preceding ones. First, definitions are not the substances of things but instead signify the substances of things. For he says "what definitions *signify* are substances." So definitions are signs and the substances of things are signified, and the sign is not the signified.

(96) Second, definitions do not signify universals. Hence, since they signify the substances of singular things, they will signify singulars. For he says "definitions are composed of universals." Therefore, the universals themselves are not signified by the definitions but are signs and parts of the definitions that signify particulars. For between the particular and the universal there is no middle ground.

(97) Third, we have the statement that universals are truly predicated of particulars. Yet they are not in particulars. For in the particular individual there is nothing but the matter and the particular form.

(98) Suppose someone says: There is no primary substance except the matter and the particular form. Yet there is in the individual a secondary substance that is neither the matter nor the particular form.

(99) This is contrary to the Philosopher's and the Commentator's meaning [*Metaphysics* VII. comm. 44, 197C–D]. For by the same reasoning it should be said that in the individual there is nothing but the universal, because there is no secondary substance there except a universal one.

(100) Likewise, if the Philosopher and the Commentator are only proving that universals are not primary substances, and that is why they prove they are not substances, then by the same reasoning they should prove that particulars are not substances because they are not secondary substances. For if animal is divided by man and ass, it should equally be proven that a man is not an animal because he is not an ass as it is proven for the same reason that an ass is not an animal because it is not a man.

(101) Fourth, we have the statement that universals are not substances, and particulars are not composed of them.

(102) Again, comm. 45, [197]: "Let us say then that it is impossible for any of what are called universals to be the substance of any thing, even though they reveal the substances of things." Therefore, universals are not substances and they do not belong to the substance of any thing. Instead they only reveal the substances of things as signs.

(103) Again, comm. 47, [198F]: "Since it has been explained that understood universals are the dispositions of substances"—and he calls 'dispositions of substances' what are predicable of substances, as in the preceding comment—"it is impossible that they be parts of substances existing *per se*."

(104) Suppose someone says: The Philosopher and the Commentator are not proving universals are not substances absolutely, but that they are not substances separated from sensibles, as Plato holds.

(105) The Philosopher's procedure goes against this. For first he proves that universals are not substances, and second that they are not exemplars such as Plato maintained.

(106) Again, the Commentator, *Metaphysics* VII. comm. 2, [210D–E] says: "It has been determined that form and its parts are substances, and that the universal is not a substance—neither is genus, because it is a universal. Then Aristotle said 'Now about exemplars,' etc. He meant this was not investigated in the preceding treatment and will be investigated later. For certain people say there are separated substances other than sensible substances." Therefore, it is part of the Commentator's meaning that the Philosopher in *Metaphysics* VII proves absolutely that universals are not substances, and *afterwards* shows there are no such separated substances.

[Against the arguments for the common view]

(107) To the first argument for the other view [(14)], I say: What is divided into true things, as a true composite is divided into the parts essentially included in it, is a true thing. In this way a body is divided into its integral parts, and a whole into its essential parts. Such division really occurs outside the soul. But when something is divided into true things as a sign is divided into its significates, this does not have to be so, any more than what is divided into substances as a sign is divided into substances, as into its significates, has to be a substance. Species is divided in this second sense, and so is genus. For the species or genus, or any universal, is not varied in any respect on account of such a division. Neither are the "parts" into which it is divided really parts any more than the several significates are parts of a significant word.

(108) To the second argument [(15)], I say: In general the superior never belongs to the essence of the inferior, or is included essentially in the inferior or in its quidditative understanding. Rather it is predicated essentially of the inferior, because it reveals the essence of the inferior or reveals the inferior itself <or a thing conveyed by the inferior>. This is what it is to be predicated *in quid*, or *per se* in the first mode and essentially.

(109) Thus just as according to some [Scotus, 4. 221–227], being indicates a concept that does not belong to the essence of God and is not an essential part of him (because then something real would be univocal to God and creature, which they deny), and yet it is predicated *in quid* and *per se* in the first mode of God and of a creature, so too I say in the present case that nothing on the part of reality is univocal to any individuals, and yet there is something predicable *in quid* of individuals.

(110) Likewise, just as they say [W 6. 359–360] that the universal that is numerically one object, predicable of each *suppositum* by a predication saying 'This is this', is not in reality (because nothing in reality is predicable like that), and yet this predication is called essential and *in quid* and *per se* in the first mode, so too I say that in general predicating a superior of an inferior is not predicating anything that is in any way in reality outside the soul. Consequently what is predicated is not a part of the thing and does not belong to the essence of the thing. Yet it is predicated *in quid* of things. The

reason for this is that it is not predicated for itself but rather for the things of which it is predicated.

(111) If someone says: In that case, to say 'Socrates is a man' would be the same as saying 'Socrates is Socrates', I reply: That does not follow. For although 'man' in the first proposition supposits for Socrates, and the proposition cannot be verified except of Socrates, nevertheless what is predicated is something else. Therefore, although there is something the same *for* which the predication occurs in each proposition, nevertheless because what is predicated is different, therefore it is not the same proposition.

(112) Likewise, although in 'Socrates is a man' the term 'man' supposits for Socrates, yet it does not supposit *precisely* for Socrates, because "potentially" (as logicians say) it supposits for any man. For it is inferred from any man. A term in such cases always supposits for the same things, because it supposits for all the things it is verified of. Nevertheless 'Socrates is a man' is not verified except of Socrates. Therefore, to say 'Socrates is a man' is not the same as saying 'Socrates is Socrates'.

(113) To the confirmation [(16)], I say and grant, as will be clear later [OT 2. 458.13–460.6], that a thing can be understood not only confusedly but even perfectly and distinctly, without understanding anything superior to it. When it is said [(16)] 'Socrates cannot be understood if animal is not understood', I say this can be distinguished. (Whether the distinction is literal or not I do not care). For 'animal' can supposit simply, and in that case the proposition is false. For then it is denoted that Socrates cannot be understood if the common animal in the mind is not understood. And that is absolutely false. Or 'animal' can supposit personally for a thing. In that sense, I grant the proposition. For in that sense Socrates cannot run unless an animal runs. For it necessarily follows: "Socrates runs; therefore, an animal runs." But the common animal in the mind does not have to run. In this sense a man cannot be understood unless a being is understood. Yet according to them a man can be understood when the common being in the mind is not understood—especially if, as they say,[67] what is common is not anything real.

(114) To the third argument [(17)], I say nothing is communicable to things by identity except only the divine essence to the three *supposita* with which it is really the same. Thus it should not properly be granted that a nature is communicated to a *suppositum*, unless perhaps it is said that a human nature is communicated to the divine Word—and even in that case it is not

---

67. The critical edition cites Henry of Harclay's first *Disputed Question*, in a Vatican manuscript. See also (109).

communicated to it by identity. Instead it should more properly be said that the nature *is* a *suppositum*, as will be shown later [OT 2. 377–378].

(115) Thus just as they have to say [see **(109)**] that the being that is common and univocal to God and creature is not communicable to anything by identity (for then something real would be univocal to God and creature, just as according to them something real is univocal to Socrates and Plato), so too I say in general that nothing univocal is communicable by identity to its univocates.

(116) To the fourth argument [**(18)**], I say: Not all items in a categorial line containing what are ordered *per se* according to superior and inferior are true things outside the soul. Rather some such items are only beings in the soul.

(117) To the first proof [**(18)**], I grant that genus is predicated *in quid* and univocally of all its inferiors. And I grant that something is predicated univocally and *in quid* and *per se* in the first mode of a real being, < or of a pronoun indicating a real being, > and of a being of reason—but not *for* the being of reason, but rather for the *thing*. For the being of reason will not have simple supposition but personal.

(118) Therefore, genus is predicated of the species, but not *for* the species (for the act should not be exercised as 'The species is the genus'). Instead it is predicated of the species for the thing. Therefore, the signate act should be exercised as: 'A man is an animal', so that both terms stand personally for a thing.

(119) So too others[68] have to say being is predicated of wisdom in general *per se* in the first mode, and likewise it is predicated of a real being, and yet wisdom in general is not something real < outside the soul >. For then there would be something real common to God and creature. Therefore, being, which is precisely univocal to real beings, is predicated univocally and *in quid* of a real being and of a being of reason. But then that being of reason does not supposit for itself but for a thing.

(120) Hence when one says 'Every wisdom is a real being', this is a predication *in quid*. Nothing is required for this except that the wisdom that is God is a real being. It is not required that the univocal common wisdom be a real being.

(121) So I say that for the truth of 'Every man is an animal' it suffices that this man be an animal and[69] that man be an animal, and so on for the other

68. Scotus and Henry of Harclay. See n. 67 above.

69. Omitting the edition's '*quod*', which suggests that either clause separately is sufficient. But the required sense is that they are sufficient only *together*.

singular things. It is not required that what is univocal to these men be an animal. So too for 'Every animal is a substance', 'Every body is a substance', 'Every color is a quality', 'Every intention is a quality', and the like.

(122) To the second proof [(19)], I say the same thing: It proceeds in terms of divisors such that the divided is verified of each of them suppositing for a thing. But when the divided does not stand for a thing but for something else, this does not have to be so. Hence if genera and species were substances, they could in no way be beings of reason. But in fact they are not substances.

(123) I say therefore: For something to be or to be contained under some genus can be understood in two senses: Either (a) because it is that of which, for itself <or of a pronoun indicating it,> the genus is verified. In this sense, only singulars are contained in a genus, because only singulars are substances and only singulars are qualities. Neither species nor genera are contained in this sense under the genus substance. In another sense (b), something is in a genus because it is that of which, not for itself, the genus is truly predicated. In this sense, genera and species are in a genus.

(124) The proposition taken as a premise [in (19)] is true for contents in the first sense, not for contents in the second sense.

(125) To the third proof [(20)], the answer will be clear in the following question [q. 8].

(126) To the fifth argument [(21)], I say: Between a nature and a *suppositum* there is sometimes even a real distinction, as between the *suppositum* of the divine Word and the assumed human nature. But sometimes there is no distinction at all on the part of reality. Yet these concepts—that is, "*suppositum*" and "nature"—are distinguished. So it can be verified of something that it is a nature but not a *suppositum*, although it was previously a *suppositum*. But this is never possible except by corruption or by real assumption.[70] This will be discussed elsewhere [**OT** 2. 377–378 & 6. 3–42].

(127) When it is said [(21)] that in that case 'Man is humanity' would be true, I say: This proposition is to be granted literally, unless some syncategorematic mode conveyed in the name 'humanity' according to the speakers' usage prevents it. Yet 'Man is humanity' is contingent, even without the corruption of a humanity.

(128) To the sixth argument [(23)], I say it is not part of Boethius's meaning that the species *is* the whole being of individuals, but that it *indicates* the whole being of individuals as in a way a sign that is not the signified. This is universally true for a most specific species, although it is not univer-

---

70. As in the Incarnation, where the *suppositum*, the second person of the Trinity, "assumed" a human nature.

sally true for a genus. How this is to be understood will be clear in the eighth distinction [**OT** 3. 217.7–218.11].

(**129**) To the seventh argument [(**24**)], I say nature does work mysteriously in the case of universals. Not that it produces the universals themselves outside the soul, as though they were real things, but because in producing its cognition in the soul it—at least <immediately or> mediately—produces the universals as it were "mysteriously," in the way they are apt to be produced. Thus every community in this sense is natural and proceeds from singularity. It is not necessary that in this sense it comes about from nature that community is outside the soul. Rather it can be in the soul.

(**130**) To the eighth argument [(**25**)], I say: "If the genus is destroyed" etc. is to be understood in the sense that whatever the genus is truly denied of, the species and individual are truly denied of the same thing. For example, if a stone is not an animal, then it is not a man, it is not an ass, it is not Socrates. Yet it does not have to be the case that if (whether this is possible or not) what is a genus did not exist, the individual would not exist either.

(**131**) To the ninth argument [(**26**)], I say the Philosopher means that demonstration is about the perpetual and incorruptible—that is, about necessary propositions.

(**132**) As for the Lincolnite [(**26**)], who wants to defend the Philosopher, one can say he means that demonstration is about universals found in singulars because those universals are truly *predicable* of singulars, so that they are "in" singulars by predication.

(**133**) To the tenth argument [(**27**)], I say: The universal is *not* everywhere and always unless because 'being somewhere' is predicated of a universal, not for itself but for a thing, whenever it is predicated of a singular. In general, whatever is predicated of a singular or of a pronoun indicating a singular is predicated of a universal taken particularly.

(**134**) To the Lincolnite [(**27**)], I reply: He means the same thing, unless he departs from the Philosopher's meaning and from the truth.

(**135**) To the eleventh argument [(**28**)], I say: Universals are said to be more known, not because they are known before singulars by an incomplex knowledge but because they are more common and in more. Common characteristics are known by more people about common terms, suppositing not for themselves but for things, than special characteristics are known about special things, as will be said later [**OT** 2. 502].

(**136**) To the twelfth argument [(**29**)], I say: According to Damascene, "being in" is in one sense the same as "being said of." The Commentator there understands that they "are in things" in the same sense, because they are said of particular things.

(137) To the thirteenth and the fourteenth arguments [(30)–(31)], I say: Real being is said of an individual and a universal, not insofar as the universal supposits or stands for itself but for a particular.

(138) To the fifteenth argument [(32)], I reply: We say the universal is in them by predication.

(139) To the sixteenth argument [(33)], I say the same thing: Socrates is not in many—that is, he is not said of many.

(140) To the seventeenth argument [(34)], I reply: It signifies what something is insofar as "what something is" is called a universal, as a superior signifies all its inferiors—however they are inferiors, whether in the first mode or the second, < and this in a certain order, > as was discussed above [(108)].

(141) To the Commentator [(35)], I say the same thing: These universals are truly more principally called beings because being is verified of them in a more worthy and noble and prior way, not insofar as they supposit simply but insofar as they supposit personally. So by such propositions signate acts are understood. I reply the same way to all the authorities [(36)–(37)].[71]

(142) Suppose someone says: What reveals the quiddity of an individual substance is a substance [Averroes, *Metaphysics* VII. comm. 45, 197K]. But what does that is a universal. Therefore, etc.

(143) I say: Here he means by that proposition a signate act—namely, that substance is predicated of such a thing, just as genus is predicated of species and yet the species is not the genus. But elsewhere, where he says that such things are not substances, he means it literally. So here (since he does not contradict himself) he explains how he understood the earlier propositions, which seem to contradict this one.

(144) To the other argument [(38)], as will be said often, the Philosopher [*Metaphysics* VII. 3, 1028^{b}33–1029^{a}9, 1029^{a}30–34; 6, 1031^{b}15–1032^{a}11; 13, 1038^{b}6–15] and the Commentator, [*Metaphysics* VII. comm. 7, 9, 21 & 44, 157K–158B, 159I–160C, 170M–171K, & 197C–F] understand by the quiddities of substances the form that is one part of the composite, as is clear in comment 21, and in comment 9 and 7, and in comment 44, and in many other places. In this sense, I grant that the quiddities of substances are substances, because these quiddities are particular parts of particulars.

(145) To the nineteenth argument [(39)], I reply: It is more perfect to know through substantial universals, etc., because these are predicable *in quid* whereas others are not.

(146) To the twentieth argument [(40)], I reply: The metaphysician con-

71. (36)–(37) contain further arguments based on the passage quoted in (35).

siders the substance a definition signifies, because that substance is what many propositions are verified of.

(147) To the other argument [(41)], I reply: Definition signifies the substance predicated, not that it is so predicated in itself, but that a sign of it is predicated, and that is the definition.

(148) To the last argument [(42)], I say the same thing: The real quiddity itself is not predicated in itself, but only insofar as it is universal—that is, its universal is predicated. This is the way the Commentator speaks. It is not *literally* true, and neither are many other ways of speaking he uses, even though their *sense* is true. He explains that sense in other places [(55), (57)–(59)].

[Reply to the main argument]

(149) To the main argument [(3)], I say: Literally it should not be granted that a definition is the same as the substance of the thing, either really or formally. Instead he understands a signate act by that proposition—namely, that being the same really and in all respects with the defined is predicated of the definition. That signate act should be exercised as: 'A rational animal is the same in all respects as a man.' And that is true.

(150) Suppose someone says: In this sense, 'A genus is the same in all respects as a species' would be true, and 'An attribute is the same in all respects as its subject' is true. For 'An animal is the same in all respects as a man' is true, and so is 'A risible thing is the same in all respects as a man'.

(151) I reply: The Commentator means still more by that proposition. He means such a signate act, which should be exercised in the way described. Besides this he understands the proposition that nothing is signified by a definition that is not signified by the defined, and conversely, although they signify in different ways. The latter fails in the examples given.

[Question 8

Is a univocal universal anything real existing anywhere subjectively?]

(1) Fifth, I ask whether a univocal universal is anything real existing anywhere subjectively.

(2) Yes it is:

(3) For the universal primarily moves the intellect. But what primarily moves the intellect is something real. Therefore, etc.

(4) To the opposite:

(5) Everything real is singular. But a universal is not singular, as has been explained [q. 7]. Therefore, etc.

[Different theories]

(6) On this question there could be different theories,[72] many of which I regard as absolutely false, but any one of which I would prefer to any theory disproved in the preceding questions [qq. 4–7].

[The first theory]

(7) The first theory could be that a universal is a concept of the mind, and that the concept is really the act of intellection itself,[73] so that then a universal would be nothing but a confused intellection of a thing. This intellection—since one singular is not more understood by it than another one is—would be indifferent and common to all singulars. So insofar as it would be more confused or less confused, it would be more universal or less universal.

[Against the first theory]

(8) Against this theory one can argue:

(9) By every intellection something is understood. Therefore, by an intellection like this one something is understood. It is not anything singular outside the soul, because it would be no more one than another, and no more

---

72. The critical edition cites passages from James of Viterbo, Durand of St. Pourçain, and Peter Aurioli.

73. Henry of Ghent, *Quodlibet* IV. 8, 98^v, & V. 14, 174^r–179^v; Godfrey of Fontaines, IX. 19, 270–281.

what does not exist than what does exist. Therefore, either no such thing or every such thing is understood by such an intellection. Not every one, <because then an infinity of them will be understood by that intellection>. Therefore, nothing like that is understood by such an intellection.

(10) Moreover, according to everyone, what terminates an act of understanding is called a "concept of the mind." But such an intellection does not primarily terminate itself. For there is no greater reason why one intellection should terminate itself than another one should. So since the intellection that understands Socrates does not terminate itself primarily, therefore neither does this intellection terminate itself primarily. Therefore, the concept is not the intellection itself.

[The second theory]

(11) A second theory could be that a universal is some species[74] that, since it is equally related to every singular, is called a universal.[75] So it is universal in representing, and yet singular in being.

[Against the second theory]

(12) But this theory seems to be false. For as will be explained elsewhere [OT 5. 268.1–276.11], such a species is not necessary.

(13) Second, because a universal is claimed to be what is understood by the intellect's abstracting. But the species is not so understood. For either it is understood in itself. And then, as will be clear elsewhere [*ibid.*], it is necessarily intuitively understood first. Or it is understood in something else. Consequently, as will be clear elsewhere [*ibid.*, 298.11–20], that something else is a universal with respect to this species. In that case, I ask about that as before. So either there will be an infinite regress or else the species will not be universal.

(14) Moreover in that case a universal is not abstracted but is truly generated, because it would be a true quality generated in the intellect.

[A third theory]

(15) There could be another theory: The universal is some true thing following on the intellect's act, which thing would be a likeness of the [con-

74. Not species as opposed to genus, but "species" in the epistemological sense, the form of the object as taken on by the knower.

75. The critical edition cites Aquinas, *Summa theologiae* 1. 85. 2–3, and Giles of Rome's *Commentary on the Sentences*.

ceived] thing. It would be universal because it would be equally related to all [things conceived by it].[76]

[Against the third theory]

(16) But this theory does not seem true, because no such thing has to be posited. For everything in the intellect is either an act or a passion or a habit [*Nichomachean Ethics* VI. 3, 1139^{b}16–17]. But none of these could be held to be the thing postulated by this theory.

[Agreement among these three theories]

(17) These theories would agree on this conclusion: The universal would be in itself a true singular thing and numerically one. Nevertheless, with respect to external things, it would be universal and common and indifferent to the singular things, and so to speak a natural likeness of those things. For this reason it could supposit for an external thing. The situation with this universal would be in a way like that of a statue with respect to what are most like it.[77] For the statue would be in itself singular and numerically one, and yet indifferent to what are most like it. It would not lead more to the knowledge of one than of another.

(18) Likewise according to this theory, one who claimed that besides the intellection there is a species or habit in the soul would be no more able to say the intellection is really a universal than that the species or habit is really a universal, or conversely. For each of these would be indifferent to all the singulars.

(19) These theories cannot be easily disproved. They are not so improbable and do not contain so evident a falsehood as do the theories disproved in the other questions [qq. 4–7].

[A fourth theory]

(20) There could be a fourth theory, that nothing is universal from its own nature, but only from institution, in the way a word is a universal.[78] For no

76. The editors cite Scotus, *On Porphyry's Universals* q. 4 (**W** 1. 90).

77. *I. e.*, represented by it. Ockham is not thinking of a statue of a particular person, but of something more like the statues of indeterminate soldiers one finds on courthouse lawns.

78. The view attributed to Roscelin. See the discussion in King.

thing can from its own nature supposit for another thing or be truly predicated of another thing, and a word cannot either. This happens only from a voluntary institution. Therefore, just as words are universals and are predicable of things through an institution, so too for all universals.

[Against the fourth theory]

(21) But this does not seem true. For then nothing would be a species or a genus from its nature, or conversely. In that case, God and a substance outside the soul could be a universal just as much as anything in the soul can, which does not seem true.

[The fictum-theory]

(22) Therefore, in another sense, it can be said[79] with some probability that the universal is not anything real having subjective being,* either in the soul or outside the soul. Instead it only has objective being* in the soul. It is a kind of fictum having being in objective being like what the external thing has in subjective being. This happens as follows: The intellect, seeing some thing outside the soul, fashions a similar thing in the mind in such a way that, if it had a productive power as it has a fictive power, it would produce such a thing externally, numerically distinct from the former thing.

(23) It would be, analogously, like the case of an artisan. For just as the artisan, seeing a house or some building externally, fashions in his soul a similar house, and afterwards produces a similar house externally, and the produced house is only numerically distinct from the former one, so too in the present case the fictum in the mind formed from the vision of some external thing would be an exemplar. For just as the fictive house, if the one who contrives it had a real productive power, is an exemplar for the artisan, so here the fictum would be an exemplar with respect to one who so contrives it.

(24) The fictum can be called a universal, because it is an exemplar and indifferently related to all external singulars. On account of this likeness in objective being, it is able to supposit for external things that have a similar being outside the intellect. In this way, the universal is not the result of generation but of abstraction—which is nothing but a kind of picturing.

---

79. The critical edition cites texts of William of Alnwick, Peter Aurioli, and Henry of Harclay. On Ockham's change of mind about the fictum-theory, see Gál, "Gualteri de Chatton."

(25) Therefore, first I shall give some arguments to prove there is something in the soul having objective being only, without subjective being.

(26) This is clear, first, because according to the philosophers [Aristotle, *Metaphysics* V. 7, 1017ª7–ᵇ9; Averroes, *Metaphysics* V. comm. 13–14, 113B–117K], in its first division being is divided into being in the soul and being outside the soul. Being outside the soul is divided into the ten categories. I ask then: How is 'being in the soul' taken here? Either it is taken for what has objective being only. And then the point is established. Or it is taken for what has subjective being. But that is not possible, because what has true subjective being in the soul is contained under the kind of being that is precisely divided into the ten categories, because it is contained under quality. For an intellection and in general every accident that informs the soul is a true quality, just as heat or whiteness is. So it is not contained under the branch divided against the kind of being divided into the ten categories.

(27) Moreover figments have being in the soul, and it is not subjective being. For then they would be true things. Hence a chimera and a goat-stag and the like would be a true thing. Therefore, there are some things that have only objective being.

(28) Likewise, propositions, syllogisms and the like—which logic deals with—do not have subjective being. Therefore, they have only objective being, so that their being is their being cognized. Therefore, there are such beings having only objective being.

(29) Likewise, artificial things in the mind of the artisan do not seem to have subjective being, and neither do creatures in the divine mind before creation.

(30) Likewise, relations of reason are generally maintained by the Doctors.[80] I ask then: Do they have only subjective being? In that case, they will be true and real things. Or do they have only objective being? In that case, the point is established.

(31) Likewise, according to those who think otherwise than I do [e. g., Scotus, 4. 221–227], being indicates a univocal concept and yet no other *thing*.

(32) Likewise, almost everyone distinguishes second intentions from first intentions [K Ch. 23]. <They do not call any real qualities in the soul "second intentions." Therefore, since they are not really outside the soul, they could only be objectively in the soul.>

(33) Second, this theory would say that the fictum is what is primarily and

---

80. *E. g.*, Aquinas, *Summa theologiae* I. 28. 1; Scotus, *Quodlibet* 13 (**W** 12. 320–321), translated in John Duns Scotus, *God and Creatures*, 295–296.

immediately denominated by the mental intention of universality. It has the aspect of an object, and is what immediately terminates the act of understanding when no singular is understood. Because it is such in objective being as the singular is in subjective being, therefore it is able from its nature to supposit for the singulars it is in some way a likeness of. Also certain predicates conveying true things are verified of the fictum, not for itself but for the things. And it is a one that is predicated of several in such a way that it itself is not varied. Otherwise no genus would be truly predicated of several species, but would necessarily have to be one thing and another, and there would be as many genera as there are species.

(34) Indeed the genus could not differ from the species in any way. Neither would the genus be in more than the species is. For if it did differ from the species, I ask: How does the genus differ from the species? Either (a) on the part of reality. But that was disproved earlier [q. 6]. Likewise, given that it is distinguished on the part of reality, I ask: (i) Is that nonvaried genus predicated of several species or (ii) not? If (i) it is, I have my point: Something not varied or multiplied is predicated of several. And that something is not in reality (except according to the view reported in the first question [q. 4]). Therefore, it is only in the mind.

(35) But if (ii) nothing not varied or multiplied is predicated of several, then the genus is not in more than the species or individual is. For the varied species is certainly predicated of several, and the varied and multiplied individual is truly predicated of several.

(36) But if (b) the genus is distinguished from the species only in the mind's concept, then either (i) the same concept is predicated of several or (ii) not, but only a varied and multiplied concept. If (i) it is, I have my point: The same concept, not varied or multiplied, is predicated of several—but not for itself, because then those several items would be one and not varied, which is impossible. If (ii) it is not, then no distinction can be given between genus and species—least of all with respect to greater and lesser community.

(37) So therefore something the same, not varied or multiplied, is predicated of several. I call what is so fashioned by the mind in the way described a "concept."

(38) Likewise, the same item is subject in a universal proposition and a particular one, not only in propositions in speech but also in propositions in the mind, which belong to no language. In the latter, no *thing* is in subject position. Therefore, only a kind of concept is in subject position. Therefore, it could be said that just as a word is universal and is a genus and a species, but only through institution, so too the concept so contrived and abstracted from pre-cognized singulars is universal from its own nature.

(39) One can use this way of speaking, calling what is contrived in this way a concept and a universal, because this seems to be how Blessed Augustine speaks. It could seem to someone to be Augustine's meaning, who had better views on this topic [than most people do]. This is clear from his statement in *On the Trinity* VIII. 6 [= VIII. 4. 7], where he says: "It is necessary that when we believe in some corporeal things we have read or heard about, but have not seen, the mind contrives for itself something with the outlines and forms of bodies, as happens to one who thinks. This fictum either is not true, or even if it is true, which can only rarely happen."[81] He adds: "For who, when he reads or hears what the Apostle Paul writes, or what things are written about him, does not contrive in his mind both the face of the Apostle himself and the faces of all whose names are mentioned there?" Later on: "And the face of the Lord himself in the flesh is varied and fashioned with the diversity of innumerable thoughts, which face nevertheless was one."

(40) From this passage one can argue: The intellect is no less able to contrive from something seen something entirely similar to it than it is able to contrive from things seen something like something *not* previously seen. But someone is able to contrive from many seen faces something like the face of the Apostle, or of Christ, or of someone else he has never seen. Therefore, it is not a problem that the mind should contrive from some seen or intuitively cognized individual something similar. Such a fictum will not be a real being but only a cognized one. Just as according to Blessed Augustine something else is insinuated by such a fictum, so too by the fictum formed from something seen all things similar to what was previously seen are so to speak insinuated and signified. This is nothing but affirming or denying something of such a fictum, not for itself but for the thing from which it is or can be fashioned.

(41) For example, one who sees a singular whiteness fashions a similar whiteness in his soul, just as the artisan from the seen or pictured house fashions a similar one in his mind. Of that fictive whiteness he predicates the following attributes: 'Whiteness is a color', 'Whiteness dazzles sight', and so on. He does not mean that such a fictum is a color or dazzles sight, but that every whiteness from which the fictum can be formed is a color or dazzles sight. Thus, since he cannot think of every external whiteness individually, he uses the fictum instead for every whiteness.

(42) Moreover Augustine, [*On the Trinity*] VIII. 7 [= VIII. 4. 7], says:

81. Augustine completes the thought by saying that even if it is true, that does not help us believe in it by faith.

"Neither in the faith we have about the Lord Jesus Christ is what the mind fashions for itself beneficial—perhaps it is fashioned far otherwise than the thing really is. Rather what is beneficial is what we think about man according to species. For we have, as it were by a rule, an imprinted knowledge of human nature, in accordance with which whatever we see like that, we know right away it is a man."

(43) From this it is clear that although, because of the diversity of shape and color and other accidents in different men, we can contrive diverse things that are not similar to every man—or perhaps are similar to none—nevertheless we can have a knowledge of some fictum equally related to all men, in accordance with which we can judge about anything whether it is a man or not.

(44) That we can also fashion something like what was previously seen (so that if I had a productive power, not just a fictive one, I could really produce such a thing) is clear from Blessed Augustine in the same book, Chapter 10 [= VIII. 6. 9], where he says: "When I heard from many people and believed the city [of Alexandria][82] was a big one, as much as it could be told to me, I contrived in my mind the image of it I could." And later [*ibid.*]: "Which image, if I could bring it forth out of my mind before the eyes of men who know Alexandria, surely either they all would say 'That is not it' or, if they said 'That is it', I would be very surprised. Looking at it with my mind—that is, at the image, as it were its picture—nevertheless, I would not know it is [Alexandria]."

(45) From this passage it is clear, first, that such ficta can be fashioned by the mind, and much more so from things seen in themselves (as he explains immediately before the passage cited) than from things not seen in themselves but in other, similar, imperfectly seen things.

(46) Second, it is clear that such a fictum is called a likeness or image or picture of the thing, and as he says in the same place, it is called a "word" of the thing.

(47) Third, it is clear that such a fictum is truly the object cognized by the intellect.

(48) Because of these facts, it can be a term of a proposition and can supposit for all the things it is an image or likeness of. This is what it is to be universal and common to them.

(49) Again, [*On the Trinity*] IX. 6. [11]—he is treating of how diverse things are fashioned by the mind from things seen, and how because of the diversity of the latter's bodily features some things so fashioned are like what

---

82. In the context, Augustine makes it clear he had never been to Alexandria.

they are fashioned from and what the one who fashions them uses these ficta for—he infers at the end of the chapter: "So we judge about these particulars according to that form, and we discern that form by the gaze of the rational mind. But these particulars we either touch with the bodily sense if they are present, or recall the images of them fixed in memory if they are absent, or fashion things in their likeness such as even we ourselves would undertake if we wanted to or could do so."

(50) From this passage it is clear that ficta like these are such in objective being as other things are in subjective being. If the intellect had a productive power, it would make them be similar in subjective being too.

(51) Moreover Blessed Augustine expressly says the mind fashions such ficta from things known beforehand, and such ficta are what are cognized, in accordance with which the intellect is able to judge about other things. He does this in *On the Trinity* X. 2. [4], where he says: "He fashions in his mind an imaginary form by which he is aroused to love. Now from what does he fashion it but from the things he already knows? Yet if he should discover that the form that was praised is unlike the form shaped in his mind and completely known in his thought, perhaps he will not love it." And immediately afterwards he explains how on account of such a likeness the singulars themselves are cognized in it and are in a way loved in it. None of these statements would be true unless such ficta had a certain community toward those singulars and others like them, from which singulars the ficta are fashioned. Such community I call "universality," < according to this theory >. < This theory > does not maintain any other kind of universality, except perhaps from institution, as a word or a sign imposed at will is called a universal.

(52) Suppose it is said in reply to all these considerations: It is not possible to fashion such ficta except about composite corporeal things—that is, from the fact that their parts are put together in different ways by the intellect. This is not possible for spiritual things or simples that do not have such a diversity of parts.

(53) Against this we have Augustine himself, *On the Trinity* Ch. 3, [= X. 3. 5], where he says the soul can even fashion a similar fictum about itself, which figment will not be the soul itself, but it will truly be cognized by the intellect. Thus he says: "Therefore, perhaps it does not love itself"—fill in: the mind—"but what it fashions *about* itself, which is perhaps quite other than it itself is, this it loves. Or if the mind does contrive something like itself, and therefore when it loves this figment it loves itself before it knows itself, because it gazes on what is like itself, in that case therefore it knows other minds from which it fashions a fictum of itself and is known to itself

in its genus." From this text it is clear that such a fictum can be had even about the soul, which is simple, and that this fictum is known and is a genus—that is, common. And that was the point.

(54) Hence <according to this view> you should know the fictum is called by Blessed Augustine an "image," a "likeness," a "phantasm" and a "species." These ficta are said by Blessed Augustine to remain in memory in the absence of sensibles, on account of a habit immediately inclining the soul to understanding them. So they are there so to speak in a near potency, inasmuch as the intellect is able to make them in the kind of objective being that pertains to them, by means of the habit left behind. But it is not able in this way, by means of the habit, to make external bodies in the kind of being that pertains to them, because the kind of being that pertains to them is real being.

[Doubts about the fictum-theory]

(55) But there are some doubts about what has just been said.

(56) First, it does not seem anything can have objective being unless it somewhere has subjective being. Therefore, such ficta truly have subjective being, at least in the mind.

(57) *Confirmation*: Everything that is is a substance or an accident [*Categories*, 4, 1^{b}25–27].

(58) Second, it seems such ficta are not like things. For no accident can be made similar to a substance. But the fictum would be further from a substance than any accident is. Therefore, it cannot be a likeness of a thing outside the soul.

(59) Third, it does not seem such ficta are universals. For it has been said [(22)] that if the intellect had a productive power, not just a fictive one, it would produce similars externally. But if it produced similars externally, the products would be no more universal than anything else would be. All of the products would be numerically distinct individuals of the same kind. This is clear in the case of the house produced from such a likeness and the house known beforehand from which its similar is fashioned by the mind. Therefore, in the same way, these ficta are not universals in fictive being.

(60) The fourth doubt is about syncategorematic, connotative and negative concepts: From where can they be taken or abstracted? If precisely from things, there appears to be no way they can be distinguished from other concepts. Now it is clear that there are such concepts, because to every proposition in speech there can correspond a similar one in the mind. Therefore, to the proposition 'Every man is an animal' and to 'Some man is

an animal' there correspond distinct propositions in the mind. Therefore, something corresponds to the quantifier-sign in the one proposition that does not correspond to the quantifier in the other.

(61) The fifth doubt concerns the claim that a spoken word is universal. This seems false. For in that case a spoken word would be a genus, and a species. Consequently a whole categorial line would be in one subalternate genus of the category of quantity.[83]

(62) Likewise, in that case numerically one accident would be a genus for many substances, because numerically one word would be.

(63) Likewise, in that case there would be innumerable most general genera, just as there are innumerable words.

(64) All these results seem absurd. Many other absurdities seem to follow too.

[Replies to these doubts]

(65) To the first of these [(56)], those who hold this theory would say there are certain beings of reason that neither have nor can have any subjective being. For just as before the creation, creatures had no subjective being and yet were truly cognized by God, so too something that has no subjective being can be fashioned by the created intellect.

(66) And when it is said [(57)] "Whatever is is a substance or an accident," it is true that whatever is outside the soul is a substance or an accident. Yet not everything that is in the soul objectively is a substance or an accident.

(67) To the second doubt [(58)], they would say such ficta are not really similar [to external things], but are more dissimilar and further from a substance than accidents are. Yet they are such in objective being as other things are in subjective being. The intellect from its own nature has the power to fashion ficta like what it cognizes externally. Hence just as it can fashion ficta like what it does *not* cognize externally, but this is because it does cognize many things on the basis of which it can fashion such ficta, so too it can fashion ficta like what it *does* cognize.

(68) To the third doubt [(59)], they would say such ficta are indeed universals. But if they were produced in real being, they would not be universals. For then they would be of absolutely the same kind as the others,

---

83. I am emending the edition's 'quality'. No variants are reported here. But in *Categories* 6, 4ᵇ20–37, Aristotle divides quantity into two subcategories, discrete quantity and continuous quantity, and explicitly includes speech under discrete quantity.

and there would be no greater reason for the one to be a universal than for the other. But because in fact they are not of the same kind as the others, since the fictum is not absolutely an animal or a man, therefore the one will be said to be more universal than the other is.

(69) Suppose it is said that according to the Lincolnite [*Commentary on the Posterior Analytics* I. 17. 121], the universal is not a figment.

(70) Likewise, in that case there would be as many universals as there are acts of understanding.

(71) To the first of these [(69)]: The universal is not a figment such that there does not correspond to it anything in subjective being like what is fashioned in objective being, as is the case with a chimera. For a chimera is fashioned as something composed of different animals, and there can be no such thing in reality. Rather the universal is a figment such[84] that there does correspond to it something similar in reality. For example, when something composed of a body and a soul is fashioned, that fictum is a universal. Likewise, if a house is fashioned in the mind before it is produced, what is so fashioned is not a figment like a chimera or anything like that.

(72) To the second objection [(70)]: I do not care for now whether the figment or concept is varied according to the variation in acts of understanding or not. They would say that the most general genus substance either is absolutely one and not varied, or else is one by equivalence. In the latter way, others say the same thing is predicated in the spoken propositions 'Socrates is a man' and 'Plato is a man'. For really it is a different word.[85] Yet it is the same by equivalence, as they say (and rightly so), because to have all the same results it would be just as good if numerically the same word as before were pronounced as it is if the other word is pronounced that is in fact pronounced, and conversely. So it is in the present case: There are only ten most general genera by equivalence, whether or not there are only ten absolutely, and whether the predicate is varied < or the genus is varied > or not.

(73) To the fourth doubt [(60)], they would say syncategorematic, connotative and negative concepts are not concepts abstracted from things and suppositing by their nature for things or signifying them in a way distinct from the way other concepts do. Therefore, they would say no concept is syncategorematic or connotative or negative except by institution only, in the way all such linguistic features are predicated by institution of a word and of other signs. In general, neither grammatical nor logical modes can

84. Following the emendation suggested in the edition.
85. *I. e.*, it is numerically different, a different token of the same type.

belong of themselves more to these concepts than to those. Rather this happens only according to the users' will. But such concepts can be imposed on or abstracted from words, and that is what in fact happens, either always or at any rate generally.

(74) For example, to the word 'man' there belongs the grammatical mode that it is in the singular number, nominative case, masculine gender, and so on. To the word 'man's' there belong other grammatical modes.

(75) Likewise to the word 'man' there belongs the fact that it determinately *per se* signifies a thing. This does not belong to the word 'every'. Instead it belongs to the latter that it signifies only together with something else. The case is similar for the word 'not', and for '*per se*', 'inasmuch as', 'if', and such syncategoremata.

(76) Then, from these words so signifying, the intellect abstracts the common concepts predicable of them and imposes those concepts to signify the same things the external words signify.

(77) In the same way, the intellect forms propositions about such things, similar to spoken propositions and having properties like the ones spoken propositions have. Just as the intellect can institute such concepts to signify in this way, so too it can institute these concepts abstracted from *things* to signify under the same grammatical modes the words signify under. Nevertheless this is better done through concepts abstracted from *words*, in order to avoid equivocation, since those concepts are as distinct as the words (although not all of them are distinct). But the other concepts[86] are not distinct. So each such mental proposition has to be distinguished—say, the mental proposition corresponding to the proposition 'A man is men', and the one corresponding to 'A man is a man's', and so on. What has just been said for these cases has to be said analogously for all connotative, negative, and syncategorematic terms, such as verbs like 'is', 'runs', and so on.

(78) To the fifth doubt [(61)]: The spoken word is truly universal, even though not from its own nature but from the will of the one who institutes it. Likewise, they would grant that a spoken word is a genus and a species and a most general genus, and so on. There is no greater problem about attributing such features to a spoken word on account of the will of the one who institutes it than there is about attributing to a spoken complex word that it is true or false, necessary or impossible. Yet it is truly said that the spoken word itself is true, and that the spoken word itself is false. For no one but a madman can deny that many false things and lies are said, and likewise many true and necessary things are reported. In the same way 'A

---

86. The ones abstracted from *things*.

man is an animal' is true *per se* in the first mode. Likewise 'A man is risible' is true *per se* in the second mode, even in speech. And the spoken proposition 'A man is an ass' is impossible. In the same way, in 'A man is an ass' a common term is in subject position and likewise another one is in predicate position. Likewise a genus is predicated of a species.

(79) Suppose someone says: A spoken proposition is not true or false except because it is a sign of a true or false proposition in the mind. Therefore, likewise no spoken word will be a genus or a species unless because it is a sign of a genus or species.

(80) Likewise, in that case the same term could be a genus and a species. For one person can impose the same word to signify all such and such individuals, and another can impose it to signify others. Therefore, etc.

(81) To the first of these [(79)], it can be granted that some proposition is true in speech even though it is not a sign of any proposition in the mind. Nevertheless in fact every such spoken proposition is *able* to be a sign of a proposition in the mind. In the same way I grant that every spoken word that is a genus or a species can be a sign of a genus or species in the mind, and is in fact even a sign ordained for some such role.

(82) The second objection [(80)] is childish. Nevertheless literally it should be granted that, because of diverse impositions, numerically the same spoken word is a genus and a species. This is no more a problem than granting that numerically the same spoken word is equivocal and univocal, and that numerically the same proposition is necessary and impossible. <All of these should be granted, unless one calls a "true proposition" precisely one that signifies what is true and *not* what is false, and so on in other cases. > For the word 'man' is absolutely univocal for Latins, and the same word could be imposed by Greeks or others to signify several things equally primarily, and so for them it would be absolutely equivocal.

(83) In the same way 'Every dog is an animal' is absolutely true, and it is also absolutely false. For it has one true sense and another false one.[87] Therefore, this numerically same proposition signifies what is true and what is false, and this is what it is for the same proposition to be true and false.

(84) To the second problem [(61)], I say: It is not a problem for a whole categorial line containing things predicable *per se* in the first mode to be in one subalternate genus with respect to all the common things contained in it, so that they are things belonging to that category, as was said earlier for

---

87. 'Dog' was a paradigm of an equivocal term, much like 'bank' in recent literature. 'Dog' means: (a) the animal that can bark (*animal latrabile*), (b) the "Dog Star" in the constellation *Canis major*, (c) the sea-monster, the "dog fish."

beings of reason [(26)]. This is not a problem, unless it is regarded as one by those who do not understand.

(85) To the third problem [(63)],[88] I say the same thing: There is no problem with one word's being a genus by convention, just as there is no problem with a word's being predicated *per se* in the first mode of another word. Hence those who regard these and similar claims as false should grant for the sake of consistency that no one can speak either what is true or what is false, nor has anyone ever heard either lies or truths, and in the same way neither truths nor falsehoods can be written, and other absurdities the whole human community shudders at.

< [The *intellectio*-theory[89]]

(86) One who does not like this theory of ficta in objective being can hold that a concept, and any universal, is a quality existing subjectively in the mind. It is the sign of an external thing just as much from its nature as a spoken word is the sign of a thing according to the will of the one who institutes it. In that case it can be said: In every respect, just as certain spoken words and other voluntarily instituted signs properly and *per se* signify external things (as categorematic terms do), and certain other ones do not signify but only consignify together with other signs (as syncategoremata do), and some signify one way and some another way insofar as there are the different accidents of the grammatical parts of speech, so too there are certain qualities existing subjectively in the mind to which from their own nature there belong (analogously) such grammatical accidents as belong to words through a voluntary institution. There seems to be no greater problem in being able to call forth in the intellect qualities that are natural signs of things than there is for brute animals and men naturally to emit sounds to which signifying other things naturally pertains.[90]

(87) Yet there is a difference, in that brutes and men do not emit such sounds except for the sake of signifying passions or accidents existing in them. But the intellect, because it is a greater power in this respect, can call forth qualities for the sake of naturally signifying any things whatever.

(88) According to this theory, it should be said that any universal, even a most general genus, is truly a singular thing existing as a thing in a determi-

---

88. The argument in (62) is never explicitly addressed.

89. All of (86)–(93) is a later addition by Ockham.

90. *E. g.*, groans and shouts, which signify pain and anger.

nate genus. Yet it is universal through predication, not for itself but for the things it signifies. So the categorial line of substance is a composite or aggregate made up of many qualities naturally related as superior and inferior—that is, one quality in that line is from its nature a sign of more and another is a sign of fewer, just as if such a hierarchy were to occur among spoken words.

(89) Yet there would be a difference, in that spoken words ordered as superior and inferior do not signify what they signify except by voluntary institution, but the others signify naturally and are from their nature genera and species.

(90) Arguments like the following do not work against this theory: A quality is not predicated of a substance, and one category is denied of everything contained under another category. Such rules[91] and many others that could be added to them have truth when the terms supposit personally. For example, 'A substance is not a quality' is true if the terms supposit personally. Yet if the subject supposits simply and the predicate personally, it is to be granted that a substance *is* a quality according to this theory. Thus many such arguments against this theory are not valid.

(91) Now this theory can be held in various forms. In one form, this quality existing subjectively in the soul would be the very act of intellection. This theory could be explained, and the arguments against it solved, as I have explained elsewhere [**OP** 2. 351–358].

(92) In another way, it could be maintained that this quality would be something other than the intellection and posterior to the intellection itself. In that case, one could reply to the motives for the theory of ficta in objective being as was treated elsewhere [*ibid.*], where I expressed this theory of the intention or concept of the soul more strongly, claiming it is a quality of the mind.

(93) I regard each of these three theories as likely.[92] But which of them is the truer I leave to the judgment of others. But I do hold this: No universal—unless perhaps it is a universal through voluntary institution—is anything existing in any way outside the soul. Rather everything that is a universal predicable from its nature of several is in the mind, either subjectively or objectively. No universal belongs to the essence or quiddity of any sub-

---

91. Adopting the variant '*regulae*' for the edition's '*replicae*'.

92. The three theories are the *intellectio*-theory **(7)**, **(86)**–**(92)**; the theory (in two forms) that a universal has subjective being but is distinct from the act of intellection **(11)**, **(15)**; and the fictum-theory **(22)**–**(24)**. The theory in **(20)** appears to be rejected.

stance. So too for the other negative conclusions I gave in the preceding questions [**qq. 4–7**]. >

[To the main argument]

(94) To the main argument [(3)], I say: What primarily moves the intellect is not a universal but a singular. Therefore, the singular is primarily understood with a primacy of generation, as will be clear later [**OT** 2. 473.8–474.18].

Glossary

The items listed here are very selective. For additional help see the references in the Introduction.

Accidents, absolute/respective or relative: Accidents in the category of quantity or quality are absolute. Those in categories like relation or orientation are "respective" or "relative."

Appellate: If *x* is called a *P*, then '*P*' is said to "appellate" *x*. See also *Nomination*.

Common sensibles: Features that can be sensed through more than one sense modality, as for instance shape can be both seen and felt.

Ell: Latin '*ulna*'. The word means both the physical elbow (the joint in the arm) and also the unit of measurement called the "ell," which was basically "an arm's length" (up to the elbow).

Entity: Throughout the text from Scotus, 'entity' has a gerundial rather than a participial force. *I. e.*, an "entity" in this sense is not something that *is*, but rather what something that is *does*. The word might sometimes be translated "way of being."

Hinnibility: The ability to neigh or whinny. It was taken as a property of horses, as risibility was of human beings.

Imposition: See *Invention*.

In quid/in quale predication: Genera were said to be predicated "*in quid*," since they indicate *what* (= *quid*) the thing is. Differences were said to be predicated "*in quale*," since they indicate *what kind* of a thing (= *quale*) it is within the genus. The distinction comes from Aristotle's distinction between *en tō ti esti* and *en tō poion ti estin*.

Induction: An "inductive argument" is an argument from *all* individual cases to a general conclusion. This is not the modern or Humean kind of induction, which proceeds from a mere *sampling* of individual cases and is subject to special problems.

Inferior: If *x* and *y* are in the same category and *x* is lower than *y* on the Porphyrian tree, then *x* is "inferior" to *y*.

Institution: See *Invention*.

Intellect, agent/possible (potential): See **K** Chs. 29–31.

Intension and remission: Increase and decrease, as for example in the intensity or brightness of a color. See **K** Ch. 27.

Invention: The conventional agreement by which spoken and written words come to mean what they do. Sometimes the term 'institution' is used in the same sense. A term is said to be "imposed" on the things of which it is truly predicable. Thus 'man' is "imposed" on Socrates, Plato, Cicero, etc. There is a close connection between the notions of "invention" and "imposition" or "institution."

Nomination: Naming. See also *Appellate*.

Object: In mediaeval Latin this term never means just "any old thing." It means an "object" of a "power" or of the "act" of such a power. In this volume, the reference is often to the objects of the *intellectual* power.

Objective/subjective being: Objective being is the reality a thought-object has, roughly the reality of a modern "intentional object." Subjective being is mind-independent reality, the reality of a "subject" of real predication. Note that modern usage just reverses these senses.

Per se predication: On the four modes of "*per se*" predication, see *Posterior Analytics* 1, 4, 73^{a}34–^{b}16. The Oxford translation renders *per se* predication as "essential" predication.

Person: In *Contra Eutychen* (4. 4–5), Boethius defined "person" as "an individual substance of a reasonable [= rational] nature." The term had a specialized use in the theology of the Trinity and the Incarnation, but also came to be used sometimes in metaphysics and logic to mean simply "individual," whether of a rational nature or not. Thus "personal supposition" has nothing necessarily to do with *people* (see **K** Ch. 9), and Abelard (**A (41)**) speaks of a "personal discreteness" among all individuals.

Personal distinction: What makes one person distinct from another. A special case of the *individual* distinction (what makes one *individual* distinct from another). See also *Person*.

Personally discrete: See *Person*.

Predication: See *In quid/in quale*, *Per se*, *Primary*.

Primary predication: See *Posterior Analytics* 1, 4, 73^{b}26–74^{a}2. The Oxford translation renders this as "commensurate and universal" predication.

Property: Do *not* understand this term in the sense current nowadays, namely as *any* metaphysical feature of a thing. The correct way of interpreting it throughout this volume is the fourth sense given in **P (56)**.

Quantum: Something with a quantity. In this volume, the reference is usually to something with a *size*.

Repetition, unnecessary: nugatio. The term is sometimes translated 'babbling'. For the technical meaning, see Aristotle, *Sophistic Refutations* 3, 165^{b}16, and 13, 173^{a}31–^{b}16.

Signify: On the authority of *On Interpretation* 3, 16^{b}19–21, a term signifies whatever it "establishes an understanding of"—that is, what it makes the hearer think of. See **K** Ch. 9.

Status (plural *status*): For Abelard, where '*x*' is replaced by a common term, the *status* of *x* is *being x*. Thus the *status* of man is *being a man*.

Subject: Metaphysically, a real substance, which is "subject" to accidents. The term is *not* restricted to minds or psychological "subjects." See also *Object*, *Objective/subjective being*.

Supposit: See *Supposition*.

Supposition: The mediaeval theory of reference and of something like quantification theory. Supposition was divided into material, simple and personal, and the latter into several subdivisions. See **K** Ch. 9.

Suppositum: **(1)** In a metaphysical sense, roughly: What does not inhere in anything else, although other metaphysical ingredients may perhaps inhere in it. Except in the theology of the Trinity and the Incarnation, a *suppositum* in this sense is just an individual substance. **(2)** In a logical sense, a referent of a term. (On the logical sense, see **K** Ch. 9.)

Understanding: The word can mean either **(a)** the *faculty* or *power* of understanding, **(b)** an *act* of understanding, or **(c)** a concept.

Unity, per se: See Aristotle, *Metaphysics* 5, 6.

Verb, substantive/accidental: A "substantive" verb is a form of the verb 'to be'. Other verbs were called "accidental" verbs.

Whole/part: **(a)** A universal is a *universal whole* with respect to its inferiors (its *subjective parts*). It is always predicable of its subjective parts. Thus man is an animal. **(b)** A quantity is a *quantitative whole* with respect to the smaller quantities it contains (its *quantitative parts*). It is never predicable of its quantitative parts. Thus a pint is not a gallon. For a basic text on the mediaeval theory of wholes and parts (although not always in the terminology of the later Middle Ages), see Boethius's *On Division*.

Bibliography

In accordance with a common practice, I have alphabetized mediaeval authors by *first* name. I have not included here certain standard works, such as Aristotle's writings, which are cited in the usual ways. Where references in the text and notes above include both a page and a line number, the two are separated by a period only, without a space.

Adams, Marilyn McCord. *William Ockham*, 2 vols., Notre Dame, IN: University of Notre Dame Press, 1987; rev. ed., 1989.

Anonymous. *Liber sex principiorum*. See Porphyry.

Averroes. *Aristotelis Opera cum Averrois Commentariis*, 10 vols. in 13, Venice: Juntas, 1562–1574. Photoreprint, Frankfurt am Main: Minerva, 1962. All references to the Latin text of Averroes will be to this edition, except for his commentary on the *De anima*. (See below.) Vol. 4 = *Physics*; 8 = *Metaphysics*; 9 includes Averroes' *On the Substance of the Sphere*. References are by folio number and marginal identifying letter. Mediaeval authors cited Averroes' commentaries by book and *comment* number, since the modern division of Aristotle's writings into chapters was not yet established.

Averroes. *Averrois Cordubensis commentarium magnum in Aristotelis De anima libros*, F. Stuart Crawford, ed., ("Corpus commentariorum Averrois in Aristotelem," Versionum latinarum, Vol. 6.1); Cambridge, MA: The Mediaeval Academy of America, 1953.

Averroes. *On the Substance of the Sphere.* = *Averroes' De Substantia Orbis: Critical Edition of the Hebrew Text with English Translation and Commentary*, Arthur Hyman, ed. & tr., Cambridge, MA: The Mediaeval Academy of America, 1986.

Avicenna. *Avicenna Latinus: Liber de philosophia prima sive scientia divina*, S. Van Riet, ed., 2 vols. Vol. 1 (I-IV), Louvain: E. Peeters, and Leiden: E. J. Brill, 1977. Vol. 2 (V-X), Louvain: E. Peeters, and Leiden: E. J. Brill, 1980. Note: This edition contains marginal references keyed to the folio numbers in the standard Venice edition of 1508 (see below). The latter references are used throughout the present volume.

Avicenna. *Opera*, Venice: Bonetus Locatellus for Octavianus Scotus, 1508. Photoreprint, Frankfurt am Main: Minerva, 1961. References are by folio number.

Boethius. *Commentary on Cicero's Topics.* = *Boethius's In Ciceronis Topica*,

Eleonore Stump, tr., Ithaca, NY: Cornell University Press, 1988. The Latin original may be found in Migne 64. 1039D–1174B.

Boethius. *In Isagogen Porphyrii commenta*, Samuel Brandt, ed., ("Corpus Scriptorum Ecclesiasticorum Latinorum," Vol. 48); Vienna: F. Tempsky, 1906.

Boethius. *In librum Aristotelis Peri Hermeneias ed. I*, Carl Meiser, ed., Leipzig: B. G. Teubner, 1877.

Boethius. *On Division.* = *De divisione*, in Migne, 64. 875D–892A. Translated in Kretzmann and Stump, *Cambridge Translations*, 11–38. The translation includes references to Migne, so that the text will be cited according to the latter.

Boethius. *The Theological Tractates, The Consolation of Philosophy*, H. F. Stewart and E. K. Rand, eds. & trs., ("The Loeb Classical Library"); London: William Heinemann, 1968. Includes *Contra Eutychen* and *On the Trinity*. References are by section and line numbers.

Courtenay, William J., ed. *Vivarium* 30. #1 (May, 1992). Special issue devoted to the papers of a conference on "The Origin and Meaning of Medieval Nominalism" held at the University of Wisconsin—Madison, October 3–5, 1991.

Gál, Gedeon. "Gualteri de Chatton et Guillelmi de Ockham controversia de natura conceptus universalis," *Franciscan Studies* 27 (1967), 191–212.

Gál, Gedeon. "Henricus de Harclay: Quaestio de significato conceptus universalis," *Franciscan Studies* 31 (1971), 178–234.

Giles of Rome. *Quodlibeta*, Bologna: Dominicus de Lapis, 1481. References are by folio number.

Godfrey of Fontaines. *Les quatre premiers Quodlibets de Godefroid de Fontaines*, M. De Wulf and A. Pelzer, eds., ("Les philosophes Belges," vol. 2), Louvain: Institut supérieur de philosophie de l'université, 1904. See the note two entries below.

Godfrey of Fontaines. *Les Quodlibets cinq, six et sept*, M. De Wulf and J. Hoffmans, eds., ("Les philosophes Belges," vol. 3), Louvain: Institut supérieur de philosophie de l'université, 1914. See the note on the following entry.

Godfrey of Fontaines. *Le huitième Quodlibet, Le neuvième Quodlibet, Le dixième Quodlibet*, ("Les philosophes Belges," vol. 4), Louvain: Institut supérieur de philosophie de l'université, 1924, 1928, 1931. Note: References to Godfrey are by *quodlibet* and question number, with a page reference to the volume containing that *quodlibet*.

Gracia, Jorge J. E. *Introduction to the Problem of Individuation in the Early Middle Ages*, Munich: Philosophia Verlag, 1984; 2nd, rev. ed., 1988.

Henry of Ghent. *Quodlibeta*, Paris: Jodicus Badius Ascensius, 1518. References are by *quodlibet*, question, and folio number.

Henry of Ghent. *Summae quaestionum ordinarium*, 2 vols., Paris: Jodicus Badius Ascensius, 1520. Photoreprint, St. Bonaventure, NY: The Franciscan Institute, 1953. References are by article and question, then volume, folio, and marginal identifying letter.

John Damascene. *Elementarium.* = *Introductio dogmatum elementaris*, in J.-P. Migne, ed., *Patrologiae cursus completus . . . series graeca*, 162 vols., Paris: J.-P. Migne, 1857–1866, Vol. 95 (1864), cols. 97–112.

John Damascene. *On the Orthodox Faith.* = *De fide orthodoxa: Versions of Burgundio and Cerbanus*, Eligius M. Buytaert, ed., ("Franciscan Institute Publications," Text Series, No. 8); St. Bonaventure, NY: The Franciscan Institute, 1955.

John Duns Scotus. *God and Creatures: The Quodlibetal Questions*, Felix Alluntis and Allan B. Wolter, trs., Princeton: Princeton University Press, 1975. Reprinted Washington, DC: The Catholic University of America Press, 1981.

John Duns Scotus. *Opera omnia*, Luke Wadding, ed., 12 vols., Lyon: Laurentius Durand, 1639. Photoreprint, Hildesheim: Georg Olms Verlagsbuchhandlung, 1968.

John Duns Scotus. *Opera omnia*, Vatican City: Vatican Polyglot Press, 1950– . Unless otherwise indicated, all references are to vol. 7, containing the text translated in the present volume.

John Duns Scotus. *Philosophical Writings*, Allan B. Wolter, tr., Indianapolis: Hackett Publishing Company, 1987. Reprint of the "Nelson Philosophical Texts" edition, 1963.

King, Peter O. *Peter Abailard and the Problem of Universals*, Ph.D. dissertation, Princeton University, 1982. (Dissertation Abstracts International, #8220415.) A revised version of this dissertation is forthcoming from Cornell University Press.

Kretzmann, Norman, Anthony Kenny, and Jan Pinborg, eds. *The Cambridge History of Later Medieval Philosophy*, New York: Cambridge University Press, 1982.

Kretzmann, Norman, and Eleonore Stump, trs. *The Cambridge Translations of Medieval Philosophical Texts*, Vol. 1: *Logic and the Philosophy of Language*, New York: Cambridge University Press, 1988.

Migne, Jacques-Paul, ed. *Patrologiae cursus completus . . . series latina*, 221 vols., Paris: J.-P. Migne, 1844-1864. References are by volume, column number, and marginal identifying letter.

Peter Abelard. *Logica 'ingredientibus'*, Bernhard Geyer, ed., ("Beiträge zur Geschichte der Philosophie und Theologie des Mittelalters," 21. 1–3), Münster i. W.: Aschendorff, 1919–1927. References include the fascicule number.

Porphyry. *Isagoge et in Aristotelis Categorias commentarium*, Adolfus Busse, ed., ("Commentaria in Aristotelem Graeca," Vol. 4.1), Berlin: George Reimer, 1887.

Porphyry. *Porphyrii Isagoge translatio Boethii et anonymi fragmentum vulgo vocatum "Liber sex principiorum,"* Lorenzo Minio-Paluello, ed., ("Aristoteles Latinus," Vol. I.6-7), Bruges-Paris: Desclée de Brouwer, 1966.

Priscian. *Institutiones grammaticae*, Martin Hertz, ed., ("Grammatici Latini," Vols. 2–3); Leipzig: Teubner, 1855–1859. Photoreprint, Hildesheim: Georg Olms, 1961. References are by volume, page, and line number.

Robert Grosseteste. *Commentarius in Posteriorum analyticorum libros*, Pietro Rossi, ed., Florence: Leo S. Olschki, 1981. References are by book, chapter, and line number.

Roland-Gosselin, M.-D. "Le Principe de l'individualité," in Roland-Gosselin, ed., *Le "De ente et essentia" de S. Thomas d'Aquin*, Paris: J. Vrin, 1948, 49–134.

Spade, Paul Vincent. "Synonymy and Equivocation in Ockham's Mental Language," *Journal of the History of Philosophy* 18 (1980), 9–22.

Tweedale, Martin M. *Abailard on Universals*, Amsterdam: North-Holland, 1976.

Walter Burley. *Burlei super artem veterem Porphirii et Aristotelis*, Venice: Otinus (de Luna) Papiensis, 1497. References are by folio number.

William of Ockham. *Opera philosophica*, 7 vols., St. Bonaventure, NY: The Franciscan Institute, 1974–1988.

William of Ockham. *Opera theologica*, 10 vols., St. Bonaventure, NY: The Franciscan Institute, 1967–1986.

William of Ockham. *Philosophical Writings*, Philotheus Boehner, ed. & tr., Indianapolis: Hackett Publishing Company, 1990. Reprint of the "Nelson Philosophical Texts" edition, 1957, with revisions by Stephen F. Brown, 1989.

Wippel, John F. *The Metaphysical Thought of Godfrey of Fontaines: A Study in Late Thirteenth-Century Philosophy*, Washington, DC: The Catholic University of America Press, 1981.

Wolter, Allan B. *The Philosophical Theology of John Duns Scotus*, Marilyn McCord Adams, ed., Ithaca, NY: Cornell University Press, 1990.